A Key into the LANGUAGE *of* AMERICA

ROGER WILLIAMS

A Key into the LANGUAGE *of* AMERICA

Edited with a critical Introduction, Notes, and Commentary by
John J. Teunissen and Evelyn J. Hinz

Wayne State University Press, Detroit, 1973

Library of Congress Cataloging in Publication Data
Williams, Roger, 1604?–1683.
A key into the language of America.
Definitive ed. of the authors work originally printed in 1643 by G. *Dexter, London.*
Bibliography: p.
1. Narragansett Indians. 2. Narraganset language. *I. Title*
E99.N16W67 1973 497'.3 72–6590
ISBN 0–8143–1490–2

Published simultaneously in Canada by the Copp Clark Publishing Company 517 Wellington Street, West Toronto 2B, Canada.
Publication of this book was assisted by the American Council of Learned Societies under a grant from the Andrew W. Mellon Foundation.

To
Alexandra and Jeremy
who helped us proofread

It is a glorious *Character* of every true *Disciple* or *Scholler* of *Christ Jesus,* to be never too *old* to *learn.*

Williams, *The Bloody Tenent*

Contents

Illustrations

Acknowledgments

A project of this kind would be impossible without the cooperation of many librarians. Without them the best scholars are well nigh helpless, and we would have been rather more so. We are indebted greatly to all those who knowledgeably and cheerfully helped us in the libraries of Brown University, Providence, Rhode Island, and especially to Mrs. Joseph Hardy of the John Carter Brown Library there. In addition, we wish to thank Mr. John Alden of the Boston Public Library and the staffs of the Library Company of Philadelphia, the Newberry Library, the Library of the Rhode Island Historical Society, the Beinecke Rare Book and Manuscript Library of Yale, the Library of the American Antiquarian Society, the Houghton Library of Harvard, the Library of the Massachusetts Historical Society, and the New York Public Library.

With much pleasure we also acknowledge the assistance of our colleagues in the preparation of this edition. We are indebted to A. W. Plumstead and Everett H. Emerson who read the manuscript in various stages of its progress and who most generously shared with us their learning and professional insights. Needless to say, any errors or infelicities which remain here are ours, not theirs.

We have been able to complete the necessary research because of generous financial assistance. Evelyn Hinz wishes to acknowledge her indebtedness to the Canada Council and John Teunissen to the University of Massachusetts.

Mrs. Carrie Bell and E. Wallace Coyle brought their own inimitable kinds of good humor to various thankless tasks involved in preparing the final version. Mrs. Marguerite Wallace, our editor at the press, has been, as Roger Williams would have put it, of "unspeakable" service.

Finally, to Christopher S. Diamond goes a large share of

our gratitude. He provided us with a much needed refuge and showed us New England from the top of a mountain one morning.

Nausauket Beach,
Killington, Vermont
Appanaug, Rhode Island
August 19, 1971

Introduction*

Roger Williams is best known in America as the liberal opponent of John Cotton in the struggle for religious toleration and as a forerunner of Thomas Jefferson in the argument for the separation of church and state. This is unfortunate, not merely because such a reputation is generally inaccurate in its implications but also because it has indirectly deprived American literature of one of its most rightful and earliest possessions—*A Key into the Language of America* (1643), Roger Williams's first published work. For, unlike many literary works of the colonial period that until recently were neglected simply because they were undiscovered, *A Key* has not been classified as literature because of misrepresentation and misinterpretation, which originated because of the reaction to the historical and political significance of its author. *A Key* is primarily an emblematic and sympathetic presentation of Indian life and an ironic and critical comment upon European civilization in general and New England in particular. Misrepresentation has consisted basically in ignoring one or both of these features, resulting in either a utilitarian appraisal of the whole or an evaluation of isolated parts.

The author

The first step in restoring the integrity of *A Key* must consist in a brief biographical sketch of the author for three reasons: first, that we might recognize and appreciate more easily the ironic dimensions of the work, a knowledge of Williams's encounters with the objects of these ironies is very valuable. Such information also helps to explain the early treatment

* Complete information on all works cited in abbreviation will be found in the bibliography at the end of this volume.

of the work. But possibly more important, the base from which Williams launches his criticisms of his contemporaries and expresses his admiration of the Indian is his personal experience. His are "observations" in the full sense of the word: they are conclusions arrived at through emotional response to and rational meditation of empirical evidence. Finally, biography helps to restore to the marble monument that is Roger Williams of Providence Plantations the humanity without which there can be no art.

Roger Williams was born in the Smithfield district of London, probably in 1603, the third of four children. His father, James, was a merchant tailor, a small shopkeeper, and a textile retailer of the old guild variety; his mother, Alice Pemberton, came from a family of tradesmen, of slightly higher rank than her husband's. Sydrach, the eldest son, followed his father's trade and advanced to become "Merchant to Turkey and Italy"; Katherine, the only daughter, married a neighbor merchant tailor; Robert, the youngest, first served as apprentice to Sydrach and then left England, following in the path of his other brother, Roger who had also become a trader, but in another country—America.

Unlike his brothers', however, Roger Williams's success was not limited to commerce because, partly at least, unlike theirs, his education was not simply that of a merchant apprentice. While he was still a boy, his skill in shorthand attracted the attention and subsequently the patronage of the famous jurist and critic of royal prerogative Sir Edward Coke, who arranged for his enrollment, first at the preparatory school Charterhouse (1621), and later at Pembroke Hall, Cambridge (1623). In 1627 Williams received the bachelor's degree and returned to the university the following term to continue studies towards the M.A., the passport of that age to honor, preferment, and establishment. That he did not obtain this degree the records clearly indicate (Winslow, p. 72); why he did not is nowhere definitely stated, although his writings suggest that the required oath and the scholastic methods of Cambridge were central factors in his decision.

Whatever the reasons, in 1629 Williams left Cambridge and was employed as household chaplain in the wealthy manor of Sir William Masham. During his year's service there he met the two men who were later to become his chief opponents in New England, John Cotton and Thomas Hooker; during this period he also became acquainted with the two women who played the leading roles in his personal life, Jane Whalley and Mary Barnard. The first was the niece of Lady Barrington; it was she to whom he proposed in the spring of 1629 by means of a "paper deputy" to the haughty aunt, who not only dismissed the plea but also dispensed with the services of the young clergyman. In December of the same year he married another member of the same household, Mary Barnard, maid and companion to the daughter of Lady Masham. One year later, December 1, 1630, the Williamses boarded the *Lyon* at Bristol bound for America.

On February 5, 1631, Roger Williams arrived in Boston and very quickly was invited to become minister. By way of refusal he castigated the congregation for not having explicitly demonstrated their separation from the Church of England, and before he left in March he aimed another blow at the "City on a Hill" by arguing that magistrates had no right to enforce the first table of the Decalogue.

Turning his back on Boston, Williams was received by Salem, much to the consternation of the Massachusetts magistrates, as they themselves speedily explained to the Salem congregation. And so Williams moved again, for the third time in less than a year.

It was at Plymouth that his career as a trader and friend to the Indians began. Not that he abandoned his ministerial duties; rather, by becoming self-supporting he became what he considered to be the ideal Christian minister—one who refused to mingle spiritual and material concerns, the preacher who preached "for nothing." It was also at Plymouth that Roger Williams's career as a writer and controversialist began. Sometime during 1632 he prepared a small treatise (no longer extant) in which he questioned the colonists' right to their land, because it depended upon the King's Charter, which in turn depended upon the "sinful opinion" that Christian rulers had a divine right to the lands of the heathen (see Winthrop, pp. 116–17). While the argument here is based upon Williams's belief in the necessary separation of spiritual and material prerogatives, his personal acquaintance with the Indian undoubtedly encouraged him to formulate his convictions.

It was not until after he had returned to Salem in 1633, however, that this treatise became a public issue, and a dangerous one, since it was ironically at that time that England, herself, was questioning the New England experiment and looking for reasons to revoke the charter. On the alert for any such treasonous playing into the hands of the transoceanic enemy, the Massachusetts magistrates demanded to see the treatise and, having done so, summoned Williams and advised him to retract. He did. But not for long.

The battle flag this time was the mutilated British ensign; the sword was Endicott's, but the idea may well have been Williams's (see *Magnalia,* p. 499). To wash their hands of the deed the General Court formulated and administered an oath of allegiance to all the freemen of the colony. Williams challenged the procedure, again arguing from his theory of total distinction between civil and religious policy: as a sacred thing an oath cannot be requested of an unregenerate person; an oath is a spiritual instrument, not a civil weapon.

Despite the turmoil generated by such unorthodox argumentation, the Salem congregation invited Williams to become their pastor upon the death of their own in the early fall of 1634. Such disregard for their authority did not go unnoticed by the Massachusetts magistrates; at a meeting of the General Court, both the Salem congregation and Williams were admonished and advised to consider the errors of their ways. As an added inducement, the Boston authorities refused to grant the Salem church a small parcel of land which they had requested. Williams struck back by encouraging the Salem church to write letters to the other churches in the colony, informing them of this action and asking them to discipline the magistrates who were in their congregations. Boston retaliated by depriving the Salem deputies of their seats in the council until the majority of the Salem freemen would disclaim such "lies."

On September 3, 1635, the General Court met and passed their first sentence upon Roger Williams: that, because of his obstinacy and erroneous opinions, he leave the jurisdiction within six weeks. On October 9 he was again before the General Court, this time to argue his charges against the Court's advocate, Thomas Hooker; and since they were unable to "reduce him from any of his errors," the previous sentence was reissued. The Salem church, on the other hand, "wrote an humble submission to the magistrates, acknowledging their fault in joining with Mr. Williams" (Winthrop, p. 163), thereby obtaining the desired piece of land but losing their pastor, who characteristically moved his pulpit to his house where he preached only to a fit audience though few.

Upon condition that he refrain from uttering his opinions, Williams was given permission to remain until spring. When he failed then to comply, the Court met in January and decided that the only way to keep him from "infecting" the body politic of the colonies would be to send him back to England, which made him in some ways a very strange colleague of Morton of Merrymount. For the purpose of so banishing him they summoned him to Boston, but he declined the invitation for reasons of ill health, "Whereupon a pinnace was sent with commission to Capt. Underhill, etc., to apprehend him and carry him aboard the ship, (which then rode at Natascutt;) but when they came at his house they found he had been gone three days before; but whither they could not learn" (Winthrop, p. 168).

Fortunately, because of his previous contact with the Indians, Roger Williams was not a stranger to the wilderness. Having been informed of the General Court's plans, he fled south from Salem to an Indian settlement on the Blackstone River. Here he was restored to health, and in the spring was joined by four other Englishmen who also felt the desirability of exile. Together they moved westward to the northern tip of Narragansett Bay and, upon land Williams had previously purchased from the Sachems, planted their crops.

Before harvest, however, they were advised by Governor Winslow of Plymouth that their land lay within his jurisdiction. Whereupon the group, enlarged to a dozen or so during the summer, moved further west across the Seekonk to the mouth of the Moshassuck River. Here, upon land later formally purchased from the Narragansett Sachems, Canonicus and Miantunomu (the spelling of whose names varies considerably), Williams founded the settlement he called Providence, "in grateful remembrance of God's merciful Providence to him in his distress."

Ironically, no sooner had Williams been completely banished from their midst than his judges began pleading for his assistance in the crisis of the Pequot War of 1636–37. Initially a tribal war between the Pequots and Narragansetts, the conflict had quickly become a struggle for survival between the English and the Pequots, with the Narragansetts—and ironically their English friend, Roger Williams—holding the balance of power. Williams's task became twofold: first, to negotiate a Narragansett-English treaty and, second, to act as mediator whenever infractions of that treaty occurred, as they were bound to. He managed to accomplish both, although not without many experiences which demonstrated for him the true nature of Christian "faithfulnesse." In 1637 the Pequots were exterminated.

Having thus helped to secure the future of the American experiment, Williams had then to turn again to protect his own. The Providence Plantations had grown in size and numbers, but the original mutual contract was still the only form of government, and the Sachems' mark still the only authorization of ownership. Two problems in particular had arisen: intestine conflict had led weaker parties to place themselves and their land under the protection—and hence jurisdiction—of Massachusetts; under-Sachems had claimed as theirs land deeded by the chief Sachems and, to make themselves more secure, placed their assumed territories under the protection of the Massachusetts Bay Colony. The latter proceeding could only antagonize the Narragansetts, and the New England colonies, fearing an ensuing Indian uprising, formed a league from which Providence was excluded. And so to ensure the independence and survival of Providence by obtaining a charter, Roger Williams was compelled to return to England.

He left New York early in 1643, being banned from Boston harbor, and arrived in England in the summer of that year. He spent his time on board ship drafting his first published work, *A Key into the Language of America,* which was printed in London shortly after his arrival. While in England he wrote four other works, three of which were printed while he was there. *Mr. Cotton's Letter Answered* is a caustic reply to a *Letter* which the Boston theocrat wrote him shortly after his banishment in order to justify that action. The *Letter* was published in early 1643, by whose agency it is not known. According to Williams's reply, Cotton's *Letter* is mere self-exculpation and his professed moderation is only masked intolerance. In *Queries of Highest Consideration,* Williams again attacks the *via media,* this time as proposed by the Westminster Assembly and expressed in the *Apologeticall Narration. The Bloudy Tenent* is his return to the battle with Cotton, but in a much more impersonal sense than previously. A letter had been sent to Cotton, supposedly from a prisoner in Newgate, complaining of his persecution because of his beliefs; Cotton's answer is a justification of persecution for the sake of conscience; Williams's *Bloudy Tenent* is an attack upon this theory and a statement of his own convictions concerning the separation of civil and religious commitments and of freedom of conscience. Introduced into *The Bloudy Tenent* as a focus for attack are excerpts from *A Model of Church and Civil Power,* a statement of the New England theory of the relationship between church and state which Williams attributed to Cotton, although it was actually a composite. Cotton was not the only one to be disturbed by *The Bloudy Tenent;* the censors included it in their list of books to be burned.

Christenings Make Not Christians is the last product of Williams's first mission to England. References to it in *A Key* suggest that it was being written at about the same time, although it was not published until 1645 when Williams was back in America. The work looks back to the offending treatise in its attack upon the application of the term *Christian* to an entire country or nation, and provides a logical justification for the negative attitude toward the process of conversion artistically presented in *A Key*: until the civilized have become truly Christianized, it is folly to convert the Indian to the same errors; until he is civilized the Indian cannot be Christianized; to baptize a savage is not to convert but to blaspheme. As a seventeenth-century reformer, Williams is only too conscious of certain inconsistencies in the church's open-armed acceptance of the barbarian hordes.

The remainder of Roger Williams's biography can, of course, have no direct bearing upon any reading of *A Key;* it is presented here, however, so that the reader can have a kind of overall view of certain events which caused changes in his attitudes and so that we can compare the ideas which he records in 1643 with his later positions. He returned to America in 1644, having obtained the desired charter, and having obtained it at least partly because of his notoriety as a man who had lived among the Indians. Upon his return he was elected "chiefe officer" of the Providence Plantations, an office he held for three years, and one of the major tasks of which was to get the charter ratified. Understandably, those who had previously submitted themselves to the benevolent protection of Massachusetts refused to accept their new political position; while Williams was away Miantunomu had been murdered by Uncas, the Mohegan, with the sanction of the Boston authorities, and his successor had been encouraged to put his mark to a deed surrendering a large tract of the newly chartered land to the crown. With the execution of King Charles in 1649, even the validity of the charter was in question.

As a result of these complications, Williams was forced to make a second trip to England, selling his trading post in order to finance the voyage. To this period belongs his friendship with John Milton, a friendship which was based upon a mutually held set of principles; and the stay in London produced another series of publications. *The Bloody Tenent Yet More Bloody* continues the Cotton controversy, being a reply to Cotton's *Bloody Tenent Washed.* Here Williams repeats his arguments for the separation of civil and religious administrations and for complete soul liberty. *Experiments of Spiritual Life and Health* was also written prior to his voyage, probably in 1650. It is a devotional work written to encourage his wife while he was away on a trading mission. *The Hireling Ministry None of Christ's* treats of a contemporary issue—the debate concerning the legal establishment of religion and the compulsory support of the clergy. Williams here demands not only dissociation of the ministry from any part of the civil service but also their expulsion from the universities. *Major Butler's Fourth Paper* is also a topical publication: Butler, a strong tolerationist, had advocated as his "fourth" point the toleration of the Jews; Williams's tract is an explanatory endorsement of Butler's position. One final pamphlet on the church-state relationship, *The Examiner Defended,* while not certainly by Williams, gives evidence both in style and content of his authorship.

In 1654 he returned to America, having again obtained safe-conduct through Massachusetts, but this time only with hopes concerning the charter (which was finally officially confirmed in 1663). Again he played a leading role in shaping the policies of the Plantations, always adhering to his publicly announced principles. Thus, when in 1656 Massachusetts closed her doors to the Quakers, Providence opened hers; partly because of this practical example of toleration, and partly because of the basic similarity between his and Quaker ideas, Williams's last major work has puzzled many readers. *George Fox Digg'd out of his Burrowes,* published in Boston in 1676, is Williams's record of a four-day public debate in which he participated shortly after the visit of the Quaker leader to Providence in 1672. The long title of the work smacks hardly at all of toleration: "As also how (G. *Fox* slily departing) the Disputation went on being managed three dayes at *Newport* on *Rode-Island,* and one day at *Providence,* between *John Stubs, John Burnet,* and *William Edmondson* on the one part, and *R. W.* on the other. In which many *Quotations* out of *G. Fox* & *Ed. Burrowes* Book in *Folio* are alleadged. With an APENDIX Of some scores of *G. F.* his simple lame Answers to his Opposites in that Book, quoted and replyed to By R. W. of *Providence* in N. E."

The origin of the debate was an interruption of Williams's dispute with a Quaker missionary the previous year. The central issue of the debate, proposed and arranged by the septuagenarian but vigorous Roger Williams, was the way in which God enlightens souls; against the Quaker theory of the inner light, Williams argued study of the

Bible, attacking the idea of an "indwelling God" from the Calvinist premise of total depravity. Just as the origin of the debate was personal, however, so also was the larger context. By making salvation a free and easy thing, the Quakers seemed to slight Williams's labors as a missionary. In his arguments with the formalistic Cotton and his cohorts, Williams had stressed the Spirit against the Letter, charity against "divinity"; now in combating the Quaker, he posits diligent study against lazy inspiration, intellectual conviction against emotional response. It is helpful also to remember that Williams was now an old man being challenged by his juniors.

His final role as a negotiator was fittingly and ironically played during the war which effectively destroyed the political power of the Indian in New England, "King Philip's War," during the crucial years, 1675–76. Like the first great Indian war in the north, the Pequot War, this final conflict was basically an Indian-English struggle, with the Narragansetts and their friend Roger Williams in the middle. In the first contest Roger Williams helped to save the English by treaty with the Narragansetts in spite of their suspicions regarding European "honor." In this struggle Williams was able to do little, because the New Englanders did not trust the Narragansetts who were giving shelter to the enemy non-combatants. Williams understood the problem but could do nothing. He watched helplessly as the Narragansetts, *his* tribe, were annihilated in the Great Swamp Fight of 1675. Providence was burned, his house destroyed, but Williams was unharmed.

Some eight months before his death (1683), Williams wrote to Governor Bradstreet requesting aid in publishing a number of "discourses," which seem to have been sermons he preached to his English congregation (*Letters,* p. 404). The sermons are no longer extant, but among his papers was found a list of twenty-two sermon subjects headed "The Contents or Heads of ye Nahigonset discourses" (Winslow,

p. 270), and the list itself provides insight into the mind of the Puritan who began his literary career by recording his observations upon the contrasting customs of the Indians and the English: his sermons included such subjects as atheism, the drowning of the old world, Job's trials and patience (a favorite in the seventeenth century in both Old and New England), and meditations on harvest, especially Indian harvest.

The literary history of "A Key"

Circumstances, to a great extent, encouraged Williams's contemporaries to view *A Key* as a political and factual document. As we have seen, Williams wrote the book during his first mission to London to obtain a charter for the Providence Plantations in order to ensure their independence from the expansionist policies and intolerant practices of the Bay Colonies. Since the conversion of the Indian and trade with him were the ostensible reasons for colonization advanced by all parties and since the granting of the charter coincided with the publication of *A Key,* it was only natural for both Williams's supporters and opponents to treat the book as evidence of his success as a colonial agent both in England and America.

Throughout the eighteenth century, the utilitarian approach persisted, accompanied by the conditioning political bias. For if, on the one hand, the way Cotton Mather describes the book—a "little relation, with observations," wherein Williams "*spiritualizes* the *curiosities*"—indicates his recognition of the more than factual value of *A Key,* his unacknowledged use of the work in the *Magnalia Christi Americana* as a source book for his "life" of John Eliot, the orthodox and hence more acceptable missionary to the Indians, continues the political and non-literary treatment of the work (*Magnalia,* p. 499).

In 1794 and 1798 the Massachusetts Historical Society printed two series of extracts from *A Key,* first, the passages dealing with the customs of the Indians and, later, the vocabulary sections. While the utilitarian approach would seem to be the rationale behind such a procedure, when one considers both the nature of the omitted passages and the editing of those included, other motives come into focus. Missing from the Massachusetts versions of *A Key* are the observations and poems which conclude the individual chapters—the sections in which Williams's criticism of the New English and admiration for the Indian are most pointedly expressed. A similar principle seems to characterize the edited sections; for example, missing from the following description of the Indian manner of salutation is the word we italicize here: "I have seen the party *reverently* doe obeysance"; or again, omitted from Williams's observation of the Edenic nature of native clothing is the phrase, "after the patterne of their and our first Parents." Numerous other examples are recorded in the textual notes to the present edition; thus suffice it to say that the work presented by these first modern publishers of Williams's book is a straightforward linguistic and cultural record of the Indian—a work in no way suggestive of either the artistic form or frequently ironic tone of the original *Key*.

Since the copy from which the Massachusetts Historical Society prepared their version was then thought to be the only one extant in America, Williams's work was known, for more than thirty years after it, only in this truncated and neutralized form. It was not until the second quarter of the nineteenth century that the original dimensions of *A Key* were restored, but again from essentially a non-literary and an understandably partisan point of view. In 1827 the Rhode Island Historical Society reprinted *A Key* as the first volume of their *Collections*. Here, speaking of Roger Williams's work in general, the editors provide the following significant assessment: "In regard to the literary attainments of Roger Williams it is deemed proper to say but little. The readers of this work will be principally such as chuse to form their *own* opinions. It will be, however, generally admitted, that his Style, abounds with the Beauties and Defects, peculiar to the Literature of his own Times. It is no small praise to say of him, that, as an author, he compares well with his great opponent, Cotton" (RIHS, p. 15).

A Key also constitutes the greater part of the first volume of the publication by the Narragansett Club of Williams's complete works (1866–74). Their choice of J. Hammond Trumbull, an accomplished linguist, as editor in itself best expresses their approach to the work, while his singling out the association of the book and the charter as of "peculiar interest" recalls the initial appraisals of *A Key*.

With Moses Coit Tyler's *History of American Literature during Colonial Times, A Key* began to be appreciated for its historical rather than utilitarian value, with ancestor worship generally replacing the former political biases: "through all, whether in verse or prose, runs a gentle and liberal tone, that note of magnanimity, compassion, personal freedom and freshness, to be heard all along the life of this man" (Tyler, p. 213). Not content with the general literary status thus given *A Key,* in *The First Century of New England Verse* Harold Jantz describes Williams as "the finest poet among the heretics," and then after pointedly lamenting the "strange fate" which Williams's verses have suffered at the hands of "literary historians," he goes on to suggest that were his poems anthologized they would certainly become favorites (Jantz, p. 7). Both Kenneth Silverman and Harrison T. Meserole have responded to this suggestion, extracting a number of poems from *A Key* for their recent anthologies.

Despite the fact that to isolate Williams's poems makes for as much misinterpretation as the earlier practice of extracting his observations, to these anthologists, and to Perry Miller who reproduces a considerable body of excerpts from *A Key* in his critical collection of selected writings of Williams, and to Josephine Piercy who refers to *A Key* in her discussion of the blend of the scientific and literary in seventeenth-century works must go the credit of bringing Williams's work into literary focus. What they have initiated, the following introduction to the literary dimensions of *A Key* attempts to bring to completion.

Concordiâ parvæ res crescunt, Discordiâ magnæ dilabuntur, in many ways the central thematic motto of *A Key,* is equally appropriate as a summary of critical approaches to the work itself, epitomizing the inadequacies of previous considerations and indicating the intentions and methods of the present edition.

General dimensions and tone

If sensitivity to diction is invaluable for any meaningful appreciation of both seventeenth-century literature in general, and work in the ironic mode in particular, for *A Key* it is prerequisite. The importance which Williams attached to words was so pronounced that he refused to use the polite address "goodman" for any but those whom he considered the regenerate (see Morgan, p. 148, n. 3), while it can be recalled that he had labeled James I a liar for his indiscriminate phraseology in granting Patents (Winthrop, pp. 116–17). Similarly, his attack upon Cotton's justification of persecution in *The Bloudy Tenent* consists largely of an almost word-by-word explication of Matt. 13:25–27. In the same way he devotes both a "proposition" and an "appendix" to prove that the Quakers' writings are "*Poor, Lame, Naked*" (*Fox*, p. 5).

But accompanying his sensitivity to connotation and etymology, and thereby frequently masking its operation, are Williams's simplicity of style and deliberate pose as naive author. His public letters characteristically conclude with "Your unworthy . . . ," while his prefaces typically include a suggestion of enforced publication: "*For the* Substance *and most of this, I suddenly drew it up, and delivered two Copies unto two eminent friends of* Jesus Christ, *and this* Nation: *But being importuned for more Copies than I was possibly able to transcribe, and being (therefore) advised by some honourable Friends, to use the help of the Press; I am thus (beyond my first* Intentions *and* Desires) *held forth in Publike*" (prefatory epistle to *The Hireling Ministry,* p. 152). And often linked with his stated reluctance to publish is a characteristic apology for the lack of artistry in his work:

> *I confess* (Madam) *it was but a* private *and* sudden discourse, *sent in private to my poor* Companion *and* Yoakfellow, *occasioned by a sudden* sickness *threatening* death, *into which, and from which it pleased the* Lord *most graciously to cast and raise her.*
>
> *The* forme *and* stile *I know will seem to this refined* Age, *too rude and barbarous: And the* truth *is, the most of it was penn'd and writ (so as seldom or never such discourses were) in the thickest of the naked* Indians *of* America, *in their very wild* houses, *and by their barbarous* fires; *when the Lord was pleased this last year (more than ordinarily) to dispose of my* abode *and* travell *amongst them. And yet, is the* Language *plaine? it is the like* Christs: *Is the composure rude? such was his outward* Beauty: *Are the tryals (seemingly) too close? such is the two edged* Sword *of his most* holy Spirit, *which pierceth between the very* Soul *and* Spirit, *and bringeth every* thought *into the* obedience *of* Christ Jesus.
>
> [Prefatory epistle to *Experiments,* p. 48]

In view of Williams's attitude to language as expressive in itself as well as being a medium for expression, it seems natural that his first work should have taken the form of a "key," at the same time that it seems logical to expect that *A Key* will demand an extra measure of attention to the subtleties of diction.

To begin, one might consider the implications of the long title of *A Key* itself, since probably it is here that many of the misconceptions concerning the work originated. While in itself the word *key* is a synonym for dictionary, the structuring of the title suggests that in this instance *key* is a metaphorical term indicating the way in which the work will use vocabulary as a means to a non-linguistic end: the movement is from language to cultural observations to spiritual observations. Language will be used as an index to a culture which in turn will function as material for spiritual insights. The *key* of the title, then, announces the metaphoric nature of the work; or as Williams says later when he more fully describes the work in his prefatory epistle: "A little *Key* may open a *Box,* where lies a *bunch of Keyes*" (p. 83). Language is a key, but *A Key* is not simply a language, a dictionary; Indian words are the language of America, but language means more than mere vocabulary.

The second valuable directive offered by the long title is the designation of the intended beneficiaries of the work and the nature of the assistance which the author proposes to provide them. Not the native but the European and all men in general, the New Englander in particular, will profit from reading *A Key;* and they will profit, again as the structuring of the title suggests, not from the language directly but rather from the "Spirituall *Observations,* Generall and Particular," arising from the "briefe *Observations* of the Customes, Manners and Worships, *&c.* of the aforesaid *Natives.*" "For want of this," says Williams about his book in the prefatory epistle, "I know what grosse *mis-takes* my selfe and others have run into" (p. 84); he has "endeavoured (as the nature of the worke would give way) to bring some short *Observations* and *Applications* home to *Europe* from *America*" (p. 87). Unlike the usual handbook for traders or missionaries, *A Key* is in large part concerned with the spiritual aids the observation of the Indian may afford the white man.

Last, by concluding with the traditional *utile et dulce* formula, Williams's title indicates that the work has been basically fashioned according to literary and artistic principles. *A Key* will be a work of art but, it must be remembered, a Puritan work of art.

The reader familiar with the "Custom House" introduction to *The Scarlet Letter* will have little difficulty in appreciating the prefatory epistle to *A Key*. Both introductions function as bridges between actual history and the imaginative reproduction of that history; both designate and define the basic artistic technique to be employed; both introduce a first-person narrator and characterize him as an isolated but humane individual at odds with his contemporaries; both operate ironically, but both have been accepted as straightforward autobiographical documents. It is here impossible to discuss these features in any great detail, but an analysis of the opening paragraphs of *A Key* will suggest the necessity of recognizing their operation throughout: "I Present you with a *Key;* I have not heard of the like, yet framed, since it pleased God to bring that mighty *Continent* of *America* to light: Others of my Countrey-men have often, and excellently, and lately written of the *Countrey* (and none that I know beyond the goodnesse and worth of it)" (p. 83). Both the formality of the opening sentence and the use of the structural term "framed" suggest that Williams's craftsmanship was careful, deliberate, and aesthetically oriented. Similarly, his allusion to the uniqueness of *A Key* may be a reference to its artistic form as well as to its linguistic content. Smith and Hariot, for example, had preceded him in describing the native; Wood had gone beyond them by including a "small Nomenclator" of Indian words in his study; the travel books of the period had popularized the observational method. *A Key* is an artistic advance over such works because Williams organizes his observations thematically instead of mechanically, because he "frames" them rather than simply recording or reporting them, and because he uses language as a means to an end.

Moreover, Williams's comment may refer to another

and equally important way in which *A Key* is unique. Although works by men such as Alexander, Hariot, Higginson, and Smith include discussions of the Indian, the tendency is to consider him as part of the exploitable potential of the country, as suggested by Smith's indiscriminate listing of the goodness of New England parts: "And surely by reason of those sandy cliffes, and cliffes of rocks, both which we saw so planted with Gardens and Corne fields, and so well inhabited with a goodly, strong and well proportioned people, besides the greatnesse of the Timber growing on them, the greatnesse of the fish, and the moderate temper of the ayre . . ." (*Description,* p. 193). Similarly, Wood presents the typical way in which the cultural habits of the Indian were viewed: "Now whereas I have written the latter part of this relation concerning the Indians, in a more light and facetious stile, than the former; because their carriage and behavior hath afforded more matter of mirth, and laughter, than gravity and wisedome; and therefore I have inserted many passages of mirth concerning them, to spice the rest of my more serious discourse, and to make it more pleasant" (Wood, "To the Reader"). *A Key* differs from these works in its positive attitude toward the Indian, in its negative opinion concerning the practices of the European, and in its expression of both through the medium of language and its adjuncts.

In the passage in which Williams claims the uniqueness of *A Key,* it is criticism of his fellow Europeans that is being expressed through an ironic comment upon their literary handling of the American subject. *A Key* will go beyond such literature by exposing it, and by expressing at the same time the true meaning of America and its inhabitants through the medium of their language: "This *Key,* respects the *Native Language* of it, and happily may unlocke some *Rarities* concerning the *Natives* themselves, not yet discovered" (p. 83). Both by punning upon "respects" and "happily" and by introducing the metaphor of the chest of mysterious treasure, Williams contrasts his motives and methods with the exploitational manner of the typical explorer and the condescension of the typical cultural reporter.

A few examples will quickly demonstrate how Williams does indeed, in his own words, "suite my endeavours to my pretences" (prefatory epistle, p. 87). Wood's description of "The Indian Squaw . . . /To dive for Cocles, and to digge for Clamms,/ Whereby her lazie husbands guts shee cramms" epitomizes the stereotypic attitude toward the role of woman in Indian society (Wood, pp. 34–35); in contrast, after describing the agricultural habits of the native, Williams goes on to observe: "The Women set or plant, weede, and hill, and gather and barne all the corne, and Fruites of the field: Yet sometimes the man himselfe, (either out of love to his Wife, or care for his Children, or being an old man) will help the Woman which (by the custome of the Countrey) they are not bound to" (p. 170). Again in contrast to Wood's comment that Indian customs are typically considered a matter for mirth, Williams mentions "*Cloth inclining to white,* Which they like not, but desire to have a sad coulour without any whitish haires, suiting with their owne naturall Temper, which inclines to sadnesse" (p. 216). Similarly, the stereotype of the uncouth and inarticulate savage is neatly undermined when Williams notices that "*their Language is exceeding copious, and they have five or six words sometimes for one thing*" and then goes on to use for his example the two Indian ways of expressing the single English phrase of police address, "*I pray your Favour*" (*Directions,* pp. 90–91). In very different fashion, Williams's respect for the native language comes into focus when one contrasts his reproduction of the Indian's broken English with the following attempt by Smith to put into English Habamok's lamentation for the sick Massasowat. "My loving *Sachem,*" Smith records Habamok as saying, "my loving *Sachem,* many have I knowne, but never any like thee, nor shall ever see the like amongst the Salvages; for he was no lier, nor bloudy and cruell like other *Indians;* in anger soone reclaimed, he would be ruled by reason, not scorning the advice of meane men, and governed his men better with a few strokes, then others with many: truly loving where he loved, yea he feared wee had not a faithfull friend left amongst all his Countreymen" (*The Generall Historie,* p. 763). In Williams's record of his conversation with the dying Wequash there is nothing of the Indian who speaks like a Stuart courtier but rather an appreciation of the concreteness and pathos of the Indian mode of expression: "said he *your words were never out of my heart to this present;* and said hee *me much pray to Jesus Christ:* I told him so did many *English, French,* and *Dutch,* who had never turned to *God,* nor loved Him: He replyed in broken English: *Me so big naughty Heart, me heart all one stone! Savory expressions* using to breath *from compunct and broken Hearts,* and a sence of *inward hardnesse* and *unbrokennesse*" (prefatory epistle, p. 88).

In his attempt to teach the Indian about God Williams similarly respects their mode of language and avoids theological abstractions:

Tasuóg Maníttowock?	*How many Gods bee there?*
Maunaúog Mishaúnawock.	*Many, great many.*
Nétop machàge.	*Friend, not so.*
Paúsuck naúnt manìt.	*There is onely one God.*
Cuppíssittone.	*You are mistaken.*
Cowauwaúnemun.	*You are out of the way.*

A phrase which much pleaseth them, being proper for their wandring in the woods, and similitudes greatly please them. [P. 195]

With equal sensitivity he notes, for example, that the native calendar has "thirteen *Moneths* according to the severall *Moones:* and they give to each of them significant names," such as "*Spring moneth,*" or "*Harvest moneth*" (p. 145). It is the emblematic nature of the Indian names that makes them significant, and in this respect Williams's attitude toward the Indian language has much in common with Emerson's attack upon "this rotten diction" and his theories concerning the origin of language as set forth in *Nature*.

Finally, "This *Key,* respects the *Native Language* of it" simply by recognizing that "Indian" is the native language of America and thus that the Indian has the native right to the land. In the chapter significantly titled, "*Of the Earth, and the Fruits thereof, &c.,*" Williams makes specific observation of this point while he also destroys one of the rationalizations of an opposing point of view:

> *Obs.* The *Natives* are very exact and punctuall in the bounds of their Lands, belonging to this or that Prince or People, (even to a River, Brooke &c.) And I have knowne them make bargaine and sale amongst themselves for a small piece, or quantity of Ground: notwithstanding a sinfull opinion amongst many that Christians have right to *Heathens* Lands: but of the delusion of that phrase, I have spoke in a discourse concerning the *Indians* Conversion. [P. 167]

It is a "sinfull opinion" in two respects: first, because the term *Christian,* by being wrongly applied to entire nations, includes many non- and even anti-Christians; second, because not even Christians have a right to dispossess the native Indian. The first, the theological issue, is discussed, as Williams points out, in the "discourse" *Christenings;* the second argument is the "Patent" controversy, and is best outlined in *Cotton's Letter* (pp. 40–47) and Smith's *Advertisements* (pp. 934–36), and best refuted practically in Williams's dealings, and artistically in *A Key*.

Having suggested the basic dimensions of *A Key* by distinguishing it from other "American" literature, Williams goes on to describe its genesis, emphasizing the non-professional and unsophisticated character of its author:

> I drew the *Materialls* in a rude lumpe at Sea, as a private *helpe* to my owne memory, that I might not by my present absence *lightly lose* what I had so *dearely bought* in some few yeares *hardship,* and *charges* among the *Barbarians;* yet being reminded by some, what pitie it were to bury those *Materialls* in my *Grave* at land or Sea; and withall, remembring how oft I have been importun'd by *worthy friends,* of all sorts, to afford them some helps this way. I resolved (by the assistance of *the most High*) to cast those *Materialls* into this *Key, pleasant* and *profitable* for *All,* but specially for my *friends* residing in those parts.
>
> [Prefatory epistle, p. 83]

While this description has its origin in fact, the reader familiar with other of Williams's writings will realize that the fact has been shaped to fit a formula—the naive and reluctant author—discussed above. Further, through the use of the extended sculpture and profit metaphors, Williams demonstrates his artistic ability and ironic bent at the same time that he presents himself as an unassuming man with a plain and practical purpose. Just as language is a means to an end in *A Key,* therefore, so behind the "unworthy Country-man" who signs the prefatory epistle stands Roger Williams.

All of which is not to say that *A Key* does not contain evangelical and linguistic directives, but that these are subordinate to the controlling artistic dimension: "A little *Key* may open a *Box,* where lies a *bunch* of *Keyes.*" To treat either the literal-lexicographic, or the prose-cultural, or the poetic-moral dimensions of the book in isolation is to forget that the individual "keys" can be legitimately obtained only by discovering the master key.

Theme and structure

Again we are aided by Williams's own directive: "A Dictionary *or* Grammer *way I had consideration of, but purposely avoided, as not so accommodate to the Benefit of all, as I hope this Forme is*" (*Directions,* p. 90). Instead of employing a lexicographic format, Williams decided to structure *A Key* as a history of the Indians "from their *Birth* to their *Burialls*," as he explains in the prefatory epistle (p. 87). Hence the first of the thirty-two chapters is entitled "*Of Salutation*," and the thirty-second chapter is headed "Of Death *and* Buriall." Upon closer observation one discovers that the chapters are also so grouped as to focus upon the Indian before and then after "civilization." An examination of this movement suggests that the structure of *A Key* could further be called elegiac and its theme could be called that of the "fall."

The first section or movement consists of chapters I through VII. As the chapter headings suggest, Williams's focus in this section—"Of *Eating* and *Entertainment*," "*Concerning* Sleepe *and* Lodging," "*Of the Family and businesse of the House*"—is upon the basic physical features of native life. But in addition to this topical arrangement, the section also evidences a logical and narrative development. In chapter I we greet and are greeted by our native host. Chapter II invites the reader to sample Indian hospitality and food. So quite naturally the third chapter finds the rested and refreshed European asleep in the Indian house. A lesson in numbers, very useful for next morning's trading, constitutes the next chapter, and by way of an observation upon the natural orientation of the natives' arithmetic, we move to the next chapter's concern with the way natural affections determine their marital and social organization. Chapter VI begins with a comment upon the communal respect for the family unit, and then goes on to deal with the division of labor among the natives. The final chapter in this section —"Of *their Persons* and *parts of body*"—is concerned with the physical virtues and natural stamina of the Indian, and moving as it does from the brain down through all parts of the body and introducing observations on aspects of Indian life related to the respective parts, this chapter also functions as a summary of the first section.

From this concrete dramatization and particular presentation of the life of the native, Williams comes to the general conclusion that from the "natural" point of view the "savage" is in no sense inferior to the civilized European, and that in respect to *natural* virtue he is undeniably superior:

> There is a savour of *civility* and *courtesie* even amongst these wild *Americans,* both amongst *themselves* and towards *strangers.* [P. 99]

> It is a strange *truth,* that a man shall generally finde more free entertainment and refreshing amongst these *Barbarians,* then amongst thousands that call themselves *Christians.* [P. 104]

> Nature knowes no difference between *Europe* and *Americans* in blood, birth, bodies, &c. God having of one blood made all mankind . . . . [P. 133]

Unlike the typical primitivist, Thomas Morton of Merrymount for example, Williams the Puritan cannot rest in his admiration for natural man. As noble as the Indian is, as humane, as handsome, he is nevertheless irretrievably damned in his natural state—an attitude that can best be defined as tragic primitivism, the only kind of primitivism allowed to the Calvinist, a primitivism in which one's intellectual commitments may be at odds with one's emotional response. For example, the following is Roger Williams's illustration of the theological point that "*No spiritual object* [can be] *seen with a natural eye*":

> But now let's descend to *Cultus Institutus* and *Cultus Naturalis,* an *Instituted,* and a natural *Worship.* Come to the light of nature worshipping this *Deity:* Come to the seven precepts of *Noah,* which some, both *Jewes,* and other ancients, talk of; and then I ask, if it be not a downright Doctrine of *Free-will,* in depraved nature? If it be not to run pointblank against all the *Histories* of the *Nations,* and all present *Experience* of mankind, in all known parts of the World, to attribute so much *Light* to any of the *Eldest* and *Gallantest* sons of Nature, as to attain a

> *Spiritual* and saving knowledge of *God,* to attain a love unto *God,* in all their knowledge; to attain the mystery of the *Father* and of the *Son, God* manifested in Flesh, by whom *Creation* and *Redemption* are wrought; to the matter of true worship, or to any thing but *Splendidum Peccatum,* without the Revelation of the *Word* and *Spirit* of *God,* out of his absolute, free, and peculiar Grace and Mercy in Christ Jesus. [*The Examiner Defended,* p. 242]

Yet but a little further in the same tract he attacks those who would interpret this doctrine too literally, who would confuse the spiritual and the material in attempting to measure precisely the means to salvation:

> And howsoever some grant that as to the visible profession of the *Christian Religion,* a distinct knowledge of Christ Jesus is necessary, Yet we know what is extant abroad of a possibility of Salvation, without an express and distinct knowledge of the name of Christ, according to that of *Heb.* 1. He that comes to *God,* must believe that *God* is, and that he is a *Rewarder* of them that diligently seek him. And I ask, Whether (although it be a duty to work out Salvation with fear and trembling, and to grow in the *Grace* and *Knowledge* of the *Lord Jesus)* yet is it not very presumptuous and dangerous to set a *Ne plus infra,* a *stint* and *bound* of so much *Knowledge,* and so much grace of Christ (as to the degrees of it) without which there is no Salvation. [P. 271]

With even greater vehemence in *Christenings,* he attacks those who would make conversion a matter of nation rather than of the individual, and in the process reveals the emotional reasons for his "relative" Calvinism:

> Now Secondly, for the hopes of CONVERSION, and turning the People of *America* unto God: There is no respect of Persons with him, for we are all the worke of his hands; from the rising of the Sunne to the going downe thereof, his name shall be great among the nations from the East & from the West, &c. If we respect their sins, they are far short of *European* sinners: They

> neither abuse such corporall mercies for they have them not; nor sin they against the Gospell light, (which shines not amongst them) as the men of *Europe* do: And yet if they were greater sinners then they are, or greater sinners then the *Europeans,* they are not the further from the great *Ocean* of mercy in that respect.
>
> [*Christenings,* p. 35; see also *Fox,* p. 130]

With all his heart Williams admires the natural Indian but, his theology tells him, that way "*Splendidum Peccatum*" lies. And in *A Key,* this tension between the head and heart is simply but poignantly expressed when in the prefatory epistle he writes, "I dare not conjecture in these *Uncertainties,* I believe they are *lost,* and yet hope (in the Lords holy season) some of the wildest of them shall be found to share in the blood of the Son of God," and a little further, "I know not with how little *Knowledge* and *Grace* of Christ, the Lord may save, and therefore neither will *despaire,* nor *report* much" (pp. 86–87).

The artistic implication of this internal conflict becomes clearer in chapter VIII of *A Key,* a chapter which functions as a most ingenious transition from the first to the second section. The chapter is entitled, "Of *Discourse* and *Newes,*" and after a brief dialogue illustrating the subject, Williams observes, "Their desire of, and delight in newes, is great, as the *Athenians,* and all men, more or lesse; a stranger that can relate newes in their owne language, they will stile him *Manittóo,* a God" (p. 134). By comparing the Indians to the Athenians (both explicitly and implicitly by paraphrasing Acts 17:21), Williams underlines the potential nobility of pre-Christian man; by noting the Indians' religious reaction to a messenger bearing good news, he implies that which the natural man lacks and for which he is constantly seeking—the "good news" of the Gospel.

Having Revelation, the civilized European is superior to the Indian, but only if he responds accordingly. That by far and large he does not is dramatized in the parable which follows: old Canonicus, well aware of European perfidy, is allowed to illustrate the fact in a most impressive manner. "He tooke a sticke, and broke it into ten pieces, and related ten instances (laying downe a sticke to every instance) which gave him cause thus to feare and say . . ." (pp. 131–37). And immediately following this removal by default of the white man's claim to moral superiority is a small dialogue which leads to the observation that the native word for "I believe you," like the Greek, also means "I will obey." Unlike the Englishman who has separate words (most conveniently) for each of these ideas, who obeys when he does not believe and who believes when he does not obey, the Indians and the Greeks are closest to the New Testament usage. Not only, then, is the Indian naturally superior, potentially he may also be spiritually superior.

Furthermore, although because of his illiteracy the savage cannot read the "Book of the Word," he can and does read the "Book of the Creatures." For, "The *Sunne* and *Moone,* and *Starres* and *seasons* of the yeere doe preach a *God* to all the sonnes of men, that they which know no letters, doe yet read an *eternall Power* and *God-head* in these" (pp. 145–46). Thus for the second stage in man's history and development —his need of, his search for, his discovery of God—Williams presents a lesson in natural theology which takes the form of an acclimatization of the Genesis story. For example, the section—chapters IX through XX—begins with a discussion of the way the native uses "those *Heavenly Lights*" to tell the time of day: "The *Sunne* and *Moone,* in the observation of all the *sonnes* of *men,* even the wildest, are the great *Directors* of the *day* and *night;* as it pleased *God* to appoint in the first *Creation*" p. 142). In similar fashion Williams reads the spiritual lessons of the seasons, the weather, the wind, and then moves from the firmament to the earth and the fruits thereof; and always in contrast to the natives' interest in and obedience to natural truths is the civilized Christians' rejection of supernatural truth. So that by virtue of contrast and innuendo, by the end of the first two sections of *A Key* Williams has created a picture, not of the "noble savage" but of the closest possible seventeenth-century approximation of the Garden and its prelapsarian attributes. Why he chose for his tribe the Narragansetts, a primarily agricultural people, now appears to have an artistic as well as a biographical answer. Instead of our modern idea that the agricultural condition is a more sophisticated one than the nomadic in the development of human society, Roger Williams believed with many of his contemporaries that the first condition of man, even before the fall, was that of *gardener,* and that the predatory and nomadic condition of the hunter was a stage in the continuing degeneration of man from the Edenic state.

> [1.] *Yeeres thousands since, God gave command*
> *(As we in Scripture find)*
> *That* Earth *and* Trees *&* Plants *should bring*
> *Forth fruits each in his kind.*
>
> [2.] *The Wildernesse remembers this,*
> *The wild and howling land*
> *Answers the toyling labour of*
> *The wildest* Indians *hand.*
>
> [3.] *But man forgets his* Maker, *who*
> *Fram'd him in Righteousnesse.*
> *A paradise in Paradise, now worse*
> *Then* Indian *Wildernesse.* [P. 172]

The prelapsarian "paradise within" (see *Paradise Lost* 12. 587) as a result of the fall has become an unweeded garden, "*worse*" than the American Wilderness, which paradoxically has not yet entirely lost its pristine immediacy to the Creator, and continues to respond to His original command, even though civilized man, removed as he is from the Wilderness, forgets his Maker. By emphasizing the harmony between the Indian and nature, Williams is able to present America as both the wilderness of Eden and the original Garden of Paradise, and the Indian consequently as both the wild and Edenic man.

And at this point one is best prepared to understand Williams's theory as to the "*Originall* and *Descent*" of the Indian. "From *Adam* and *Noah* that they spring, it is granted on all hands," he writes in the prefatory epistle (p. 85). Since Adam was the first man, and since only the family of Noah survived the Deluge, and since, as he continues his observation, he passes over more scientific and historical theories, such as their northern Asiatic origin, and proceeds to notice the affinity of their customs with those of the Old Testament Jews, one concludes that Williams's purpose is to make the Hebraic descent of the Indian a direct one. And when one considers Williams's "Indian" version of the creation of man one begins to understand his logic:

Wuttàke wuchè wuckee-sittin pausuck Enìn, *or,* Eneskéetomp Wuche mishquòck,	*Last of all he made one Man* *Of red Earth,*
Ka wesuonckgonnakaûnes Adam, túppautea mishquòck. Wuttàke-wuchè, Câwit míshquock,	*And call'd him Adam,* or *red Earth.* *Then afterward, while Adam,* or *red Earth slept,*
Wuckaudnúmmenes manìt peetaúgon wuchè Adam,	*God tooke a rib from Adam,* or *red Earth,*
Kà wuchè peteaúgon Wukkeesitínnes pausuck squàw, Kà pawtouwúnnes Adâm-uck.	*And of that rib he made One woman,* *And brought her to Adam.*

[P. 196]

The importance of Williams's emphasis upon the meaning of the name *Adam* cannot be overstressed. First, biblical scholars regard the derivation of the word as doubtful. One school of thought derives it from a root meaning "red" (see *Edom*, Gen. 25:30), another follows Gen. 2:7, where there is a play on the word for "ground." In combining these two interpretations to describe the origin of the first man, Williams is clearly asserting the Adamic nature of the "red" Indian. This is not simply a bow to the Indian's sensibilities; it is one of the cornerstones of Williams's primitivism; it is what *allows* him as a Puritan Englishman to be a primitivist.

Through the Hebraic descent of the Indian, then, Williams defines the role of the native in his brief American epic; through noting their affinity with another pre-Christian people, the Athenians, he is able to define his own role as missionary. "Yet againe I have found a greater *Affinity* of their Language with the *Greek* Tongue," Williams writes in the prefatory epistle (p. 86). And as we have seen, in describing the Indians' desire for news—both profane and spiritual—and in discussing their word for believe-obey, he has already compared them to the Athenians, the noblest of pre-Christians. The Indian, in short,—"*As wise, as faire, as strong, as personall*" (p. 133)—is the American counterpart of the Athenian; Roger Williams, in bringing to them the Pauline "Glad tidings," is the seventeenth-century Apostle to the Gentiles. In his typological view of things, Roger Williams and the Narragansett Indians form the American spiritual antitype to the New Testament type of Paul and the Athenian Greeks.

In the first place, while Williams's narratives of his physical hardships have autobiographical foundation, they also seem to indicate his awareness that the parallels to those of Paul which he sees in his own experiences have prophetic and typological significance; they represent for him the working-out in America of the pattern of the voyages of conversion at the beginning of Christianity. In the prefatory epistle, for example, Williams writes: "I have run through varieties of *Intercourses* with them Day and Night, Summer and Winter, by Land and Sea" (p. 87); Paul's famous narrative of his sufferings as the Apostle to the Gentiles reads: "In journeyings often, in perils of waters, in perils of robbers, in perils by mine own countrymen, in perils by the heathen, in perils in the city, in perils in the wilderness, in perils in the sea, in perils among false brethren; In weariness and painfulness, in watchings often, in hunger and thirst, in fastings often, in cold and nakedness" (2 Cor.11: 26–27). In chapter XI, "Of *Travell*," Williams observes of the Indian word for "*We are distrest undone,* or *in misery,*" "They use this word properly in wandring toward Winter night, in which case I have been many a night with them, and many times also alone, yet always mercifully preserved" (p. 15). Chapters XIV and XVIII continue the Pauline parallels, now on the water. In the former, entitled "Of the Winds," the reference to "*dreadfull stormes*" in the concluding poem reminds one of Jonah and Paul and their perilous sea voyages on the Lord's business; in the latter, it is the narrative of Paul's voyage and shipwreck in Acts 27 that is evoked by both the dialogue and then the observation: "I having been necessitated to passe waters diverse times with them, it hath pleased God to make them many times the instruments of my preservation: and when sometimes in great danger I have questioned safety, they have said to me: Feare not, if we be overset I will carry you safe to Land" (p. 178). But if that parallel holds, then the fact that in Acts 27:23 it is the "angel of God" who appears to Paul in a dream, "Saying, fear not," must contain certain implications regarding Williams's attitude toward his Indian companions. Thus on two accounts it comes as no surprise that Williams should conclude this Pauline chapter with a paraphrase of Romans 11:33, the very epistle in which Paul defines his role as the Apostle to the Gentiles and argues that both Israelites and Gentiles can be saved. Paul's voyage across the Mediterranean to the Romans was arduous enough, but Williams seems uninclined to yield place to Paul in view of his own three-thousand mile ocean journey to these latter-day Gentiles: "How unsearchable are the depth of the Wisedome and Power of God in separating from *Europe, Asia* and *Africa* such a mightie vast continent as *America* is? and that for so many ages? as also, by such a Westerne Ocean of about three thousand of *English* miles breadth in passage over?" (p. 179). The irony of Williams's paraphrase, however, points to a crucial difference between his position and that of Paul's. The Athenians were civilized (Greece was part of the mainland and there had been contact between Greece and Old Testament Palestine; and in both the geographical and cultural areas Paul was consequently much less separated initially from his converts than was Williams) and not the least of Paul's advantages was that he could speak an understood language; Roger Williams had to learn Narragansett, and the Indians were not civilized. Believing as he did, that "Christenings make not Christians," that an Indian cannot be truly converted until he is civilized, and being all too aware of the barbarousness of European civilization, Williams here rhetorically enunciates his tragic primitivism once more.

In the succeeding chapter, suitably concerned with "Of *Fish* and *Fishing*," he brings his American "idyll" to an end by empirically observing that in the case of "*Sturgeon*," for example, "the Natives for the goodnesse and greatnesse of it, much prize it, and will neither furnish the *English* with so many, nor so cheape, that any great trade is like to be made of it, untill the *English* themselves are fit to follow the fishing" (p. 180), and by concluding that:

[3.] *Christs little ones must hunted be,*
Devour'd, yet rise as Hee.
And eate up those which now a while
Their fierce devourers be. [P. 184]

Chapter XX begins the final movement of *A Key*, being concerned with the fall as is suggested by its symbolic title—"Of *their nakednesse* and *clothing*"—and with the fall from a natural to a European civilized state as Williams's observation indicates. When "within doores" they are "wholly naked" except "their secret parts, covered with a little Apron, after the patterne of their and our first Parents." Their outdoor clothing, on the other hand, consists of a "Beasts skin, or an English mantle" (p. 185). To continue with the Genesis parallel, it should be remembered that indoors, that is in the Garden, Adam and Eve were naked, and that it was not until the fall that they recognized their nakedness and clothed themselves, however, in aprons of fig leaves, and that later God took pity upon their poor naked condition and clothed them in garments made of the skins of beasts. One question arises: what role might the European play in this modern correspondence to the story of the fall of man?

"While they are amongst the *English* they keep on the *English* apparell, but pull of all, as soone as they come againe into their owne Houses, and Company" (p. 187). In man's continuing degeneration since the fall, Williams sees three stages of clothing: first, aprons as the Indians wear; second, "coats of skins" with which the Lord clothed Adam and Eve later (Gen. 3:21), and which the Indians also wear; third, fashionable European clothes which the Indians reject as impractical; one might also conjecture that since the Indian is in the second stage of sartorial degeneration at worst, he is closer morally to the Adamic condition. Of related significance is Milton's comparison of Adam and Eve's nakedness to that of the Indian:

> Such of late
> *Columbus* found th'*American* so girt
> With feathered Cincture, naked else and wild
> Among the Trees on Iles and woodie Shores.
> [*Paradise Lost* 9. 1115–18]

This is not to say that to Roger Williams civilization was by definition evil. On the contrary, as we have seen, his premise is that civilization is essential to christianization, and that the Athenian to whom he positively refers in his discussion of the natural virtues of the Indian was highly civilized. Rather it is Europe's type of civilization that constitutes the fall, a civilization in which Christianity is as superficial as clothing. To civilize the Indian under such circumstances is to corrupt him, and yet without it there can be no conversion. Consequently, in his attitude toward civilization we find the split we also found in his attitude toward the moral situation of the native. On the lighter side, one might notice that in the description in chapter VI of the careful locking of the "artificiall" door made of "*English* boards and nailes," it is not the stupidity of the native but the ludicrous aspects of natural man's being induced to ape civilized man's customs that is illustrated in the comic climax—the exit from the chimney (p. 122). More seriously, one might consider what Williams has to say in chapter IX after observing that the Indians make a God of the Sun:

> 2. *They have no helpe of* Clock *or* Watch,
> *And* Sunne *they* overprize.
> *Having those artificiall helps, the* Sun
> *We unthankfully despise.* [Pp. 142–43]

The English undervalue God's creation while the Indian overvalues it and becomes an idolator. Of the two evils, asks Williams, which is worse?

But whatever his feelings about it, civilization has entered the American wilderness, and from chapter XX till the end of the work we explore the pathology of the European infection of America. Whereas the first two sections of the work focused upon the natural virtues and environment of the native American, this last section is concerned with the less admirable and more "civilized" characteristics of the Indian in seventeenth-century New England, which nevertheless are yet preferable to the English in Old England.

For example, in "*Of Religion, the soule, &c.*," the first chapter after the "fall," we find both a description of the "papist-like" idolatry of the Indian form of worship and an indictment of orthodox missionary activities. It concludes with the general observation: "The wandring Generations of *Adams* lost posteritie, having lost the true and living God their Maker, have created out of the nothing of their owne inventions many false and fained Gods and Creators" (p. 200). Yet in the same chapter we are told, "He that questions whether God made the World, the *Indians* will teach him" (p. 189), suggesting that belief in even a false God is preferable to sophisticated European skepticism (see also *Bloudy Tenent,* p. 290).

Thus while the contrast between English and Indian is present in both the first and last sections of *A Key,* in the later chapters a second contrast is also in operation that doubles the satiric and tragic tone and at the same time universalizes Williams's theme. This is the contrast between the Indian before and after the fall, since *A Key* is so structured that subjects treated in the first section are treated from another point of view in the later sections. For example, in chapter XVI one finds the following description of communal living: "With friendly joyning they breake up their fields, build their Forts, hunt the Woods, stop and kill fish in the Rivers, it being true with them as in all the World in the Affaires of Earth or Heaven: By concord little things grow great, by discord the greatest come to nothing . . ." (p. 170). Like Eden before the fall, so America before the arrival of the English—a perfectly natural and idyllic existence. But so also the dream of the first New England settlements, and in particular the organizational principle of the Providence Plantation itself. In chapter XXII, following "religion" as a prelapsarian subject, one finds such entirely different observations on government as "The *Sachims,* although they have an absolute Monarchie over the people; yet they will not conclude of ought that concernes all, either Lawes, or Subsides, or warres, unto which the people are averse, and by gentle perswasion cannot be brought" (p. 202). While still better than the English, then, the Indian now, however, is less naturally sociable than before: "The most usuall Custome amongst them in executing punishments, is for the *Sachim* either to beat, or whip, or put to death with his owne hand, to which the common sort most quietly submit: though sometimes the *Sachim* sends a secret Executioner, one of his chiefest Warriours to fetch of a head, by some sudden unexpected blow of a Hatchet, when they have feared Mutiny by publike execution" (p. 203). And thus the chapter comes to the following general observation: "The wildest of the sonnes of Men have ever found a necessity, (for preservation of themselves, their Families and Properties) to cast themselves into some Mould or forme of Government" (p. 204).

This passage is an instance of the basic agreement between the theological naturalism of the American Puritan and the political naturalism of Hobbes, who makes a very similar statement in *Leviathan.* For Hobbes, the natural condition of man is one of constant warfare, which is as good a definition as any of the Christian idea of the fallen state of man. In the natural condition there is no opportunity for any kind of civilization, "and which is worst of all, continuall feare, and danger of violent death; and the life of man, solitary, poore, nasty, brutish, and short." And thus the necessity of the individual's yielding up a large part of his personal power to a newly created central Authority. At least in the case of the Narragansetts, however, Williams would not agree that "the savage people in many places of *America,* except the government of small Families, the concord whereof dependeth on naturall lust, have no government at all; and live at this day in that brutish manner . . ." (*Leviathan,* chap. XIII). It comes as no surprise, then, that the first "social contract" recorded in modern times was drawn up at Plymouth in 1620, "for our better ordering and preservation and furtherance of the ends aforesaid. . . . After this they chose . . . their Governor for that year" (Bradford, p. 76).

Another way in which the contrast between the first and later sections of *A Key* is emphasized is in the shift from the pre-Christian people Williams uses as a type for the Indian: in the first part, as we have seen, the Indian was compared with the Athenian; in the final chapters it is the Old Testament that provides the pattern: "They have an exact forme of King, Priest, and Prophet, as was in Israel typicall of old in that holy Land of *Canaan,* and as the Lord *Jesus* ordained in his spirituall Land of *Canaan* his Church throughout the whole World . . ." (p. 192). These observations suggest again his paradoxical attitude toward the Indian: on the one hand, America is the antitype of "that holy Land of *Canaan*"; on the other, the Americans are like the "lost" tribes of Israel, still awaiting the advent of Christ and his transformation of the "exact forme" into its spiritual antitype. But what is understandable, even admirable, in the Indian, is quite the opposite in the civilized and Christian world. Thus by establishing a theocracy, the Massachusetts Bay Colonies are not only hopelessly literal-minded but they are also anti-Christian worldlings (see *Bloudy Tenent,* p. 416; and *The Examiner Defended,* p. 251).

The marriage customs of the Narragansetts similarly reflect the Old Testament laws: "Generally the Husband gives these payments for a Dowrie, (as it was in *Israell*) to the Father or Mother, or guardian of the Maide" (p. 206). The sexual morality of the Narragansetts is also like that of the Old Testament Jews, with whom "if a man entice a maid that is not betrothed, and lie with her, he shall surely endow her to be his wife. If her father utterly refuse to give her unto him, he shall pay money according to the dowry of virgins" (Exod. 22:16–17). But for adultery, the death penalty is exacted of both parties (Lev. 20:10):

Obs. Single fornication they count no sin, but after Mariage (which they solemnize by consent of Parents and publique approbation publiquely) then they count it hainous for either of them to be false.

Mammaûsu.	*An adulterer.*
Nummam mógwun ewò.	*He hath wronged my bed.*
Pallè nochisquaûaw.	*He* or *She hath committed adultery.*

Obs. In this case the wronged party may put away or keepe the party offending: commonly, if the Woman be false, the offended Husband will be solemnly revenged upon the offendor, before many witnesses, by many blowes and wounds, and if it be to Death, yet the guilty resists not, nor is his Death revenged. [P. 205]

And while the need for such regulations was not mentioned in the early chapter on marriage, even greater than this difference is that between the "esteeme of the Mariage bed" by the pagan Indian and by the Christian European:

[1.] *When Indians heare that some there are,*
(That Men the Papists call)
Forbidding Mariage Bed and yet,
To thousand Whoredomes fall. [P. 208]

In Milton's description of the prelapsarian Adam and Eve a similar difference is noted:

Handed they went; and eas'd the putting off
These troublesom disguises which wee wear,
Strait side by side were laid, nor turnd I ween
Adam from his fair Spouse, nor *Eve* the Rites
Mysterious of connubial Love refus'd:
Whatever Hypocrites austerely talk
Of puritie and place and innocence,
Defaming as impure what God declares
Pure, and commands to som, leaves free to all.
Our Maker bids increase, who bids abstain
But our Destroyer, foe to God and Man?
Hail wedded Love . . . . [*Paradise Lost* 4. 739–50]

Between Williams and Milton, however, there is this difference: in attempting to describe what was, Milton cannot forget what is; in attempting to record what is, Williams cannot forget what was. Milton's readers are encouraged to debate "*felix culpa*" versus "*infelix malus*"; Williams's readers are given less choice:

> O the infinite wisedome of the most holy wise *God,* who hath so advanced *Europe,* above *America,* that there is not a sorry *Howe, Hatchet, Knife,* nor a rag of cloth in all *America,* but what comes over the dreadfull *Atlantick* Ocean from *Europe:* and yet that *Europe* be not proud, nor *America* discouraged. What treasures are hid in some parts of *America,* and in our *New-English* parts, how have foule hands (in smoakie houses) the first handling of those Furres which are after worne upon the hands of Queens and heads of Princes? [P. 220]

As in the work of many of his contemporaries, the conclusion of *A Key* is apocalyptic; but unlike the traditional apocalyptic vision it is also very ironic. America has proved to be not the "New English Canaan" but the "Old English Egypt" writ large. The American Garden, through the process of discovery and exploitation, has *become* the American Wilderness; the dream has become the nightmare. This is the boxed secret that has been revealed and, accordingly, in the concluding lines of the work the key to a continent is exchanged for the keys of the heavenly door.

Chapter structure and the emblematic mode

After explaining, in "Directions for the use of the Language," why he has not structured *A Key* according to a "Dictionary *or* Grammer *way,*" Wiliams goes on to suggest the organizational principle of the individual chapter: "*A* Dialogue *also I had thoughts of, but avoided for brevities sake, and yet (with no small paines) I have so framed every Chapter and the matter of it, as I may call it an Implicite Dialogue*" (p. 90).

Each chapter of *A Key* consists of three basic and integrated parts: the vocabulary, the observations, and the poem. The vocabulary reveals an "*Implicite Dialogue*" in two ways. First, since "*The* English *for every* Indian *word or phrase stands in a straight line directly against the* Indian" (p. 90), and because the English translation is italicized, the vocabulary sections visually suggest a dramatic interchange, a formal conversation between an Indian and an Englishman. Realizing this one understands why it is necessary to retain the original format and to print both sides of the conversation. But in addition to this horizontal and visual type of dialogue, the vocabulary sections also present a vertical and verbal type of exchange. Instead of focusing upon the grammatical variations of single words, Williams's method is to concentrate upon phrases, questions, and sentences, then to organize these elements so as to create the impression either of two speakers engaged in interchange or of a speaker addressing and responding to an implied audience. This dialogue principle explains why the vocabulary sections vary in length from chapter to chapter and why words and phrases are repeated in different contexts. Frequently, furthermore, the vocabulary quite explicitly takes a narrative or dramatic form. By way of example one might consider the hunting dialogue in chapter XXVII which has for its anticlimax the prototypic American hunting accident followed by the proverbial tall tale:

Ntauchaûmen.	*I goe to hunt.*
Ncáttiteam weeyoùs.	*I long for Venison.*
Auchaûtuck.	*Let us hunt.*
Nowetauchaûmen.	*I will hunt with you.*
Anúmwock.	*Dogs.*
Kemehétteas.	*Creepe.*
Pìtch nkemehétteem.	*I will creepe.*
Pumm púmmoke.	*Shoote.*
Uppetetoûa.	*A man shot accidentally.*
Ntaumpauchaûmen.	*I come from hunting.*

Cutchashineánna?	*How many have you kild?*
Nneesnneánna.	*I have kild two.*
Shwinneánna.	*Three.*
Nyowinneánna.	*Foure.*
Npiuckwinneánna.	*Ten, &c.*
Nneesneechecttashín-neánna.	*Twentie.*

[Pp. 224–25]

As another and more sober example of the dramatic nature of the vocabulary sections one might consider the interchange presented in chapter XXV, "*Of buying and selling*":

Natouashóckquittea.	*A Smith.*
Kuttattaúamish aûke.	*I would buy land of you.*
Tou núckquaque?	*How much?*
Wuche wuttotânick.	*For a Towne,* or, *Plantation.*
Nissékineam.	*I have no mind to sell.*
Indiánsuck sekineámwock.	*The Indians are not willing.*
Noonapúock naûgum.	*They want roome themselves.*
Cowetompátimmin.	*We are friends.*
Cummaugakéamish.	*I will give you land.*
Aquìe chenawaûsish.	*Be not churlish.*

[Pp. 219–20]

The climax of this dialogue dramatizes Williams's own experience: "I have acknowledged (and have and shall endeavor to maintain) the rights and property of every inhabitant of Rhode Island in peace; yet, since there is so much sound and noise of purchase and purchasers, I judge it not unseasonable to declare the rise and bottom of the planting of Rhode Island in the fountain of it: It was not price nor money that could have purchased Rhode Island. Rhode Island was purchased by love; by the love and favor which that honorable gentleman Sir Henry Vane and myself had with that great Sachem, Miantonomo . . ." (*Letters,* pp. 305–06).

The second major part of each chapter consists of two kinds of "*observations.*" The first of these may be described as specific and experiential, and takes the form of anecdote or explanation; consequently, it may either precede or follow the vocabulary as the context requires. Its function is twofold: first, to expand, clarify, and comment upon the subject of the vocabulary in the friendly tones of the expert addressing the layman; and second, by recourse to personal experience, to establish the credentials of the commentator and thus to qualify him for his succeeding role as explicator of the spiritual significance of the issue dramatized in the chapter.

And here arises something of a problem for Williams. His purpose, which he pointedly suggests in the prefatory epistle, is to "present (not mine opinion, but) my *Observations*" (p. 86), and his favorite technique, in general, is to silence his erudite opponents by empirically questioning their armchair arguments: "I mused in myself (being much acquainted with the *Natives*) what *G. Fox* should mean, he not having been in *N. England* when he wrote that passage . . ." (*Fox,* p. 309). On the other hand, if he described too vividly the pagan ceremonies and heathenish habits of the Indian, his opponents could conclude that he was himself of the Devil's party. Williams's tactic is to introduce the problematic issue by relating the Indian habit to the practice of so-called civilized man and then to anticipate criticism by emphasizing that his observation preceded his awareness of the moral implications. In chapter XXVIII, "Of *their* Gaming, *&c,*" he begins with the comparison: "Their *Games,* (like the *English*)," and after describing them goes on, "none of which I durst ever be present at, that I might not countenance and partake of their folly, after I once saw the evill of them" (p. 229). Or again, in chapter XXI, it is only after noting that the Dionysiac aspects of the Indians' feasting resemble the preservation of such pagan practices in the Christian world, such as the Papist observation of Christmas, and that these ceremonies are instigated and conducted by their "*Priests,*" that he explains: "I confesse to have most of these their customes by their owne Relation, for after once being in their Houses and beholding what their Worship was, I durst never bee an eye witnesse, Spectatour, or looker on, least I should have been partaker of Sathans Inventions and Worships, contrary to *Ephes.* 5. 11" (p. 192). Consequently, initially, instead of the uncivilized heathen it is the heathenish civilized European that appears in a bad light; ultimately, instead of losing face as a firsthand observer or as a true Christian, Roger Williams augments his empirical authority by acquiring a tried and tested virtue.

In addition to establishing the credentials of the commentator, the empirical observations also expand and explain the vocabulary sections. Further, by establishing a context, these observations frequently serve to transform what might appear to be isolated words into organic parts of a thematic development. Chapter VIII provides us with the best example in this respect. After an observation upon the similarities between the Greek, Indian, and New Testament way of saying "I will obey you," the vocabulary resumes with:

Yo aphéttit.	*When they are here.*
Yo peyáhettit.	*When they are com.*

> This Ablative case absolute they much use, and comprise much in little. [P. 137]

What seems to be merely a linguistic detail, however, begins to appear as something of a stage direction as the dialogue continues, and in three steps we watch the way "*they are com,*" or the three stages in the natives' personal and historical apprehension of the white man:

> Awaunaguss, suck. *English-man, men.*
>
> This they call us, as much as to say, These strangers.
>
> Waútacone -nûaog. *Englishman, men.*
>
> That is, Coat-men, *or* clothed.
>
> Cháuquaqock. *English-men,* properly sword-men.
>
> [P. 137]

If one did not consider the interjected explanations or the order of presentation, one might conclude that the passage is designed merely to present three different Indian words for Englishman; while if one did not appreciate Williams's dialogue technique one might conclude that he was being redundant since in the preceding two chapters we have been given the words *cháuquaqock* and *Waútacone,* respectively. Considered organically, however, the interchange presents; first, the Indian's initial and distant view of the white man ("strangers") next, his recognition at closer range of the physical cultural characteristic of the English ("Coat-men"); and finally, at close-up, his appreciation of a further defining characteristic ("properly sword-men"). In turn, Williams seems to be relying upon the reader's remembering his earlier explanation that Indians call the English sword-men because they have introduced knives of all varieties into a stone-age culture and call them coat-men because of the contrast between the physical appearance of the Indian and English.

After the series of words for Englishman, the vocabulary continues by way of the root term *Waútacon-* to introduce the clothed English woman and youth; and then, the presence of the English in America having been established, the climactic question is asked: "*Why come they hither?*"

which elicits the following observation before the vocabulary continues with the answer:

> *Obs.* This question they oft put to me: Why come the *Englishmen* hither? and measuring others by themselves; they say, It is because you want *firing:* for they, having burnt up the *wood* in one place, (wanting draughts to bring *wood* to them) they are faine to follow the *wood;* and so to remove to a fresh new place for the *woods* sake.

Matta mihtuckqunnûnno?	*Have you no trees?*
Mishàunetash, Màunetash.	*Great store.*
Maunâuog, Wussaumemaunâuog.	*They are too full of people.*
Noonapúock.	*They have not roome one by another.* [P. 138]

On the one hand, Williams recounts the ingenuousness of the Indians' assuming that the English are in America in search of firewood, based upon their own primitive experience. On the other, in view of the discussion of belief and faithfulness earlier in the chapter, Williams also may be implying, first, that many English are in America indeed because, as a result of religious persecution, the trees in England are too full of people (a macabre but topical joke that gains impact when one remembers the pun on "Hangings" in chapter VI) and, second, that many English have come to America to find "a fresh new place" wherein to make a new beginning. Whereas the Indian moves from wood to wood for natural reasons, the English move from country to country because of spiritual devastation.

The second kind of observations in each chapter of *A Key* is "Generall," in the sense of abstract and universally applicable. Their function is not to add material but to reveal the spiritual truth sacramentally present in the specific and concrete dialogue, to transform an episode into a parable, the factual into the allegorical, the shadowy type into the truth. Consequently, these observations are not only organically related to the other parts of each chapter but they also serve to unify each chapter and, retrospectively, to transform simple observations into emblematic ones. Chapter XVII, for example, is concerned with the kinds of beasts to be found in the native environment. Singled out for special admiration in the first empirical observation is the beaver, "a Beast of wonder" (p. 173) because of his industry and independence. Two other such observations note the Indian tendency to label as "Divine powers" such animals as they are unable to capture, and to have a "reverend esteeme" for the "Conie" and to "conceive there is some Deitie in it" (p. 174). The vocabulary which precedes the "Generall" observation on this chapter acquires symbolic significance from the allegorical moral that follows:

Askùg.	*A Snake.*
Móaskug.	*Black Snake.*
Sések.	*Rattle Snake.*
Natúppwock.	*They feed.*
Téaqua natuphéttit?	*What shall they eat?*
Natuphéttitch yo sanáukamick.	*Let them feed on this ground.*

The general Observation *of the Beasts.*

> The Wildernesse is a cleere resemblance of the world, where greedie and furious men persecute and devoure the harmlesse and innocent as the wilde beasts pursue and devoure the Hinds and Roes. [P. 175]

In short, what began as a factual description of the literal American wilderness has become an observation on the beasts of the moral wilderness.

One explanatory observation from the chapter "Of *Beasts, &c.*" not mentioned above should be introduced here, since it is explicitly cross-referenced with the later "Of *their Hunting,* &c." and thus enables us to appreciate the difference between the pre- and postlapsarian treatments of the same subject, between the empirical and "Generall" observations, and between the satirical and spiritual dimensions of *A Key*. With retrospective irony, one learns in the early chapter about "A wild beast of a reddish haire about the bignesse of a *Pig*, and rooting like a *Pig;* from whence they give this name to all our *Swine*" (p. 173–74). The "General" observation, as we have seen, moves from the American to the universal moral wilderness. In the later chapter, however, we find the following dialogue and personal observation:

> *Obs.* They are very tender of their Traps where they lie, and what comes at them; for they say, the Deere (whom they conceive have a Divine power in them) will soone smell and be gone.
>
> Npunnowwáumen. *I must goe to my Traps.*
> Nummíshkommin. *I have found a Deere;*
>
> Which sometimes they doe, taking a Wolfe in the very act of his greedy prey, when sometimes (the Wolfe being greedy of his prey) they kill him: sometimes the Wolfe having glutted himselfe with the one halfe, leaves the other for his next bait; but the glad *Indian* finding of it, prevents him.
>
> And that wee may see how true it is, that all wild creatures, and many tame, prey upon the poore Deere (which are there in a right Embleme of Gods persecuted, that is, hunted people, as I observed in the Chapter of Beasts according to the old and true saying:
>
> *Imbelles Damæ quid nisi præda sumus?*
>
> To harmlesse *Roes* and *Does,*
> Both wilde and tame are foes.)
>
> I remember how a poore Deere was long hunted and chased by a Wolfe, at last (as their manner is) after the chase of ten, it may be more miles running, the stout Wolfe tired out the nimble Deere, and seasing upon it, kill'd: In the act of devouring his prey, two *English* Swine, big with Pig, past by, assaulted the Wolfe, drove him from his prey, and devoured so much of that poore Deere, as they both surfeted and dyed that night.

> The Wolfe is an Embleme of a fierce bloodsucking persecutor.
>
> The Swine of a covetous rooting worldling, both make a prey of the Lord Jesus in his poore servants.
>
> [Pp. 225–26]

One would suspect that, at the same time that he is preparing in this observation for the spiritual reading of the episode in his "Generall" observation, Roger Williams points to an autobiographical reading of this passage. If the deer, which the Indians conceive to have a "Divine power" and which they reclaim from its predator, represents Williams, then Boston in banishing him might well be the wolf, and Plymouth and Salem the succeeding two English Swine.

The third basic part of each chapter is a short poem, usually of three four-line stanzas, and always found at the end. They do not have titles; instead they are preceded by the note, "More Particular." This in itself would seem to indicate that these poems were not composed as autonomous additions, but that they were conceived of as the structural conclusions and thematic climaxes of each chapter. Each chapter, in short, presents a three-part movement from the empirical and specific to the spiritual and general to the poetic and particular. The structure of each unit is an organic representation of the controlling thematic perspective —the metaphoric nature of the material world, an informing point of view which we later encounter in Jonathan Edwards and Ralph Waldo Emerson.

The poems, moreover, are related to the chapters in a traditional way. They are emblematic, following a favorite seventeenth-century mode, and thus rely in part upon the didactic conventions popularized in England by Francis Quarles. The emblem as practiced in the early years of the century was a tripartite composition, consisting of a symbolic engraving, a moral motto or epigram drawn from the Bible or the classics, and an explicatory poem which frequently milked an amazing amount of meaning from the often simple allegory of the engraving. In *A Key,* the engraving is replaced by the dialogue. Both the typological theme and the metaphoric use of language provide the allegorical dimension to the printed material in much the same manner that Herbert's "Church Floor," for example, dispenses with the necessity for a pictorial representation. And in Williams's handling of the emblematic, the observations can be seen to replace the conventional moral appended to the engraving. Although usually the emblematic concept is implicit, in some of the passages we have discussed, and in chapter XXVIII specifically, the tradition is explicitly evoked: "As I have often told them in their gamings, and in their great losings (when they have staked and lost their money, clothes, house, corne, and themselves, if single persons) they will confesse it, being weary of their lives, and ready to make away themselves, like many an *English* man: an Embleme of the horrour of conscience, which all poore sinners walk in at last, when they see what wofull games they have played in their life, and now find themselves eternall Beggars" (p. 230). Following this graphic description is the "Generall" observation which adds the requisite allegorical touches: "how many vaine inventions and foolish pastimes have the sonnes of men in all parts of the world found out, to passe time & post over this short minute of life, untill like some pleasant River they have past into *mare mortuum,* the dead sea of eternall lamentation" (p. 231).

The function of the poem, of course, remains the same as in the more traditional emblem books: it explicates the general and symbolic picture provided in the dialogue and observations, and in the process makes it specifically relevant, i.e., "More Particular." To continue with the "Gaming" chapter, the poem begins:

> *Our* English *Gamesters scorne to stake*
> *Their clothes as* Indians *do,*

Nor yet themselves, alas, yet both
Stake soules and lose them to. [P. 231]

Finally, also associated with the emblematic tradition (although possibly more with Quarles and the age than with the genre itself) are such metaphysical devices as paradox and word play. Williams's controlling use of these devices, of course, lies in his ironic reversal of roles in the missionary legend: it is not the civilized man who points the way for the savage but the Indian who shows the white man the "way"—"I have heard of many *English* lost, and have oft been lost my selfe, and my selfe and others have often been found, and succoured by the *Indians*" (p. 148); it is not America but Europe that is the wilderness, not the Indian but the Englishman who is literally and metaphorically the barbarian, the "bearded outsider":

2. *When* Indians *heare the horrid filths,*
Of Irish, English *Men,*
The horrid Oaths and Murthers late,
Thus say these Indians *then:*

[3.] *We weare no Cloaths, have many Gods,*
And yet our sinnes are lesse:
You are Barbarians, Pagans wild,
Your Land's the Wildernesse. [P. 204]

To illustrate by example both the emblematic character of *A Key* and the typical integration of the parts of the individual chapters, one might examine chapter XXX, "*Of their paintings.*" In the customary fashion, the unit begins with the dialogue between the Indian and the New Englander, and Williams provides us with brief stage directions, explaining when and why the natives paint themselves—"in Warre" and "for pride." Out of context the mention of this custom would suggest the barbarousness of the Indian, but when one appreciates that this scene takes place in the final act of this American tragedy, one is prepared for deeper implications and looks back to what has been said before on the subject. In general, one recalls that in the observation upon their mourning habits in chapter VI, the Indian practice of painting themselves was mentioned with, if anything, a note of respect for their sense of propriety. More specifically, as Williams goes on in chapter XXX to observe their particular "delight in" their "red painting," the pigment for which they obtain from "the Barke of the Pine, as also a red Earth," one remembers his description of the creation of Adam from red earth in his relation of Genesis. And even more pointedly, after noting the word for "*A painted Coat,*" he specifically refers the reader to the central thematic chapter of *A Key:* "Of this and *Wússuck-wheke,* (the English Letters, which comes neerest to their painting) I spake before in the Chapter of their clothing" (p. 240). Thus the emphasis is shifted from the practice of painting as simply a sign of a barbarous nature to cosmetics as a sign of a fallen and degenerate condition, in preparation for the general observation of this chapter: "It hath been the foolish Custome of all barbarous Nations to paint and figure their Faces and Bodies (as it hath been to our shame and griefe, wee may remember it of some of our Fore-Fathers in this Nation.) How much then are we bound to our most holy Maker for so much knowledge of himselfe revealed in so much Civility and Piety? and how should we also long and endeavour that *America* may partake of our mercy" (p. 241). Through the two not wholly rhetorical questions Williams restates the problem at the heart of the book: civilization should mean the cessation of barbarous practices which in turn would identify the true Christian, and it is in this sense that one desires the civilization of a pagan land; when the generalization is particularly applied to the relations between Europe and America, however, the proposition becomes questionable as emotional experience confronts theological logic. Instead of discouraging the Indian from painting his face, the white man brings him "*A*

Looking Glasse," as Williams observed in chapter XXV, "*Of buying and selling*": "It may be wondred what they do with Glasses, having no beautie but a swarfish colour, and no dressing but nakednesse; but pride appeares in any colour, and the meanest dresse: and besides generally the women paint their faces with all sorts of colours" (p. 219). With the implied comparison to European female cosmetic fashion, the irony is biting, especially when one recalls, "I am black, but comely, O ye daughters of Jerusalem . . ." (Song of Solomon 1:5–6).

To return to chapter XXX, having thus generalized upon the Indian custom and in spiritualizing his observation made it an ironic comment upon the moral condition of his fellow men, Williams caps off his emblematic scene with a poetic "More particular":

> [1.] *Truth is a Native, naked Beauty; but*
> *Lying Inventions are but Indian Paints;*
> *Dissembling hearts their Beautie's but a Lye.*
> *Truth is the proper Beauty of Gods Saints.* [P. 241]

What, if isolated from the context, would be a rather conventional contrast between truth and hypocrisy, the saint and the sinner, now appears as a vivid depiction of the moral issue and a paradoxical exploration of a political theological situation. The paradox of the stanza lies in its association of truth with both the native and the saint, a paradox which is resolvable only if one has come to understand Williams's basic attitude toward the Indian—that he is not by definition irrevocably damned—and his concomitant attitude toward the civilized Christian—that hypocrisy is more hideous than any kind of physical disfiguration.

> 2. *Fowle are the* Indians *Haire and painted Faces,*
> *More foule such Haire, such Face in* Israel.
> England *so calls her selfe, yet there's*
> Absoloms *foule Haire and Face of* Jesabell [P. 241]

Again, one recalls that Williams has made an observation on the Indians' hair in the early section of the work: in chapter V he observed that "Their Virgins are distinguished by a bashfull falling downe of their haire over their eyes" (p. 115), a description which reminds one of the prelapsarian Eve: "Shee as a vail down to the slender waste/Her unadorned golden tresses wore/Dissheveld." In self-revelatory contrast to this appreciation of the natural modesty of the Indian is John Eliot's fifth commandment for converted natives: "If any woman shall not have her haire tied up but hang loose or be cut as mens haire, she shall pay five shillings" (*The Day-Breaking,* p. 20). In short, to appreciate Williams's comment on the Indians' hair in this chapter, one must recognize that his observation has changed and understand why.

To appreciate the political satire in the stanza in question one need only picture the long-haired English court of the time and remember the biblical episode which Williams typologically evokes. Absalom was the son of King David; he was killed by his enemies when his long hair caught in the branches of an oak under which he was riding in flight (2 Sam. 18:9–15). Jezebel was the wife of King Ahab; she caused him to worship the false god, Baal (1 Kings 16: 31–33), she slew the prophets of Jehovah (1 Kings 18:4, 19:2), and she painted her face just before her violent death (2 Kings 9:30–37). The parallels to the son and wife of Charles I would be only too obvious to the good Puritan.

The popish Protestant, then, is much more in need of repentance than the unregenerate pagan; indeed, to remove the taint contracted by ritual baptism, it is necessary to return to the "natural" waters of repentance:

[3.] *Paints will not bide Christs washing Flames of fire,*
Fained Inventions will not bide such stormes:
O that we may prevent him, that betimes,
Repentance Teares may wash of all such Formes. [P. 241]

And as this final stanza illustrates, Williams, unlike so many of his contemporary "American" versifiers, deserves the name of poet for literary as well as historical reasons. The three things which make this stanza effective are also indexes to the best features of his poetry in general: first, the complete naturalness and organicism of the resolution in terms of the central image; second, the picturesque conceit of "*washing Flames*"; and third, the homeliness and realism of the verb "wash," used instead of more "poetic" terms such as cleanse or purge.

A final way of pointing out the necessity of treating Williams's poems as emblematic and hence in terms of both their immediate and remote contexts is to consider two representative criticisms of his poetry: "Williams' full capabilities as a poet are not, perhaps, revealed in his slight quantity of verse" (Meserole, p. 177); "He was too turgid a writer to submit to the discipline of poetry, and his rhymes are not memorable art" (Miller, p. 55). When isolated from their contexts, Williams's poems do merit these criticisms, but an assessment of his poetry must begin with the recognition that his poems were not designed to be read as autonomous pieces and that his achievement demands to be measured by way of seventeenth-century criteria. It must be remembered that Williams was a contemporary of both Quarles in England and Edward Taylor in America, both relatively minor poets. Still Quarles's emblematic poems would appear slighter if separated from their contexts; Edward Taylor's poetry is undisciplined when compared to Pope's, but assumes entirely different qualities of "masculine ruggedness" when read with the works of Donne, his immediate predecessor, in mind.

Literary directions

The purpose of the present introduction is a reappraisal and perhaps a rehabilitation of Roger Williams by demonstrating that at least one of his works, *A Key into the Lan-*

guage of America, deserves to be approached as an organic and artistic work. Other approaches have led not only to neglect but also to misrepresentation. Treating the work as an evangelical tract, Perry Miller describes it as "In structure, simply a dictionary":

> The fact that the book has no formal continuity, that it consists merely of a list of words and phrases punctuated by seemingly random observations, has prevented it from being studied by any but anthropologists (who certify its scientific reliability). Most students miss the point of Williams' "directions for use [sic] of the language," in which he says that he purposely intended something more than a dictionary "as not so accommodate to the benefit of all." He was hoping that others might also move as fellow citizens among the savages! [Pp. 54–55]

Ola Winslow treats *A Key* in a chapter entitled "Linguist"; her emphasis is upon the autobiographical elements of the work, completely understandable in a biography but responsible for some questionable conclusions: "He meant exactly what he said. There is not a shadow of ambitious authorship, of literary consciousness, or more than a hint of the importance such a book might have for later times or for a wider audience" (p. 162). Harrison Meserole approaches *A Key* as a book which has "interspersed throughout" a number of poems; thus neglecting the structural argument of the work, he comes to the conclusion that "The recurrent theme is that the faults of the savage Indians are all the more egregious when manifested by supposedly civilized 'Christian' Englishmen" (p. 177).

When the work is not appreciated as an artistic product, furthermore, there is danger of misconstruing the character of Williams himself. Callender, for example, suggests that Williams's view of the Indian changed drastically from that presented in *A Key:* "on longer acquaintance and more experience, he seems to have altered his opinion of them; as appears by some expressions in a manuscript of his, yet remaining" (Callender, p. 140). Similarly, Lawrence Wroth, one of Williams's most realistically sympathetic critics, sees an inconsistency in the author because of the difference between the positive attitude toward the Indian of *A Key* and the typical attitude expressed in his political dealings with them and his later decision to trade with them instead of single-mindedly pursuing his missionary activities. He concludes that "The fundamental cause was that he did not truly love the Indians" (p. 27).

A Key is not a great work of art; nor did Williams exert in any definable sense an influence upon the American literary tradition. At the same time in *A Key into the Language of America* are to be found some of the earliest expressions of qualities that have come to be regarded as characteristic of American literature, such as the self-reliance of an Emerson, the symbolic perspective of a Hawthorne, the tragic primitivism of a Melville, and the pragmatic empiricism of a Twain. In this sense, whereas most colonial writing must be described as literature written in or about America, Roger Williams's *Key* can be described as an early example of American literature.

A Note on the Text

The copy text

Editors of *A Key into the Language of America* have no difficulty in choosing a copy text, since the only edition published during Roger Williams's lifetime—and thus the only edition with any authority—is the small octavo printed in 1643 on the press of Gregory Dexter in London. This volume (hereafter referred to as O) is collated A-O^8, made up of fourteen sheets, 224 pages including the title page. There are errors in pagination: 77 is misnumbered 67, 80 is misnumbered 86, 84 is not numbered, 92–93 are interchanged with 94–95, 96–97 are omitted, 115 is misnumbered 105 and the error is followed to the end of the volume, the last page, 207, being misnumbered 197.

O is arranged as follows: title page; epistle to the reader, fourteen pages; directions for the use of the language, two pages; thirty-two chapters of text, B-O^7; a table of contents, O^8; an appended license signed Io. Langley, which reads, "I *have read over these thirty Chapters of the* American Language, *to me wholly unknowne, and the* Observations, *these I conceive inoffensive; and that the Worke may conduce to the happy end intended by the* Author . . . . Printed according to this Licence; and entred into *Stationers Hall.*"

O is a moderately well printed book thoroughly representative of the practices of the period. There are errors in chapter numbering and page headings besides the customary occurrence of repeated words, broken, turned, transposed, and omitted letters, mixed roman and italic fonts particularly in upper-case letters, in addition to typographical variants resulting from printer's corrections to be discussed below; from a combination of some or all of which errors no London printing of the period appears to be free.

The printer—good Puritan that he evidently was—seems to have given more care to his setting of the prose, especially in the vocabulary sections, than to the verse. The poems are generally badly and irregularly set, with little adherence to the format which Williams evidently intended.

Typographical variants

Lawrence C. Wroth was the first to note variations in the typography of O. He concluded, rightly in the cases of the minor variants, that "somebody . . . was standing by as the sheets were being printed and insisting upon the press being stopped and corrections made in the form." He is correct, too, in suggesting that since the errors did not greatly affect the meaning, the incorrect sheets were bound along with the corrected ones as an economy measure; and his conjecture that Roger Williams himself might have supervised the printing and correcting is not without foundation. For Williams was only too aware of printing problems. For example, after noting a typographical error in George Fox's book, he goes on: "And abundance more of this Boyes English all his Book over, which I cannot impute to his *Northern Dialect* (having been so long in the South, and London, and read and answered (as he dreams) so many English Books: nor to the Printer (the faults of that kinde being so numerous) but to the finger of the most High . . ." (*Fox,* p. 279).

Furthermore, we know from his own statement in his "Directions" that he was concerned about the placing of the accents in the Narragansett vocabulary and that he examined at least one of the sheets before he wrote those directions, since he makes explicit reference to the printed second page, incidentally revealing his unfamiliarity with printer's jargon in calling it the "*second leafe.*" It is very likely, however, that he examined only the first sheet as it came from the press and that, satisfied, he went his busy way to write his introduction and to engage in London politics. If this is so, then the minor variants were corrected by the printer and the one major variant, about which we disagree with Wroth, was allowed to go uncorrected.

The fifteen copies of O which we have examined are as follows:

O^1, O^2, O^3:	John Carter Brown Library.
O^4:	Library Company of Philadelphia.
O^5:	Newberry Library.
O^6:	John Hay Library.
O^7, O^8:	Library of the Rhode Island Historical Society.
O^9:	Beinecke Rare Book and Manuscript Library, Yale.
O^{10}:	Library of the American Antiquarian Society.
O^{11}:	Houghton Library, Harvard.
O^{12}:	Library of the Massachusetts Historical Society.
O^{13}:	New York Public Library.
O^{14}, O^{15}:	Boston Public Library.

Of these, O^{10} is of only limited use in comparing variants since large parts of it ($A - C^8$, $K^3 - K^5$, L^8, $O^5 - O^8$) are in manuscript in a fine nineteenth-century hand which besides being very legible also corrects obvious typographical errors.

The minor variants and their distribution are as follows:

p. 21 (Catchword), Cha	O^2;	Chap	all others
p. 94 (Catchword), 8epuo?	O^1, O^5, O^{13};	Sepuo?	all others
p. 94 (l. 18), *Rivelet*	O^1, O^5, O^{13};	*Rivulet*	all others
p. 143 (page number) omit	O^1, O^5, O^6, O^{11}, O^{13};		others print.

The first and last variants noted can be regarded conceivably as simple failures to print. The second and third, which significantly occur on the same sheet, clearly are cases of correction.

The major variant on page 12, however, which Wroth treats as a case of badly set type corrected, appears rather to be a case of the progressive degeneration of the line due to a broken form. This can be demonstrated by noting that of the fourteen usable copies of O consulted, only O^{3} and O^{14} present what Wroth would take to be the corrected reading, *water coole?* But let us assume for the moment that O^{3} and O^{14} have provenance and range the variants in descending order of adherence in this manner:

O^{3}, O^{14}:	*Is the water coole?*
O^{9}, O^{13}:	*Is the water coole*
O^{7}:	*Is the water co ol e*
O^{1}, O^{5}, O^{6}, O^{11}, O^{15}:	*Is the water coo*
O^{4}:	*Is the w a t er coo*
O^{12}:	*Is the wa ter coo*
O^{8}:	*Is the wa t er coo*
O^{2}:	*Is the wa t coo*

The number and variety of "uncorrected" printings of this line clearly argue for degeneration, and thus we are left with only one sheet in the entire volume where the correcting hand of the printer can conclusively be seen at work. It becomes even less likely that Williams oversaw the printing of the whole book, and so the editor is left to his task of presenting a text as close as possible to the one the author would have printed had he been there.

Editions

There are four "modern" editions of *A Key*. The first of these was published a century and a half after O by the

Massachusetts Historical Society in its *Collections,* 1st series, vols. III and V (1794 and 1798); hereafter referred to as MHS. Volume III reprints very little of the vocabulary, concentrating almost exclusively upon Williams's observations upon the customs of the Indian, and completely avoiding the general observations and poems, as does volume V. Volume V, "In compliance with the request of Dr. Barton . . . and of other gentlemen whose opinions we respect," reprints the rest of the vocabulary (p. 80).

MHS is admittedly a series of extracts and makes little effort to preserve either the format of O or its typography, although the long s is retained and the English portions of the vocabulary are italicized. Apparently aware that O was unreliable in its accenting of the Narragansett, MHS prints the Indian words without accents. MHS used the Society's own copy of O, then thought to be unique, as copy text, that copy to which we refer above as O^{12}. O^{12} still reveals the inked editorial signs of MHS, and particularly interesting are the brackets which enclose words, phrases, and sections to be omitted from the reprint.

The third edition of *A Key* was published as volume I of the Rhode Island Historical Society *Collections* in 1827 (hereafter referred to as RIHS). It is the product of a collation of O^{12} with a manuscript copy made from an O in the Bodleian Library. An editorial advance over MHS by way of collation, it reproduces Williams's text in full, although in a modernized form. Understandably, RIHS is in avowed competition with MHS, and clearly wishes to do Williams that editorial justice which was denied him earlier. This competitive spirit is evidenced in RIHS's assertion that *A Key* "preceded Elliot's publications on the same subject, and was highly commended by the Board of Trade, at the time it was published" (p. 14). RIHS continues the modernizing trend, restoring O's original format, but abandoning most of the original italicization and capitalization. And, as with MHS, RIHS allowed errors to creep into its text in the modernizing of it.

The two subsequent editions of *A Key* demonstrate a strong editorial reaction against modernizing the text. J. Hammond Trumbull edited the first of these as volume I of the Narragansett Club standard edition of *The Complete Writings of Roger Williams.* Trumbull attempts a facsimile of O, "after the collation of several copies," with "the constant aim of the editor, to ensure the literal accuracy of the reprint,—even to the reproduction of typographical errors—of the original" (pp. 15–16). As the textual notes below will demonstrate, however, Trumbull was not consistent in his adherence to the text of O, for he made a number of unconscious corrections, while drawing the reader's attention to many more possible ones in his footnotes.

The Narragansett Club edition is invaluable for its thorough annotations; the only annotated edition to date, it provides the student with much that is of interest to the historian and linguist. For this reason alone it is far and away the best of the four modern editions. And since the present editors do not consider themselves to be primarily historians or in any sense linguists, the reader is referred to Trumbull's notes for such information.

The most recent edition of *A Key* is the 1936 publication by The Rhode Island and Providence Plantations Tercentenary Committee, with an introduction by Howard Chapin. It is with this edition that Lawrence C. Wroth was associated. Another attempt at a facsimile, this edition deviates from facsimile principles by modernizing the long s; it is based upon a collation of O^1, O^2, O^3, O^7, or O^8, and a fifth copy "in the library of the late Tracy W. McGregor, of Detroit" (Wroth, "Variations," p. 120). This edition is without editorial apparatus, and, as the textual notes below will demonstrate, it is much less trustworthy than Trumbull's, particularly in its tendency to misread the long s for f and to mistake broken ligature long s's for i's, although this occurs fortunately only in the Indian part of the vocabulary.

The text

The text which follows is our attempt to present for the first time a definitive edition of *A Key into the Language of America.* In so doing we have tried to thread a middle way between the photographic facsimile—never a very satisfactory way of reprinting scarce but important texts—and the definitive edition which bristles with such scholarly apparatus that it frequently impedes rather than facilitates rapport between the modern reader and the seventeenth-century writer. What we have aimed at is a perfectly clear text augmented by a body of textual notes and a commentary; we hope that the text and textual notes are of such quality and authority that another edition of *A Key* will not be needed; and we hope further that only a distant generation from ours will need more informational help than is provided in the commentary.

For our copy text we used a photographic copy of the volume held by the Library Company of Philadelphia (O^4), primarily because this is the copy of O which seems in the best state of preservation and would be least injured by being photographed. We sight collated O^4 with the six copies of O held in the libraries of Brown University and the Rhode Island Historical Society (O^1, O^2, O^3, O^6, O^7, O^8). The text arrived at by this method has been compared with the eight remaining copies of O listed above, and the resulting text has then been compared to the texts provided in the four modern editions. The text presented here, then, is both the most recent and the most ambitious attempt—in the absence of a manuscript of *A Key*—to provide the reader with an authoritative text. And whether that reader be a scholar of the seventeenth century in England and America, or a beginning student, or a "common reader," we have tried to provide him with a readable text, with one necessary exception: whenever we have made a conjectural insertion into the text we have enclosed it within brackets. The text is normalized but not modernized in the usual meaning. By *normalization,* we mean that to the best of our ability we have reproduced a text in keeping with the conventions of seventeenth-century spelling and printers' practices; in the absence of a manuscript, the edition must be an attempt to reproduce (barring his errors) the individual peculiarities of the printer, but of course not allowing his idiosyncrasies to stand between what the editor believes the author intended and what the printer finally produced. The text is a "modernized" one only in that we have replaced certain now archaic seventeenth-century typographical devices with their twentieth-century equivalents, again in the interest of facilitating the reading without affecting the meaning. In that sense every editing task is unique.

Consequently, we have substituted the short s for the long, j for i, v for u, w for vv, etc., and we have silently corrected such obvious printing errors as turned letters, broken letters, transposed letters, wrong fonts, repeated words, etc. But in every case where our deviation from a reading of O is in any sense questionable, hypothetical, or a matter of editorial opinion rather than obvious universal practice, we so indicate in the notes, and the interested reader will then be able to make his own decision.

In an effort not to appear pedantic while at the same time providing the reader with every possible piece of information concerning the text, we have been more economical in reporting certain deviations from the text of O made by subsequent editors. Our basic assumption, stated above, regarding MHS and RIHS is that they tend, not always consistently, to modernize spelling and that they do not necessarily follow O's format or typography, and consequently we note only what we consider to be important deviations in these areas. For example, we have considered it important to note that MHS does not follow O in paragraphing at p. 83, l. 21, and again at p. 85, l. 12, since it seems that paragraphs are needed here to indicate significant shifts in thought. In the same way we note, again for example, that where O prints "*English* men" at p. 85, l. 23, RIHS modernizes to "Englishmen." Our reasoning here is that almost certainly Williams had italicized *English,* and that quite possibly he had used the word adjectivally also, to emphasize the cultural difference between the English and the Indian; we feel that here RIHS's modernization served to weaken the point made by Williams. Where such deviations do not, in our opinion, affect the reader's comprehension of Williams's thought, we do not record them.

We do, however, note every case in which MHS omits parts of O—even to single words—for reasons which have already been made clear in our general introduction. It is our contention that many of the omissions made by MHS were not made solely for the sake of economy, but that they were made in a fairly consistent effort to disguise what would then have been regarded as Williams's heretical position with regard to the Indian and his relations to the European. The major example is, of course, the wholesale omission by MHS of the General Observations and poems which conclude each chapter; we have noted this occurrence at p. 99, l. 16. A minor example of this tendency we note at p. 94, l. 12, where MHS omits the word "reverently" from Williams's description of Indian social behavior.

According to the same principles our assumption about Trumbull and Chapin is that they tend, but not always consistently, to follow the text of O even to the extent of reproducing obvious typographical errors. We do not record the numerous cases in which both editors reproduce the typographical errors of O, even when, for example, we silently correct a turned or broken letter. In the cases of these facsimile editions we do report, however, every deviation from the text of O so that the reader may know where these editions are not facsimiles. This is not done in any way to belittle the admirable work of these editors who loved Roger Williams as we do and who labored to make *A Key* available to a wider audience; it is done—and they would agree with us—to present the reader with the most reliable text possible and to demonstrate that to him. We think, therefore, that it is important to record the fact that Trumbull, for example, unconsciously corrects the spelling of "seperate" (p. 86, l. 12), and that for "And" (p. 86, l. 34) he prints "and." We also record Chapin's printing of "mistakes" for "*mis-takes*" (p. 84, l. 3), "wellhead" for "Wellhead" (p. 85, l. 13), "wildernesse" for "Wildernesse" (p. 85, l. 18), and "Conversion" for "*Conversion*" (p. 87, ll. 12–13).

As a general rule we have amended the punctuation of O only in cases where that punctuation results in wholly ambiguous readings, and we have reported every such case in our notes. We have not, however, reported the many cases in which we have altered the punctuation in the dialogue sections. When, for example, the English translation of a Narragansett phrase indicates clearly that the phrase is a question, we have inserted the question mark even when O has no punctuation or, say, a period. And in some cases (for example, the long dialogue-catechism in chapter XXI) we have altered the punctuation to give the reader a better idea of the free-flowing vertical development of the dialogue. One may wish to compare a short section of our text (p. 196, ll. 1–22), with the original as reproduced here:

The fourth day he made
the Sun and the Moon.
Two great Lights.
And all the Starres.
The fifth day hee made
all the Fowle.
In the Ayre, or Heavens.

And all the Fish in the
Sea.
The sixth day hee made
all the Beasts of the
Field.
Last of all he made one
Man
Of red Earth,
And call'd him Adam,
or *red Earth.*

A Key into the LANGUAGE *of* AMERICA

A KEY into the

LANGUAGE

OF

AMERICA:

OR,

An help to the *Language* of the *Natives* in that part of AMERICA, called *NEW-ENGLAND.*

Together, with briefe *Observations* of the Customes, Manners and Worships, *&c.* of the aforesaid *Natives*, in Peace and Warre, in Life and Death.

On all which are added Spirituall *Observations*, Generall and Particular by the *Authour*, of chiefe and speciall use (upon all occasions) to all the *English* Inhabiting those parts; yet pleasant and profitable to the view of all men:

BY ROGER WILLIAMS
of *Providence* in *New-England.*

LONDON,
Printed by *Gregory Dexter*, 1643.

Facsimile of Title page. (*By courtesy of the John Carter Brown Library, Boston University.*)

To my Deare and Welbeloved Friends *and* Countrey-men, *in old and new* England

I Present you with a *Key;* I have not heard of the like, yet framed, since it pleased God to bring that mighty *Continent* of *America* to light: Others of my Country-men have often, and excellently, and lately written of the *Countrey* (and none that I know beyond the goodnesse and worth of it.)

This *Key,* respects the *Native Language* of it, and happily may unlocke some *Rarities* concerning the *Natives* themselves, not yet discovered.

I drew the *Materialls* in a rude lumpe at Sea, as a private *helpe* to my owne memory, that I might not by my present absence *lightly lose* what I had so *dearely bought* in some few yeares *hardship,* and *charges* among the *Barbarians;* yet being reminded by some, what pitie it were to bury those *Materialls* in my *Grave* at land or Sea; and withall, remembring how oft I have been importun'd by *worthy friends,* of all sorts, to afford them some helps this way.

I resolved (by the assistance of *the most High*) to cast those *Materialls* into this *Key, pleasant* and *profitable* for *All,* but specially for my *friends* residing in those parts:

A little *Key* may open a *Box,* where lies a *bunch* of *Keyes.*

With this I have entred into the secrets of those *Coun-*

tries, where ever *English* dwel about two hundred miles, betweene the *French* and *Dutch* Plantations; for want of this, I know what grosse *mis-takes* my selfe and others have run into.

There is a mixture of this *Language North* and *South,* from the place of my abode, about six hundred miles; yet within the two hundred miles (aforementioned) their *Dialects* doe exceedingly differ; yet not so, but (within that compasse) a man may, by this *helpe,* converse with *thousands* of *Natives* all over the *Countrey:* and by such converse it may please the *Father* of *Mercies* to spread *civilitie,* (and in his owne most holy season) *Christianitie;* for *one Candle* will light *ten thousand,* and it may please *God* to blesse a *little Leaven* to season the *mightie Lump* of those *Peoples* and *Territories.*

It is expected, that having had so much converse with these *Natives,* I should write some litle of them.

Concerning them (a little to gratifie expectation) I shall touch upon *foure Heads:*

First, by what *Names* they are distinguished.

Secondly, Their *Originall* and *Descent.*

Thirdly, their *Religion, Manners, Customes,* &c.

Fourthly, That great *Point* of their *Conversion.*

To the first, their *Names* are of two sorts:

First, those of the *English* giving: as *Natives, Salvages, Indians, Wild-men,* (so the *Dutch* call them *Wilden*) *Abergeny men, Pagans, Barbarians, Heathen.*

Secondly, their *Names,* which they give themselves.

I cannot observe, that they ever had (before the comming of the *English, French* or *Dutch* amongst them) any *Names* to difference *themselves* from strangers, for they knew none; but two sorts of *names* they had, and have amongst *themselves.*

First, *generall,* belonging to all *Natives,* as *Ninnuock, Ninnimissinnûwock, Eniskeetompaúwog,* which signifies *Men, Folke,* or *People.*

Secondly, particular *names,* peculiar to severall *Nations* of them amongst *themselves,* as, *Nanhigganéuck, Massachusêuck, Cawasumsêuck, Cowweséuck, Quintikóock, Qunnipiéuck, Pequttóog,* &c.

They have often asked mee, why wee call them *Indians, Natives,* &c. And understanding the reason, they will call themselves *Indians,* in opposition to *English,* &c.

For the second Head proposed, their *Originall* and *Descent.*

From *Adam* and *Noah* that they spring, it is granted on all hands.

But for their later *Descent,* and whence they came into those parts, it seemes as hard to finde, as to finde the *Wellhead* of some fresh *Streame,* which running many miles out of the *Countrey* to the salt *Ocean,* hath met with many mixing *Streames* by the way. They say themselves, that they have *sprung* and *growne* up in that very place, like the very *trees* of the *Wildernesse.*

They say that their *Great God Cawtántowwit* created those parts, as I observed in the Chapter of their *Religion.* They have no *Clothes, Bookes,* nor *Letters,* and conceive their *Fathers* never had; and therefore they are easily perswaded that the *God* that made *English* men is a greater *God,* because Hee hath so richly endowed the *English* above *themselves:* But when they heare that about sixteen hundred yeeres agoe, *England* and the *Inhabitants* thereof were like unto *themselves,* and since have received from *God, Clothes, Bookes,* &c. they are greatly affected with a secret hope concerning *themselves.*

Wise and *Judicious* men, with whom I have discoursed, maintaine their *Originall* to be *Northward* from *Tartaria:* and at my now taking ship, at the *Dutch Plantation,* it pleased the *Dutch* Governour, (in some discourse with mee about the *Natives*), to draw their *Line* from *Iceland,* because the name *Sackmakan* (the name for an *Indian* Prince, about the *Dutch*) is the name for a *Prince* in *Iceland.*

Other opinions I could number up: under favour I shall present (not mine opinion, but) my *Observations* to the judgement of the Wise.

[1.] First, others (and my selfe) have conceived some of their words to hold affinitie with the *Hebrew.*

Secondly, they constantly *annoint* their *heads* as the *Jewes* did.

Thirdly, they give *Dowries* for their wives, as the *Jewes* did.

Fourthly (and which I have not so observed amongst other *Nations* as amongst the *Jewes,* and *these:*) they constantly seperate their Women (during the time of their monthly sicknesse) in a little house alone by themselves foure or five dayes, and hold it an *Irreligious thing* for either *Father* or *Husband* or any *Male* to come neere them.

They have often asked me if it bee so with *women* of other *Nations,* and whether they are so separated: and for their practice they plead *Nature* and *Tradition.*

2. Yet againe I have found a greater *Affinity* of their Language with the *Greek* Tongue. As the *Greekes* and other *Nations,* and our selves call the seven *Starres* (or Charles Waine) the *Beare,* so doe they *Mosk* or *Paukunnawaw* the Beare.

3. They have many strange Relations of one *Wétucks,* a man that wrought great *Miracles* amongst them, and *walking upon the waters,* &c. with some kind of broken Resemblance to the *Sonne of God.*

[4.] Lastly, it is famous that the *Sowwest* (*Sowaniu*) is the great Subject of their discourse. From thence their *Traditions.* There they say (at the *South-west*) is the Court of their *great God Cautántouwit:* At *the South-west* are their *Forefathers* soules: *to the South-west* they goe themselves when they dye; From the *South-west* came their *Corne,* and Beanes out of their Great *God Cautántowwits* field: And indeed the further *Northward* and *Westward* from us their Corne will not grow, but to the *Southward* better and better. I dare not conjecture in these *Uncertainties,* I believe they are *lost,* and yet hope (in the Lords holy season) some of the wildest of them shall be found to share in the blood of the Son of God.

To the third *Head,* concerning their *Religion, Customes, Manners* &c. I shall here say nothing, because in those 32. Chapters of the whole Book, I have briefly touched those of all sorts, from their *Birth* to their *Burialls,* and have endeavoured (as the nature of the worke would give way) to bring some short *Observations* and *Applications* home to *Europe* from *America.*

Therefore fourthly, to that great Point of their *Conversion* so much to bee longed for, and by all *New-English* so much pretended, and I hope in Truth.

For my selfe I have uprightly laboured to suite my endeavours to my pretences: and of later times (out of desire to attaine their Language) I have run through varieties of *Intercourses* with them Day and Night, Summer and Winter, by Land and Sea; particular passages tending to this, I have related divers, in the Chapter of their Religion.

Many solemne discourses I have had with all *sorts of Nations* of them, from one end of the Countrey to another (so farre as opportunity, and the little Language I have could reach.)

I know there is no small *preparation* in the hearts of Multitudes of them. I know their many solemne *Confessions* to my self, and one to another of their lost *wandring Conditions.*

I know strong *Convictions* upon the *Consciences* of many of them, and their desires uttred that way.

I know not with how little *Knowledge* and *Grace* of Christ, the Lord may save, and therefore neither will *despaire,* nor *report* much.

But since it hath pleased some of my Worthy *Countrymen* to mention (of late in print) *Wequash,* the *Pequt Captaine,* I shall be bold so farre to second their *Relations,* as to relate mine owne Hopes of Him (though I dare not be so confident as others.)

Two dayes before his Death, as I past up to *Qunníhticut* River, it pleased my worthy friend Mr. *Fenwick* (whom I visited at his house in *Say-Brook* Fort at the mouth of that River) to tell me that my old friend *Wequash* lay very sick: I desired to see him, and Himselfe was pleased to be my Guide two miles where *Wequash* lay.

Amongst other discourse concerning his *sicknesse* and *Death* (in which hee freely bequeathed his son to Mr. *Fenwick*) I closed with him concerning his *Soule:* Hee told me that some two or three yeare before, he had lodged at my House, where I acquainted him with the *Condition* of *all mankind,* & his *Own* in particular, how *God* created *Man* and *All things:* how *Man* fell from *God,* and of his present *Enmity* against *God,* and the *wrath of God* against *Him* untill *Repentance:* said he *your words were never out of my heart to this present*; and said hee *me much pray to Jesus Christ:* I told him so did many *English, French,* and *Dutch,* who had never turned to *God,* nor loved Him: He replyed in broken English: *Me so big naughty Heart, me heart all one stone! Savory expressions* using to breath *from compunct and broken Hearts,* and a sence of *inward hardnesse* and *unbrokennesse.* I had many discourses with him in his Life, but this was the summe of our last parting untill our generall meeting.

Now because this is the great Inquiry of all men what *Indians* have been converted? what have the *English* done in those parts? what hopes of the *Indians* receiving the Knowledge of Christ!

And because to this Question, some put an edge from the boast of the Jesuits in *Canada* and *Maryland,* and especially from the wonderfull conversions made by the Spaniards and Portugalls in the *West-Indies;* besides what I have here written, as also, beside what I have observed in the Chapter of their Religion! I shall further present you with a briefe

Additionall discourse concerning this Great Point, being comfortably perswaded that that Father of Spirits, who was graciously pleased to perswade *Japhet* (the Gentiles) to dwell in the Tents of *Shem* (the Jewes) will in his holy season (I hope approaching) perswade these Gentiles of *America* to partake of the mercies of *Europe,* and then shall bee fulfilled what is written, by the Prophet *Malachi,* from the rising of the Sunne (in *Europe*) to the going down of the same (in *America*) my Name shall [be] great among the Gentiles. So I desire to hope and pray,

Your unworthy Country-man
ROGER WILLIAMS.

Directions for the use of the Language.

1. A Dictionary *or* Grammer *way I had consideration of, but purposely avoided, as not so accommodate to the Benefit of all, as I hope this Forme is.*

2. *A* Dialogue *also I had thoughts of, but avoided for brevities sake, and yet (with no small paines) I have so framed every Chapter and the matter of it, as I may call it an Implicite Dialogue.*

3. *It is framed chiefly after the* Narroganset *Dialect, because most spoken in the Countrey, and yet (with attending to the variation of peoples and Dialects) it will be of great use in all parts of the Countrey.*

4. *Whatever your occasion bee either of Travell, Discourse, Trading &c. turne to the Table which will direct you to the Proper Chapter.*

5. *Because the Life of all Language is in the Pronuntiation, I have been at paines and charges to Cause the Accents, Tones, or sounds to be affixed, (which some understand acoording to the* Greeke *Language) Acutes, Graves, Circumflexes: for example, in the second leafe in the word* Ewò *He: the sound or Tone must not be put on* E, *but* wò *where the grave Accent is.*

In the same leafe, in the word Ascowequássin, *the Sound must not be on any of the Syllables, but on* quáss, *where the Acute or sharp sound is.*

In the same leafe, in the word Anspaumpmaûntam, *the sound must not be on any other syllable but* Maûn, *where the* Circumflex *or long sounding Accent is.*

6. *The* English *for every* Indian *word or phrase stands in a straight line directly against the* Indian: *yet sometimes there are two words for the same thing (for their Language*

is exceeding copious, and they have five or six words sometimes for one thing) and then the English *stands against them both: for example in the second leafe,*

Cowáunckamish & Cuckquénamish.	*I pray your Favour.*

An Helpe to the native Language of that part of *America* called New-England.

CHAP. I.
Of *Salutation.*

Observation.

he Natives are of two sorts, (as the English are.) Some more Rude and Clownish, who are not so apt to Salute, but upon *Salutation* resalute lovingly. Others, and the generall, are *sober* and *grave,* and yet chearfull in a meane, and as ready to begin a Salutation as to Resalute, which yet the English generally begin, out of desire to Civilize them.

What cheare Nétop? *is the generall salutation of all English toward them.* Nétop *is friend.*

Netompaûog. *Friends.*

They are exceedingly delighted with Salutations in their own Language.

Neèn, Keèn, Ewò.	*I, you, he.*
Keén ka neen.	*You and I.*
Asco wequássin, Asco wequassunnúmmis.	*Good morrow.*
Askuttaaquompsìn?	*How doe you?*
Asnpaumpmaûntam.	*I am very well.*
Taubot paumpmaúntaman.	*I am glad you are well.*
Cowaúnckamish.	*My service to you.*

Observation.

This word upon speciall Salutations they use, and upon some offence conceived by the *Sachim* or Prince against any: I have seen the party reverently doe obeysance, by stroking the Prince upon both his sholders, and using this word,

Cowaúnckamish & Cuckquénamish.	*I pray your favour.*
Cowaúnkamuck.	*He salutes you.*
Aspaumpmáuntam sachim?	*How doth the Prince?*
Aspaumpmáutam Commíttamus?	*How doth your Wife?*
Aspaumpmaúntummwock cummuckiaûg?	*How do your children?*
Konkeeteâug.	*They are well.*
Táubot ne paumpmaunthéttit.	*I am glad they are well.*
Túnna Cowâum, Tuckôteshana?	*Whence come you?*
Yò nowaûm.	*I came that way.*
Náwwatuck nóteshem.	*I came from farre.*
Mattaâsu nóteshem.	*I came from hard by.*
Wêtu.	*An House.*
Wetuômuck nóteshem.	*I came from the house.*
Acâwmuck notéshem.	*I came over the water.*
Otàn.	*A Towne.*
Otânick notéshem.	*I came from the Towne.*

Observation.

In the Narigánset Countrey (which is the chief people in the Land:) a man shall come to many Townes, some bigger, some lesser, it may be a dozen in 20. miles Travell.

Observation.

Acawmenóakit, *Old England,* which is as much as *from the Land on t'other side:* hardly are they brought to believe that that Water is three thousand English mile over, or thereabouts.

Tunnock kuttòme?	*Whither goe you?*
Wékick nittóme.	*To the house.*
Nékick.	*To my house.*
Kékick.	*To your house.*
Tuckowêkin?	*Where dwell you?*
Tuckuttîin?	*Where keep you?*
Matnowetuómeno.	*I have no house.*

Observation.

As commonly a single person hath no house, so after the death of a Husband or Wife, they often break up house, and live here and there a while with Friends, to allay their excessive Sorrowes.

Tou wuttîin?	*Where lives he?*
Awânick ûchick?	*Who are these?*
Awaùn ewò?	*Who is that?*
Túnna úmwock, Tunna Wutshaûock?	*Whence come they?*
Yo nowêkin.	*I dwell here.*
Yo ntîin.	*I live here.*
Eîu *or* Nnîu?	*Is it so?*

Nùx. — *Yea.*
Mat nippompitámmen. — *I have heard nothing.*
Wésuonck. — *A name.*
Tocketussawêitch? — *What is your name?*
Taantússawese? — *Doe you aske my name?*
Ntússawese. — *I am called, &c.*
Matnowesuónckane. — *I have no name.*

Observation.

Obscure and meane persons amongst them have no Names: *Nullius numeri, &c.* as the Lord Jesus foretells his followers, that their Names should be cast out, *Luk.* 6. 22. as not worthy to be named, *&c.* Againe, because they abhorre to name the dead (Death being the King of Terrours to all naturall men: and though the Natives hold the Soule to live ever, yet not holding a Resurrection, they die, and mourn without Hope.) In that respect I say, if any of their *Sáchims* or neighbours die who were of their names, they lay down those Names as dead.

Nowánnehick nowésuonck. — *I have forgot my Name.*

Which is common amongst some of them, this being one Incivilitie amongst the more rusticall sort, not to call each other by their Names, but Keen, *You,* Ewò, *He, &c.*

Tahéna? — *What is his name?*
Tahossowêtam? — *What is the name of it?*
Tahéttamen? — *What call you this?*
Teáqua? — *What is this?*
Yò néepoush. — *Stay* or *stand here.*
Máttapsh. — *Sit down.*
Noónshem, Nonànum. — *I cannot.*
Tawhitch kuppeeyaúmen? — *What come you for?*
Téaqua kunnaúntamen? — *What doe you fetch?*
Chenock cuppeeyâumis? — *When came you?*

Maìsh, kitummâyi.	*Just, even now.*
Kitummâyi nippeéam.	*I came just now.*
Yò Commíttamus?	*Is this your Wife?*
Yo cuppáppoos?	*Is this your Child?*
Yó cummúckquachucks?	*Is this your Son?*
Yò cuttaûnis?	*Is this your Daughter?*
Wunnêtu.	*It is a fine Child.*
Tawhitch neepouweéyean?	*Why stand you?*
Pucqúatchick.	*Without dores.*
Tawhítch mat petiteáyean?	*Why come you not in?*

Observ.

In this respect they are remarkably free and courteous, to invite all Strangers in; and if any come to them upon any occasion, they request them to *come in,* if they come not in of themselves.

Awássish.	*Warme you.*
Máttapsh yóteg.	*Sit by the fire.*
Tocketúnnawem?	*What say you?*
Keén nétop?	*Is it you friend?*
Peeyàush nétop.	*Come hither friend.*
Pétitees.	*Come in.*
Kunnúnni?	*Have you seene me?*
Kunnúnnous.	*I have seen you.*
Taubot mequaunnamêan.	*I thank you for your kind remembrance.*
Taûbot neanawáyean.	*I thank you.*
Taûbot neaunanamêan.	*I thank you for your love.*

Observ.

I have acknowledged amongst them an heart sensible of kindnesses, and have reaped kindnesse again from many, seaven yeares after, when I my selfe had forgotten, *&c.* hence the Lord Jesus exhorts his followers to doe good for evill; for otherwise, sinners will do good for good, kindnesse for kindnesse, &c.

Cowàmmaunsh.	*I love you.*
Cowammaûnuck.	*He loves you.*
Cowámmaus.	*You are loving.*
Cowâutam?	*Understand you?*
Nowaûtam.	*I understand.*
Cowâwtam tawhitche nippeeyaûmen?	*Doe you know why I come?*
Cowannántam?	*Have you forgotten?*
Awanagusàntowosh.	*Speake English.*
Eenàntowash.	*Speake Indian.*
Cutehanshishaùmo?	*How many were you in Company?*
Kúnnishishem?	*Are you alone?*
Nníshishem.	*I am alone.*
Naneeshâumo.	*There be 2. of us.*
Nanshwishâwmen.	*We are 4.*
Npiuckshâwmen.	*We are 10.*
Neesneechecktashaûmen.	*We are 20.* &c.
Nquitpausuckowashâwmen.	*We are an 100.*
Comishoonhómmis?	*Did you come by boate?*
Kuttiakewushaùmis?	*Came you by land?*
Mesh nomishoonhómmin.	*I came by boat.*
Meshntiauké wushem.	*I came by land.*
Nippenowántawem.	*I am of another language.*
Penowantowawhettûock.	*They are of a divers language.*
Mat nowawtau hettémina.	*We understand not each other.*
Nummaúchenèm.	*I am sicke.*
Cummaúchenem?	*Are you sicke?*
Tashúckqunne cummauchenaûmis?	*How long have you been sicke?*

Nummauchêmin *or* Ntannetéimmin.	*I will be going.*
Saûop Cummauchêmin.	*You shall goe to morrow.*
Maúchish *or* ànakish.	*Be going.*
Kuttannâwshesh.	*Depart.*
Mauchéi *or* ànittui.	*He is gone.*
Kautanaûshant.	*He being gone.*
Mauchéhettit *or* Kautanawshàwhettit.	*When they are gone.*
Kukkowêtous.	*I will lodge with you.*
Yò Cówish.	*Do, lodge here.*
Hawúnshech.	*Farewell.*
Chénock wonck cuppeeyeâumen?	*When will you be here againe?*
Nétop tattà.	*My friend I can not tell.*

From these courteous *Salutations* Observe in generall: There is a savour of *civility* and *courtesie* even amongst these wild *Americans,* both amongst *themselves* and towards *strangers.*

More particular:

1. *The Courteous* Pagan *shall condemne*
Uncourteous Englishmen,
Who live like Foxes, Beares and Wolves,
Or Lyon in his Den.

2. *Let none sing* blessings *to their soules,*
For that they Courteous are:
The wild Barbarians *with no more*
Then Nature, goe so farre:

3. *If Natures Sons both* wild *and* tame,
Humane and Courteous be:
How ill becomes it Sonnes of God
To want Humanity?

CHAP. II.
Of *Eating* and *Entertainment.*

Ascúmetesímmis?	*Have you not yet eaten?*
Matta niccattuppúmmin.	*I am not hungry.*
Niccàwkatone.	*I am thirstie.*
Mannippêno?	*Have you no water?*
Nip, *or* nipéwese.	*Give me some water.*
Nàmitch, commetesímmin.	*Stay, you must eat first.*
Téaquacumméich?	*What will you eat?*
Nókehick.	*Parch'd meal,* which is a

readie very wholesome food, which they eate with a little water, hot or cold; I have travelled with neere 200. of them at once, neere 100. miles through the woods, every man carrying a *little Basket* of this at his back, and sometimes in a hollow *Leather Girdle* about his middle, sufficient for a man three or foure daies:

With this readie provision, and their *Bow* and *Arrowes,* are they ready for *War,* and *travell* at an *houres* warning. With a *spoonfull* of this *meale* and a *spoonfull* of water from the *Brooke,* have I made many a good dinner and supper.

Aupúmmineanash.	*The parch'd corne.*
Aupúminea-nawsaùmp.	*The parc'd meale boild with water at their houses, which is the wholesomest diet they have.*
Msíckquatash.	*Boild corne whole.*
Manusqussêdash.	*Beanes.*
Nasàump.	*A kind of meale pottage, unpartch'd.*

From this the *English* call their *Samp,* which is the *Indian* corne, beaten and boild, and eaten hot or cold with milke or butter, which are mercies beyond the *Natives* plaine water, and which is a dish exceeding wholesome for the *English* bodies.

Puttuckqunnége.	*A Cake.*
Puttuckqunnêgunash puttúckqui.	*Cakes* or *loves round.*
Teâgun kuttiemaûnch?	*What shall I dresse for you?*
Assámme.	*Give me to eate.*
Ncàttup.	*I am hungrie.*
Wúnna ncáttup.	*I am very hungry.*
Nippaskanaûntum.	*I am almost starved.*
Pàutous notatàm.	*Give me drinke.*
Sókenish.	*Powre forth.*
Cosaûme sokenúmmis.	*You have powred out too much.*
Wuttàttash.	*Drinke.*
Nquitchetàmmin.	*Let me taste.*
Quítchetash.	*Taste.*
Saúnqui nip?	*Is the water coole?*
Saunkopaûgot.	*Coole water.*
Chowhêsu.	*It is warme.*
Aquie wuttàttash.	*Doe not drinke.*
Aquie waúmatous.	*Do not drinke all.*
Necáwni mèich teàqua.	*First eat something.*
Tawhitch mat mechóan?	*Why eat you not?*
Wussaúme kusópita.	*It is too hot.*
Teâguun numméitch?	*What shall I eate?*
Mateàg keesitàuano?	*Is there nothing ready boyld?*
Mateàg mécho ewò.	*He eats nothing.*
Cotchikésu assamme.	*Cut me a piece.*
Cotchekúnnemi weeyoùs.	*Cut me some meat.*
Metesíttuck.	*Let us goe eate.*

Pautiínnea méchimucks. *Bring hither some victualls.*
Numwàutous. *Fill the dish.*
Mihtukméchakick. *Tree-eaters.* A people so called (living between three and foure hundred miles West into the land) from their eating only *Mihtúchquash,* that is, Trees: They are *Men-eaters,* they set no corne, but live on the *bark* of *Chesnut* and *Walnut,* and other fine trees: They dry and eat this *bark* with the fat of Beasts, and sometimes of men: This people are the *terrour* of the neighbour *Natives;* and yet these *Rebells,* the Sonne of God may in time subdue.

Mauchepweéean.	*After I have eaten.*
Maúchepwucks.	*After meales.*
Maúchepwut.	*When he hath eaten.*
Paúshaqua maúchepwut.	*After dinner.*
Wàyyeyant maúchepwut.	*After supper.*
Nquittmaûntash.	*Smell.*
Weetimóquat.	*It smells sweet.*
Machemóqut.	*It stinks.*
Weékan.	*It is sweet.*
Machíppoquat.	*It is sowre.*
Aúwusse weékan.	*It is sweeter.*
Askùn.	*It is raw.*
Noónat.	*Not enough.*
Wusàume wékissu.	*Too much* either *boyled* or *rosted.*
Waûmet, Taûbi.	*It is enough.*
Wuttattumútta.	*Let us drinke.*
Neesneechàhettit taúbi.	*Eenough for twentie men.*
Mattacuckquàw.	*A Cooke.*
Mattacúcquass.	*Cooke* or *dresse.*
Matcuttàssamíin?	*Will you not give me to eate?*
Keen méitch.	*I pray eate.*

They generally all take *Tobacco;* and it is commonly the only plant which men labour in; the women managing all the rest: they say they take *Tobacco* for two causes; first, against the rheume, which causeth the toothake, which they are impatient of: secondly, to revive and refresh them, they drinking nothing but water.

Squuttame.	*Give me your pipe.*
Petasínna, *or,* Wuttàmmasin.	*Give mee some* Tabacco.
Ncattaûntum, *or,* Ncàttiteam.	*I long for that.*
Màuchinaash nowépiteass.	*My teeth are naught.*
Nummashackquneaûmen.	*Wee are in a dearth.*
Mashackquineâug.	*We have no food.*
Aúcuck.	*A Kettle.*
Míshquockuk.	*A red Copper Kettle.*
Nétop kuttàssammish.	*Friend, I have brought you this.*
Quàmphash quamphomíinea.	*Take up for me out of the pot.*
Eíppoquat.	*It is sweet.*
Teàqua aspúckquat?	*What doth it taste of?*
Nowétipo.	*I like this.*
Wenómeneash.	*Grapes* or *Raysins.*
Waweécocks.	*Figs,* or some strange sweet meat.
Nemaúanash.	*Provision for the way.*
Nemauanínnuit.	*A snapsacke.*
Tackhúmmin	*To grind corne.*
Tackhumíinnea.	*Beat me parch'd meale.*
Pishquéhick.	*Unparch'd meale.*
Nummaùchip nup mauchepúmmin.	*We have eaten all.*
Cowàump?	*Have you enough?*

Nowâump. — *I have enough.*

Mohowaúgsuck, *or,* Mauquàuog, *from* móho *to eate.* — *The* Canibals, *or* Men-eaters, *up into the west two, three or foure hundred miles from us.*

Cummóhucquock. — *They will eate you.*

Whomsoever commeth in when they are eating, they offer them to eat of that which they have, though but little enough prepar'd for themselves. If any provision of *fish* or *flesh* come in, they make their neighbours partakers with them.

If any stranger come in, they presently give him to eate of what they have; many a time, and at all times of the night (as I have fallen in travell upon their houses) when nothing hath been ready, have themselves and their wives, risen to prepare me some refreshing.

The observation generall from their eating, &c.

It is a strange *truth,* that a man shall generally finde more free entertainment and refreshing amongst these *Barbarians,* then amongst thousands that call themselves *Christians.*

More particular:

1. *Course* bread *and* water's *most their fare,*
   O Englands *diet fine;*
   Thy cup *runs ore with plenteous store*
   Of wholesome beare *and* wine.

2. *Sometimes* God *gives them* Fish *or* Flesh,
   Yet they're content *without;*
   And what comes in, they part *to* friends
   And strangers *round about.*

3. *Gods* providence *is rich to his,*
Let none distrustfull *be;*
In wildernesse, *in great* distresse,
These Ravens *have fed me.*

CHAP. III.

Concerning Sleepe *and* Lodging.

Nsowwushkâwmen.	*I am weary.*
Nkàtaquaum.	*I am sleepie.*
Kukkowetoùs?	*Shall I lodge here?*
Yo nickowémen?	*Shall I sleepe here?*
Kukkowéti?	*Will you sleepe here?*
Wunnégin, cówish.	*Welcome, sleepe here.*
Nummouaquômen.	*I will lodge abroad.*

Puckquátchick nickouêmen. *I will sleepe without the doores,* Which I have knowne them contentedly doe, by a fire under a tree, when sometimes some *English* have (for want of familiaritie and language with them) been fearefull to entertaine them.

In Summer-time I have knowne them lye abroad often themselves, to make roome for strangers, *English,* or others.

Mouaquómitea.	*Let us lye abroad.*
Cowwêtuck.	*Let us sleepe.*
Kukkóuene?	*Sleepe you?*
Cowwêke.	*Sleepe, sleepe.*
Cowwêwi.	*He is asleepe.*
Cowwêwock.	*They sleepe.*
Askukkówene?	*Sleepe you yet?*
Takitíppocat.	*It is a cold night.*
Wekitíppocat.	*It is a warme night.*
Wauwháutowaw ánawat, *&* Wawhautowâwog.	*Ther is an alarme,* or, *there is a great shouting:*

Howling and shouting is their Alarme; they having no Drums nor Trumpets: but whether an enemie approach, or fire breake out, this Alarme passeth from house to house; yea, commonly, if any *English* or *Dutch* come amongst them, they give notice of strangers by this signe; yet I have knowne them buy and use a *Dutch* Trumpet, and knowne a *Native* make a good Drum in imitation of the *English.*

Matànnauke, *or* Mattannàukanash.	*A finer sort of mats to sleep on.*
Maskítuash.	*Straw to ly on.*
Wudtúckqunash ponamâuta.	*Let us lay on wood.*

This they doe plentifully when they lie down to sleep winter and summer, abundance they have, and abundance they lay on: their Fire is instead of our bedcloaths. And so, themselves and any that have occasion to lodge with them, must be content to turne often to the Fire, if the night be cold, and they who first wake must repaire the Fire.

Mauataúnamoke.	*Mend the fire.*
Mauataunamútta.	*Let us mend the fire.*
Tokêtuck.	*Let us wake.*
Askuttokémis?	*Are you not awake yet?*
Tókish, Tókeke.	*Wake, wake.*
Tókinish.	*Wake him.*
Kitumyái tokéan.	*As soone as I wake.*
Ntunnaquômen.	*I have had a good dream.*
Nummattaquômen.	*I have had a bad dream.*

When they have a bad Dreame, which they conceive to be a threatning from God, they fall to prayer at all times of the night, especially early before day: So *Davids* zealous heart to the true and living God: *At midnight will I rise* &c. *I prevented the dawning of the day,* &c. Psal. 119. &c.

Wunnakukkússaqùaum.	*You sleep much.*
Peeyaûntam.	*He prayes.*
Peeyâuntamwock.	*They pray.*
Túnna kukkowémis?	*Where slept you?*
Awaun wékick kukkouémis?	*At whose house did you sleep?*

I once travailed to an Iland of the wildest in our parts, where in the night an Indian (as he said) had a vision or dream of the Sun (whom they worship for a God) darting a Beame into his Breast, which he conceived to be the Messenger of his Death: this poore Native call'd his Friends and neighbours, and prepared some little refreshing for them, but himselfe was kept waking and Fasting in great Humiliations and Invocations for 10. dayes and nights: I was alone (having travailed from my Barke, the wind being contrary) and little could I speake to them to their understandings, especially because of the change of their Dialect, or manner of Speech from our neighbours: yet so much (through the help of God) I did speake, of the *True* and *living only Wise God,* of the Creation: of Man, and his *fall* from God, &c. that at parting many burst forth, *Oh when will you come againe, to bring us some more newes of this God?*

From their Sleeping: The Observation generall.

Sweet rest is not confind to soft Beds, for, not only God gives his beloved sleep on hard lodgings: but also Nature and Custome gives sound sleep to these Americans on the Earth, on a Boord or Mat. Yet how is *Europe* bound to God for better lodging, *&c.*

More particular.

1. *God gives them sleep on Ground, on Straw,*
On Sedgie Mats or Boord:
When English softest Beds of Downe,
Sometimes no sleep affoord.

2. *I have knowne them leave their House and Mat*
To lodge a Friend or stranger,
When Jewes and Christians oft have sent
Christ Jesus *to the Manger.*

3. *'Fore day they invocate their Gods,*
Though Many, False and New:
O how should that God worshipt be,
Who is but One and True?

CHAP. IV.
Of *their Numbers.*

Nquít.	*One.*
Neèsse.	2.
Nìsh.	3.
Yòh.	4.
Napànna.	5.
Qútta.	6.
Énada.	7.
Shwosúck.	8.
Paskúgit.	9.
Piùck.	10.
Piucknabna quìt.	11.
Piucknab nèese.	12.
Piucknab nìsh.	13.
Piucknab yòh.	14.
Piucknab napànna.	15.
Piucknab naqútta.	16.
Piucknab énada.	17.
Piucknabna shwósuck.	18.
Piucknabna paskúgit.	19.
Neesneéchick.	20.
Neesneéchick nab naquìt, *&c.*	21, *&c.*
Shwíncheck.	30.
Swíncheck nab naquìt, *&c.*	31, *&c.*
Yowínicheck.	40.
Yówinicheck nab naquìt, *&c.*	41, *&c.*
Napannetashincheck.	50.
Napannetashincheck nabna quìt.	51, *&c.*
Quttatashìncheck.	60.

Quttatashincheck nabna quìt.	61, *&c.*
Enadatashìncheck.	70.
Enadatashincheck nabna quìt.	71, *&c.*
Swoasuck ta shin check.	80.
Shwoasuck ta shincheck nebna quìt.	81, *&c.*
Paskugit tashìncheck.	90.
Paskugit tashin check nabna quìt, *&c.*	91, *&c.*
Nquit pâwsuck.	100.
Nees pâwsuck.	200.
Shweepâwsuck.	300.
Yówe pâwsuck.	400.
Napannetashe pâwsuck.	500.
Qúttatashe pâwsuck.	600.
Enadatashe pâwsuck.	700.
Shoasucktashe pâwsuck.	800.
Paskugittashe pâwsuck.	900.
Nquittemittànnug.	1000.
Neese mittànnug.	2000.
Nishwe mittànnug.	3000.
Yowe mittànnug.	4000.
Napannetashe mittànnug.	5000.
Quttàtashe mittànnug.	6000.
Enadatashe mittànnug.	7000.
Shoasucktashe mittánnug.	8000.
Paskugittashe mittánnug.	9000.
Piuckque mittánnug.	10000.
Neesneechecktashe mittânnug.	20000.
Shwinchecktashe mittánnug.	30000.
Yowinchecktashe mittánnug.	40000.
Napannetashinchecktashe mittánnug.	50000.

Quttatashinchecktashe mittànnug.	60000.
Enadatashinchecktashe mittánnug.	70000.
Shoasucktashinchecktashe mittánnug.	80000.
Pàskugittashinchecktashe mittànnug.	90000.
Nquit pausuckóemittànnug, *&c.*	100000.

Having no Letters nor Arts, 'tis admirable how quick they are in casting up great numbers, with the helpe of graines of Corne, instead of *Europes* pens or counters.

Numbers of the masculine gender.

Pawsuck.	1.	
Neéswock.	2.	Skeetomp *a Man.*
Shúog.	3.	
Yówock.	4.	*as,* Skeetom Paúog, *Men.*
Napannetasúog.	5.	
Quttasúog.	6.	
Enada tasúog.	7.	
Shoasuck tasúog.	8.	
Paskugit tasúog.	9.	
Piucksúog.	10.	
Piucksúog nabnaquìt.	11.	

Of the *Feminine* Gender.

Pâwsuck.	1.	
Neénash.	2.	
Swínash.	3.	
Yowúnnash.	4.	*as,* Wauchò *Hill.* Wauchóash *Hills.*
Napannetashínash.	5.	
Quttatashínash.	6.	
Enadatashínash.	7.	

Shoasucktashínas. 8.
Paskugittashínash. 9.
Piúckquatash. 10.
Piúckquatash nabnaquìt. 11.

From their Numbers, *Observation* Generall.

Let it be considered, whether *Tradition* of ancient *Forefathers,* or *Nature* hath taught them *Europes Arithmaticke.*

More particular:

1. *Their* Braines *are quick, their* hands,
   Their feet, *their* tongues, *their* eyes:
   God may fit objects *in his time,*
   To those quicke faculties.

2. Objects *of higher nature make them tell,*
   The holy number *of his Sons* Gospel:
   Make them and us to tell *what* told *may be;*
   But stand amazed *at* Eternitie.

CHAP. V.

Of their relations *of* consanguinitie *and* affinitie, *or*, Blood *and* Marriage.

Nnìn -nnínnuog, & Skeétomp -aûog.	*Man -men.*
Squàws -suck.	*Woman -women.*
Kichize, &	*An old man,*
Kichîzuck.	*Old men.*
Hômes, &	*An old man,*
Hômesuck.	*Old men.*
Kutchínnu.	*A middle-aged-man.*
Kutchínnuwock.	*Middle-aged-men.*
Wuskeène.	*A youth.*
Wuskeeneésuck.	*Youths.*
Wénise &	*An old woman,*
Wenîsuck.	*Old women.*
Mattaûntum.	*Very old and decrepit.*
Wásick.	*An Husband.*
Weéwo, & Mittúmmus, & Wullógana.	*A Wife.*
Nowéewo, Nummíttamus, &c.	*My Wife.*
Osh.	*A Father.*
Nòsh.	*My father.*
Còsh.	*Your father.*
Cuttòso?	*Have you a father?*
Okásu, & Witchwhaw.	*A mother.*
Nókace, nitchwhaw.	*My mother.*
Wússese.	*An Unckle.*

Nissesè. *My Unckle.*
Papoòs. *A childe.*
Nippápoos, & Nummúckiese. *My childe.*
Nummúckquáchucks. *My sonne.*
Nittaûnis. *My daughter.*
Non ânese. *A sucking child.*
Muckquachuckquêmese. *A little boy.*
Squásese. *A little girle.*
Weémat. *A brother.*

They hold the band of brother-hood so deare, that when one had commited a murther and fled, they executed his brother; and 'tis common for a brother to pay the debt of a brother deceased.

Neémat. *My brother.*
Wéticks, & Weésummis. *A sister.*
Wematíttuock. *They are brothers.*
Cutchashematítin? *How many brothers have you?*
Natòncks. *My cousin.*
Kattòncks. *Your cousin.*
Watòncks. *A cousin.*
Nullóquaso. *My ward* or *pupill.*
Wattonksíttuock. *They are cousins.*
Kíhtuckquaw. *A virgin marriageable.*

Their Virgins are distinguished by a bashfull falling downe of their haire over their eyes.

Towiúwock. *Fatherlesse children.*

There are no beggars amongst them, nor fatherlesse children unprovided for.

Tackqíuwock. *Twins.*

Their *affections,* especially to their children, are very strong; so that I have knowne a *Father* take so grievously the losse of his *childe,* that hee hath cut and stob'd himselfe with *griefe* and *rage.*

This extreme *affection,* together with want of *learning,* makes ther children sawcie, bold, and undutifull.

I once came into a *house,* and requested some *water* to drinke; the *father* bid his sonne (of some 8. yeeres of age) to fetch some *water*: the *boy* refused, and would not stir; I told the *father,* that I would correct my *child,* if he should so disobey me, &c. Upon this the *father* took up a sticke, the *boy* another, and flew at his *father*: upon my perswasion, the poore *father* made him smart a little, throw down his stick, and run for *water,* and the *father* confessed the benefit of *correction,* and the evill of their too indulgent *affections.*

From their Relations *Observation generall.*

In the *ruines* of depraved *mankinde,* are yet to be founde *Natures distinctions,* and *Natures affections.*

More particular:

[1.] *The* Pagans *wild confesse the* bonds
Of married chastitie:
How vild are Nicolâitans *that hold*
Of Wives *communitie?*

[2.] *How kindly flames of* nature *burne*
In wild humanitie?
Naturall affections *who wants, is sure*
Far from Christianity.

[3.] *Best nature's vaine, he's blest that's made*
A new and rich partaker
Of divine Nature of his God,
And blest eternall Maker.

CHAP. VI.

Of the Family and businesse of the House.

Wetu.	*An House.*
Wetuômuck.	*At home.*
Nékick.	*My house.*
Kékick.	*Your house.*
Wékick.	*At his house.*
Nickquénum.	*I am going home:*

Which is a solemne word amongst them; and no man wil offer any hinderance to him, who after some absence is going to visit his Family, and useth this word *Nicquénum* (confessing the sweetnesse even of these short temporall homes.)

Puttuckakàun. *A round house.*
Puttuckakâunese. *A little round house.*
Wetuomémese. *A little house;* which their women and maids live apart in, foure, five, or six dayes, in the time of their monethly sicknesse, which custome in all parts of the Countrey they strictly observe, and no *Male* may come into that house.

Neés quttow. *A longer house with two fires.*
Shwíshcuttow. *With three fires.*
Abockquósinash. *The mats of the house.*
Wuttapuíssuck. *The long poles,* which commonly men get and fix, and then the women cover the house with mats, and line them with embroydered mats which the women make, and call them *Munnotaúbana,* or *Hangings,*

which amongst them make as faire a show as Hangings with us.

Nòte, *or* Yòte, Chíckot & Sqútta.	*Fire.*
Notáwese & chickautáwese.	*A little fire.*
Púck.	*Smoke.*
Puckíssu.	*Smokie.*
Nippúckis.	*Smoke troubleth me.*
Wuchickapêuck.	*Burching barke,* and *Chesnut barke*

which they dresse finely, and make a Summer-covering for their houses.

Cuppoquiíttemin.	*I will divide house with you,* or *dwell with you.*

Two Families will live comfortably and lovingly in a little round house of some fourteen or sixteen foot over, and so more and more families in proportion.

Nuckqusquatch, Nuckqusquatchímin.	*I am cold.*
Potouwássiteuck.	*Let us make a fire.*
Wudtúckqun.	*A piece of wood.*
Wudtúckquanash, Ponamâuta.	*Lay on wood.*
Pawacómwushesh.	*Cut some wood.*
Maumashinnaunamaûta.	*Let us make a good fire.*
Npaacómwushem.	*I will cut wood.*
Aséneshesh.	*Fetch some small sticks.*
Wònck, & Wónkatack.	*More.*
Wonckatáganash nàus.	*Fetch some more.*
Netashìn & newucháshinea.	*There is no more.*
Wequanántash.	*Light a fire.*
Wequanantíg.	*A Candle,* or *Light.*
Wequanantíganash.	*Candles.*

Wékinan.	*A light fire.*
Awâuo?	*Who is at home?*
Mat Awawanúnno.	*There is no body.*
Unháppo Kòsh?	*Is your father at home?*
Túckiu Sáchim?	*Where is the Sachim?*
Mát-apeù.	*He is not at home.*
Peyàu.	*He is come.*
Wéche-peyàu-keémat.	*Your brother is come with him.*
Pótawash.	*Make a fire.*
Potâuntash.	*Blowe the fire.*
Peeyâuog.	*They are come.*
Wâme, paúshe.	*All, some.*
Tawhìtch mat peyáyean?	*Why came,* or, *come you not?*
Mesh noónshem peeyaùn.	*I could not come.*
Mocenanippeéam.	*I will come by and by.*
Aspeyàu, asquàm.	*He is not come yet.*
Yò aútant mèsh nippeéam.	*I was here the Sunne so high.*

And then they point with the hand to the Sunne, by whose highth they keepe account of the day, and by the Moone and Stars by night, as wee doe by clocks and dialls, &c.

Wúskont peyâuog.	*They will come.*
Teáqua naúntick ewò?	*What comes hee for?*
Yo áppitch ewò.	*Let him sit there.*
Unhappò kòsh?	*Is your father at home?*
Unnàugh.	*He is there.*
Npépeyup náwwot.	*I have long been here.*
Tawhìtch peyáuyean?	*Why doe you come?*
Téaguun kunnaúntamun?	*What come you for?*
Awàun ewò?	*Who is that?*
Nowéchiume.	*He is my servant.*
Wécum, naus.	*Call, fetch.*
Petiteaûta.	*Let us goe in.*

Noonapúmmin autashéhettit.	*There is not roome for so many.*
Taubapímmin.	*Roome enough.*
Noónat.	*Not enough.*
Asquam.	*Not yet.*
Náim, námitch.	*By and by.*
Mòce, unuckquaquêse.	*Instantly.*
Máish, kitummây.	*Just, even now.*
Túckiu, tíyu.	*Where.*
Kukkekuttokâwmen?	*Would you speake with him?*
Nùx.	*Yea.*
Wuttammâuntam.	*He is busie.*
Nétop notammâuntam.	*Friend, I am busie.*
Cotámmâuntam?	*Are you busie?*
Cotámmish.	*I hinder you.*
Cotammúmme, Cotamme.	*You trouble me.*

Obs. They are as full of businesse, and as impatient of hinderance (in their kind) as any Merchant in *Europe.*

Nqussûtam.	*I am removing.*
Notámmehick ewò.	*He hinders me.*
Maumachíuash.	*Goods.*
Aúquiegs.	*Housholdstuffe.*
Tuckíiuash?	*Where be they?*
Wenawwêtu.	*Rich.*
Machêtu.	*Poore.*
Wenawetuónckon.	*Wealth.*
Kúphash.	*Shut the doore.*
Kuphómmin.	*To shut the doore.*
Yeaùsh.	*Shut doore after you.*

Obs. Commonly they never shut their doores, day nor night; and 'tis rare that any hurt is done.

Wunêgin.	*Well,* or *good.*
Machit.	*Naught,* or *evill.*

Cowaûtam? *Do you understand?*
Macháug. *No,* or *not.*
Wunnâug. *A Tray.*
Wunnauganash. *Trayes.*
Kunàm. *A Spoone.*
Kunnamâuog. *Spoones.*

Obs. In steed of shelves, they have severall baskets, wherein they put all their housholdstuffe: they have some great bags or sacks made of *Hempe,* which will hold five or sixe bushells.

Táckunck, *or,* Wéskhunck. *Their pounding Morter.*

Obs. Their women constantly beat all their corne with hand: they plant it, dresse it, gather it, barne it, beat it, and take as much paines as any people in the world, which labour is questionlesse one cause of their extraordinary ease of childbirth.

Wunnauganémese. *A little Tray.*
Téaqua cunnátinne? *What doe you looke for?*
Natínnehas. *Search.*
Kekíneas. *See here.*
Machàge cunna miteôuwin? *Doe you find nothing?*
Wónckatack. *Another.*
Tunnatì? *Where?*
Ntauhaunanatinnehómmin. *I cannot looke* or *search.*
Ntauhaunanamiteoûwin. *I cannot find.*
Wíaseck, Eiássunck, Mocôtick, Punnêtunck, Chaúqock. *A Knife.*

Obs. Whence they call *English-men* Chauquaquock, that is, *Knive-men,* stone formerly being to them in stead of *Knives, Awle-blades, Hatchets* and *Howes.*

Namacówhe, Cówíaseck. *Lend me your Knife.*
Wonck Commêsim? *Wil you give it me again?*
Mátta nowáuwone. *I knew nothing.*
Matta nowáhea, Mat meshnowáhea. *I was innocent.*
Paútous, Pautâuog. *Bring hither.*
Maúchatous. *Carry this.*
Niâutàsh, & Wéawhush. *Take it on your backe.*

Obs. It is almost incredible what burthens the poore women carry of *Corne,* of *Fish,* of *Beanes,* of *Mats,* and a childe besides.

Awâùn. *There is some body.*
Kekíneas. *Goe and see.*
Squantâumuck. *At the doore.*
Awàun keèn? *Who are you?*
Keèn nétop? *Is it you?*
Pauquanamíinnea. *Open me the doore.*

Obs. Most commonly their houses are open, their doore is a hanging *Mat,* which being lift up, falls downe of it selfe; yet many of them get *English* boards and nailes, and make artificiall doores and bolts themselves, and others make slighter doores of *Burch* or *Chesnut* barke, which they make fast with a cord in the night time, or when they go out of town, and then the last (that makes fast) goes out at the Chimney, which is a large opening in the middle of their house, called:

Wunnauchicómock. *A Chimney.*
Anúnema. *Helpe me.*
Neenkuttánnũmous. *I will helpe you.*
Kuttánnummi? *Will you helpe me?*
Shookekíneas. *Behold here.*
Nummouekékineam. *I come to see.*
Tou autèg? *Know you where it lies?*

Tou núckquaque?	*How much?*
Yo naumwâuteg.	*Thus full.*
Aquíe.	*Leave off,* or *doe not.*
Waskéche.	*On the top.*
Náumatuck.	*In the bottome.*
Aûqunnish.	*Let goe.*
Aukeeaseíu.	*Downewards.*
Keesuckqíu.	*Upwards.*
Aumàunsh, Ausàuonsh, Aumáunamòke.	*Take away.*
Nanóuwetea, Naunóuwheant.	*A Nurse,* or *Keeper.*
Nanowwúnemum.	*I looke to,* or *keepe.*

Obs. They nurse all their children themselves; yet, if she be an high or rich woman, she maintaines a Nurse to tend the childe.

Waucháunama.	*Keep this for me.*
Cuttatashiínnas.	*Lay these up for me.*

Obs. Many of them begin to be furnished with *English* Chests; others, when they goe forth of towne, bring their goods (if they live neere) to the *English* to keepe for them, and their money they hang it about their necks, or lay it under their head when they sleepe.

Peewâuqun.	*Have a care.*
Nnowauchâunum.	*I will have a care.*
Kuttaskwhè.	*Stay for me.*
Kúttasha, & Cowauchâunum?	*Have you this or that?*
Pókesha, & Pokesháwwa.	*It is broke.*
Mat Coanichégane?	*Have you no hands?*
Tawhìtch?	*Why aske you?*
Nóonshem Pawtuckquámmin.	*I cannot reach.*

Aquie Pokesháttous.	*Doe not breake.*
Pokesháttouwin.	*To breake.*
Assótu, & Assóko.	*A foole.*

Obs. They have also amongst them naturall fooles, either so borne, or accidentally deprived of reason.

Aquie assókish.	*Be not foolish.*
Awânick.	*Some come.*
Niáutamwock, Pauchewannâuog.	*They are loden.*
Máttapeu & Qushenáwsui.	*A woman keeping alone in her monethly sicknesse.*
Moce ntúnnan.	*I will tell him by and by.*
Cowequetúmmous.	*I pray* or *intreat you.*
Wunniteóuin.	*To mend any thing.*
Wúnniteous, *or,* Wússiteous.	*Mend this.*
Wúskont nochemúckqun.	*I shall be chidden.*
Nickúmmat.	*Easie.*
Siúckat.	*Hard.*
Cummequâwname?	*Do you remember me?*
Mequaunamíinnea.	*Remember me.*
Puckqúatchick.	*Without doores.*
Nissawhócunck ewò.	*He puts me out of doores.*
Kussawhóki?	*Doe you put mee out of doores?*
Kussawhocowóog.	*Put them forth.*
Tawhítch kussawhokiêan?	*Why doe you put mee out?*
Sáwwhush, Sawhèke.	*Goe forth.*
Wussauhemútta.	*Let us goe forth.*
Matta nickquéhick.	*I want it not.*
Machagè nickquehickômina.	*I want nothing.*

Ob. Many of them naturally Princes, or else industrious persons, are rich; and the poore amongst them will say, they want nothing.

Páwsawash.	*Drie* or *ayre this.*
Pawsunnúmmin.	*To drie this* or *that.*
Cuppausummúnnash.	*Drie these things.*
Apíssumma.	*Warme this for me.*
Paucótche.	*Already.*
Cutsshitteoùs.	*Wash this.*
Tatágganish.	*Shake this.*
Napònsh.	*Lay downe.*
Wuchè machaùg.	*About nothing.*
Puppuckshácкhege.	*A Box.*
Paupaqúonteg.	*A Key.*
Mowáshuck.	*Iron.*
Wâuki.	*Crooked.*
Saûmpi.	*Strait.*
Aumpaniímmin.	*To undoe a knot.*
Aúmpanish.	*Untie this.*
Paushinúmmin.	*To divide into two.*
Pepênash, Nawwuttùnsh.	*Take your choyce.*
Pawtáwtees.	*Throw hither.*
Negáutowash.	*Send for him.*
Negauchhúwash.	*Send this to him.*
Nnegáuchemish.	*Hee sends to mee.*
Nowwêta.	*No matter.*
Mâuo.	*To cry and bewaile;*

Which bewailing is very solemne amongst them morning and evening, and sometimes in the night they bewaile their lost husbands, wives, children, brethren or sisters, &c. Sometimes a quarter, halfe, yea, a whole yeere, and longer, if it be for a great Prince.

In this time (unlesse a dispensation be given) they count it a prophane thing either to play (as they much use to doe) or to paint themselves, for beauty, but for mourning; or to be angry, and fall out with any, &c.

Machemóqut.	*It stincks.*
Machemóqussu.	*A vile* or *stinking person.*

Wúnníckshaas.	*Mingled.*
Wúnnickshan.	*To mingle.*
Nesick, *&* nashóqua.	*A Combe.*
Tetúpsha.	*To fall downe.*
Ntetúpshem.	*I fall downe.*
Tou anúckquaque?	*How big?*
Wunnáshpishan.	*To snatch away.*
Tawhìtch wunnash-pisháyean?	*Why snach you?*
Wuttùsh.	*Hitherward, & give me.*
Enèick, *or,* áwwusse.	*Further.*
Nneickomásu, *&* awwassése.	*A little further.*
Wuttushenaquáish.	*Looke hither.*
Yo anaquáyean.	*Looke about.*
Máuks, máugoke.	*Give this.*
Yo comméish.	*I will give you this.*
Qussúcqun -náukon.	*Heavie, light.*
Kuckqússaqun.	*You are heavie.*
Kunnàuki.	*You are light.*
Nickáttash, *singular.* Nickáttammoke, *plur.*	*Leave,* or *depart.*
Nickattamútta.	*Let us depart.*
Yówa.	*Thus.*
Ntowwaukâumen.	*I use it.*
Awawkáwnì.	*It is used.*
Yo awáutees.	*Use this.*
Yo wéque.	*Thus farre.*
Yo meshnowékeshem.	*I went thus farre.*
Ayátche, *&* Cónkitchea.	*As Often* [*as*].
Ayátche nippéeam.	*I am often here.*
Pakêtash.	*Fling it away.*
Npaketamúnnash.	*I will cast him away.*
Wuttámmasim.	*Give me* Tobaco.
Mat nowewuttámmo.	*I take none.*

Obs. Which some doe not, but they are rare Birds; for

generally all the men throughout the Countrey have a *Tobacco-bag,* with a *pipe* in it, hanging at their back: sometimes they make such great *pipes,* both of *wood* and *stone,* that they are two foot long, with men or beasts carved, so big or massie, that a man may be hurt mortally by one of them; but these comonly come from the *Mauquáuwogs,* or the *Men eaters,* three or foure hundred miles from us: They have an excellent Art to cast our *Pewter* and *Brasse* into very neate and artificiall *Pipes:* They take their *Wuttammâuog* (that is, a weake *Tobacco*) which the men plant themselves, very frequently; yet I never see any take so excessively, as I have seene men in *Europe;* and yet excesse were more tolerable in them, because they want the refreshing of *Beare* and *Wine,* which God hath vouchsafed *Europe.*

Wuttámmagon, Hopuònck. — *A Pipe.*
Chicks. — *A Cocke,* or *Hen:* A name taken from the *English* Chicke, because they have no Hens before the *English* came.

Chícks ánawat. — *The Cocke crowes.*
Neesquttónckqussu. — *A babler,* or *prater.*
Cunneesquttonckqussímmin. — *You prate.*

Obs. Which they figuratively transferre from the frequent troublesome clamour of a Cocke.

Nanótateem. — *I keepe house alone.*
Aquìe kuttúnnan. — *Doe not tell.*
Aquìe mooshkishâttous. — *Doe not disclose.*
Teàg yo augwháttick? — *What hangs there?*
Yo augwháttous. — *Hang it there.*
Pemisquâi. — *Crooked,* or *winding.*
Penâyi. — *Crooked.*
Nqussútam. — *I remove house:* Which they doe upon these occasions: From thick warme vallies, where

they winter, they remove a little neerer to their Summer fields; when 'tis warme Spring, then they remove to their fields where they plant Corne.

In middle of Summer, because of the abundance of Fleas, which the dust of the house breeds, they will flie and remove on a sudden from one part of their field to a fresh place: And sometimes having fields a mile or two, or many miles asunder, when the worke of one field is over, they remove house to the other: If death fall in amongst them, they presently remove to a fresh place: If an enemie approach, they remove into a Thicket, or Swampe, unlesse they have some Fort to remove unto.

Sometimes they remove to a hunting house in the end of the yeere, and forsake it not until Snow lie thick, and then will travel home, men, women and children, thorow the snow, thirtie, yea, fiftie or sixtie miles; but their great remove is from their Summer fields to warme and thicke woodie bottomes where they winter: They are quicke; in halfe a day, yea, sometimes at few houres warning to be gone and the house up elsewhere; especially, if they have stakes readie pitcht for their *Mats*.

I once in travell lodged at a house, at which in my returne I hoped to have lodged againe there the next night, but the house was gone in that interim, and I was glad to lodge under a tree:

The men make the poles or stakes, but the women make and set up, take downe, order, and carry the *Mats* and housholdstuffe.

Observation in generall.

The sociablenesse of the nature of man appeares in the wildest of them, who love societie; Families, cohabitation, and consociation of houses and townes together.

More particular:

1. *How busie are the sonnes of men?*
How full their heads and hands?
What noyse and tumults in our owne,
And eke in Pagan *lands?*

2. *Yet I have found lesse noyse, more peace*
In wilde America,
Where women quickly build the house,
And quickly move away.

[3.] English *and* Indians *busie are,*
In parts of their abode:
Yet both stand idle, *till God's call*
Set them to worke for God. Mat. 20.7.

CHAP. VII.

Of *their Persons* and *parts of body*.

Uppaquóntup.	*The head.*
Nuppaquóntup.	*My head.*
Wésheck.	*The hayre.*
Wuchechepúnnock.	*A great bunch of hayre bound up behind.*
Múppacuck.	*A long locke.*

Obs. Yet some cut their haire round, and some as low and as short as the sober *English;* yet I never saw any so to forget nature it selfe in such excessive length and monstrous fashion, as to the shame of the *English* Nation, I now (with griefe) see my Countrey-men in *England* are degenerated unto.

Wuttìp.	*The braine.*

Ob. In the braine their opinion is, that the soule (of which we shall speake in the Chapter of *Religion)* keeps her chiefe seat and residence:

For the temper of the braine in quick apprehensions and accurate judgements (to say no more) the most high and soveraign God and Creator, hath not made them inferiour to *Europeans.*

The *Mauquaúogs,* or *Men-eaters,* that live two or three [hundred] miles West from us, make a delicious monstrous dish of the head and brains of their enemies; which yet is no barre (when the time shall approach) against Gods call, and their repentance, and (who knowes but) a greater love to the Lord Jesus? great sinners forgiven love much.

Mscáttuck.	*The fore-head.*
Wuskeésuck -quash.	*Eye,* or *eyes.*

Tiyùsh kusskeésuckquash?	*Can you not see,* or *where are your eyes?*
Wuchaûn.	*The nostrills.*
Wuttówwog -guàsh.	*Eare, eares.*
Wuttòne.	*The mouth.*
Wéenat.	*The tongue.*
Wépit -teash.	*Tooth, teeth.*
Pummaumpiteùnck.	*The tooth-ake.*

Obs. Which is the onely paine will force their stout hearts to cry; I cannot heare of any disease of the stone amongst them (the corne of the Countrey, with which they are fed from the wombe, being an admirable cleanser and opener:) but the paine of their womens childbirth (of which I shall speake afterward in the Chapter of *Marriage*) never forces their women so to cry, as I have heard some of their men in this paine.

In this paine they use a certaine root dried, not much unlike our *Ginger.*

Sítchipuck.	*The necke.*
Qúttuck.	*The throat.*
Timeqúassin.	*To cut off,* or *behead,* which

they are most skilfull to doe in fight: for, when ever they wound, and their arrow sticks in the body of their enemie, they (if they be valourous, and possibly may) they follow their arrow, and falling upon the person wounded, and tearing his head a little aside by his Locke, they in the twinckling of an eye fetch off his head though but with a sorry knife.

I know the man yet living, who in time of warre, pretended to fall from his owne campe to the enemie, proffered his service in the front with them against his own Armie from whence he had revolted. Hee propounded such plausible advantages, that he drew them out to battell, himselfe keeping in the front; but on a sudden, shot their chiefe Leader and Captaine, and being shot, in a trice fetcht off his head, and returned immediatly to his own againe, from whom in pretence (though with this trecherous intention) hee had revolted: his act was false and trecherous, yet herein appeares policie, stoutnesse and activitie, &c.

Mapànnog.	*The breast.*
Wuppíttene -énash.	*Arme, Armes.*
Wuttàh.	*The heart.*
Wunnêtu nittà.	*My heart is good.*

Obs. This speech they use when ever they professe their honestie; they naturally confessing that all goodnesse is first in the heart.

Mishquínash.	*The vaines.*
Mishquè, néepuck.	*The blood.*
Uppusquàn.	*The backe.*
Nuppusquánnick.	*My back,* or *at my back.*
Wunnícheke.	*Hand.*
Wunnickégannash.	*Hands.*
Mokássuck.	*Nayles.*

Ob. They are much delighted after battell to hang up the hands and heads of their enemies: (Riches, long Life, and the Lives of enemies being objects of great delight to all men naturall; but *Salomon* begg'd Wisedome before these.)

Wunnáks.	*The bellie.*
Apòme, Apòmash.	*The thigh, the thighs.*
Mohcònt, tash.	*A legge, legs.*
Wussète, tash.	*A foot, feet.*
Wunnichéganash.	*The toes.*
Tou wuttínsin?	*What manner of man?*
Tou nùckquaque?	*Of what bignesse?*
Wompésu.	*White.*
Mowêsu, & Suckêsu.	*Blacke,* or *swarfish.*

Obs. Hence they call a *Blackamore* (themselves are tawnie, by the Sunne and their annoyntings, yet they are borne white:)

Suckáutacone.	*A cole blacke man.*

For, *Sucki* is black, and *Waûtacone,* one that weares clothes, whence *English, Dutch, French, Scotch,* they call *Wautaconâuog,* or *Coatmen.*

Cummínakese.	*You are strong.*
Minikêsu.	*Strong.*
Minioquêsu.	*Weake.*
Cummíniocquese.	*Weake you are.*
Qunnaúqussu.	*A tall man.*
Qunnauqussítchick.	*Tall men.*
Tiaquónqussu.	*Low and short.*
Tiaquonqussíchick.	*Men of lowe stature.*
Wunnêtu-wock.	*Proper and personall.*

The generall Observation from the parts of the bodie.

Nature knowes no difference between *Europe* and *Americans* in blood, birth, bodies, &c. God having of one blood made all mankind, *Acts* 17. and all by nature being children of wrath, *Ephes.* 2.

More particularly:

[1.] *Boast not proud* English, *of thy birth & blood,*
Thy brother Indian *is by birth as Good.*
Of one blood God made Him, and Thee & All,
As wise, as faire, as strong, as personall.

[2.] *By nature wrath's his portion, thine no more*
Till Grace his *soule and* thine *in Christ restore,*
Make sure thy second birth, else thou shalt see,
Heaven ope to Indians *wild, but shut to thee.*

CHAP. [V]III.
Of *Discourse* and *Newes.*

Aunchemokauhettíttea.	*Let us discourse,* or *tell newes.*
Tocketeáunchim?	*What newes?*
Aaunchemókaw.	*Tell me your newes.*
Cuttaunchemókous.	*I will tell you newes.*
Mautaunchemokouêan.	*When I have done telling the newes.*
Cummautaunchemókous.	*I have done my newes.*

Obs. Their desire of, and delight in newes, is great, as the *Athenians,* and all men, more or lesse; a stranger that can relate newes in their owne language, they will stile him *Manittóo,* a God.

Wutaunchemocouôog.	*I will tell it them.*
Awaun mesh aunchemókau?	*Who brought this newes?*
Awaun mesh kuppíttouwaw?	*Of whom did you heare it?*
Uppanáunchim.	*Your newes is true.*
Cowawwunnâunchim.	*He tells false newes.*
Nummautanùme.	*I have spoken enough.*
Nsouwussánneme.	*I am weary with speaking.*

Obs. Their manner is upon any tidings to sit round, double or treble, or more, as their numbers be; I have seene neer a thousand in a round, where *English* could not well neere halfe so many have sitten: Every man hath his pipe of their *Tobacco,* and a deepe silence they make, and attention give to him that speaketh; and many of them will deliver themselves, either in a relation of news, or in a consultation, with very emphaticall speech and great action, commonly an houre, and sometimes two houres together.

Npenowauntawâumen.	*I cannot speak your language.*
Matta nippánnawem.	*I lie not.*
Cuppánnowem.	*You lie.*
Mattanickoggachoùsk, Matntiantacómpaw, Matntiantásampáwwa.	*I am no lying fellow.*
Achienonâumwem.	*I speake very true.*
Kukkita.	*Hearken to me.*
Kukkakittoùs.	*I heare you.*

Obs. They are impatient (as all men and God himselfe is) when their speech is not attended and listened to.

Cuppíttous, Cowàutous.	*I understand you.*
Machagenowâutam.	*I understand not.*
Matnowawtawatémina.	*Wee understand not each other.*
Wunnâumwash.	*Speake the truth.*
Coanâumwem.	*You speake true.*

Obs. This word and the next are words of great flattery which they use each to other, but constantly to their Princes at their speeches, for which, if they be eloquent, they esteeme them Gods, as *Herod* among the *Jewes*.

Wunnâumwaw ewò.	*He speaks true.*
Cuppannawâutous.	*I doe not believe you.*
Cuppannawâuti?	*Doe you not believe?*
Nippannawâutunck ewò.	*He doth not believe me.*
Michéme nippannowâutam.	*I shall never believe it.*

Obs. As one answered me when I had discoursed about many points of God, of the creation, of the soule, of the danger of it, and the saving of it, he assented; but when I spake of the rising againe of the body, he cryed out, I shall never believe this.

Pannóuwa awàun, awaun keesitteóuwin.	*Some body hath made this lie.*
Tattâ, Pìtch.	*I cannot tell, it may so come to passe.*
Nni, eíu.	*It is true.*
Mat enâno, *or,* mat eâno.	*It is not true.*
Kekuttokâunta.	*Let us speake together.*
Kuttókash.	*Speake.*
Tawhitch mat cuttôan?	*Why speake you not?*
Téaqua ntúnnawem, *or,* ntéawem?	*What should I speake?*
Wetapímmin.	*To sit downe.*
Wetapwâuwwas.	*Sit and talke with us.*
Taúpowaw.	*A wise speaker.*
Enapwáuwwaw, Eississûmo.	*He speaks* Indian.
Matta nowawwâuon, matta nowáhea.	*I know nothing of it.*
Pitchnowáuwon.	*I shall know the truth.*
Wunnaumwâuonck, Wunnaumwáyean.	*If he say true.*

Obs. Canounicus, the old high *Sachim* of the *Nariganset Bay* (a wise and peaceable Prince) once in a solemne Oration to my self, in a solemne assembly, using this word, said, I have never suffered any wrong to be offered to the *English* since they landed; nor never will: he often repeated this word, *Wunnaumwáyean, Englishman;* if the *Englishman* speake true, if hee meane truly, then shall I goe to my grave in peace, and hope that the *English* and my posteritie shall live in love and peace together. I replied, that he had no cause (as I hoped) to question *Englishmans, Wunnaumwaúonck,* that is, faithfulnesse, he having had long experience of their friendlinesse and trustinesse. He tooke a sticke, and broke it into ten pieces, and related ten instances (laying downe a sticke to every instance) which gave him cause thus to feare and say; I satisfied him in some presently, and presented the rest to the Governours of the *English,* who, I hope, will be far from giving just cause to have *Barbarians* to question their *Wunnaumwâuonck,* or faithfulnesse.

Tocketunnántum, Tocketunáname, Tocketeántam?	*What doe you thinke?*
Ntunnántum, Nteántum.	*I thinke.*
Nánick nteeâtum.	*I thinke so to.*
Nteatámmowonck.	*That is my thought,* or *opinion.*
Matntunnantámmen, Matnteeantámmen.	*I thinke not so.*
Nowecóntam, Noweeteántam.	*I am glad.*
Coanáumatous.	*I believe you.*

Obs. This word they use just as the *Greeke* tongue doth that verbe, πιςένειν: for believing or obeying, as it is often used in the new *Testament,* and they say *Coannáumatous,* I will obey you.

Yo aphéttit.	*When they are here.*
Yo peyáhettit.	*When they are com.*

This Ablative case absolute they much use, and comprise much in little;

Awaunaguss, suck.	*English-man, men.*

This they call us, as much as to say, These strangers.

Waútacone -nûaog.	*Englishman, men.*

That is, Coat-men, *or* clothed.

Cháuquaqock.	*English-men,* properly sword-men.
Wautacónisk.	*An English woman.*
Wautaconémese.	*An English youth.*

Wáske peyáeyan.	*When you came first.*
Wáske peyáhetit, Wautaconâuog.	*When English-men came first.*
Táwhitch peyáhettit?	*Why come they hither?*

Obs. This question they oft put to me: Why come the *Englishmen* hither? and measuring others by themselves; they say, It is because you want *firing:* for they, having burnt up the *wood* in one place, (wanting draughts to bring *wood* to them) they are faine to follow the *wood;* and so to remove to a fresh new place for the *woods* sake.

Matta mihtuckqunnûnno?	*Have you no trees?*
Mishàunetash, Màunetash.	*Great store.*
Maunâuog, Wussaumemaunâuog.	*They are too full of people.*
Noonapúock.	*They have not roome one by another.*
Aumáumuwaw, Páudsha.	*A messenger comes.*
Wawwhawtowâuog.	*They hollow.*
Wauwhaûtowaw ánawat.	*'Tis an Alarme.*

Obs. If it be in time of *warre,* he that is a *Messenger* runs swiftly, and at every towne the *Messenger* comes, a fresh *Messenger* is sent: he that is the last, comming within a mile or two of the Court, or chiefe house, he *hollowes* often, and they that heare answer him, untill by mutuall *hollowing* and answering hee is brought to the place of *audience,* where by this meanes is gathered a great confluence of people to entertaine the *newes.*

Wussuckwhèke,
Wussúckwhonck. *A letter* which they so call from Wussuckwhómmin, *to paint;* for, having no letters, their painting comes the neerest.

Wussúckquash.	*Write a Letter.*
Wussúckwheke, yímmi.	*Make me a Letter.*

La Pendasion from Jacques Callot, *Les Grandes misères de la guerre* (1633). (*By courtesy of the Houghton Library, Harvard University.*)

Obs. That they have often desired of me upon many occasions; for their good and peace, and the *English* also, as it hath pleased God to vouchsafe opportunitie.

Quenowâuog.	*They complaine.*
Tawhitch quenawáyean?	*Why complaine you?*
Muccò.	*It is true you say.*
Tuckawntéawem?	*What should I say to it?*

The generall *Observation* from their *Discourse* and *Newes.*

The whole race of *mankind* is generally infected with an *itching desire* of hearing *Newes.*

more particular:

1. Mans *restlesse soule hath restlesse eyes and eares,*
Wanders in change *of sorrows, cares and feares.*
Faine would it (Bee-like) *suck by the ears, by the eye*
Something that might his hunger satisfie:
The Gospel, *or* Glad tidings *onely can,*
Make glad the English, *and the* Indian.

CHAP. IX.
Of *the time of the day.*

Obs. They are punctuall in measuring their *Day* by the *Sunne,* and their *Night* by the *Moon* and the *Starres;* and their lying much abroad in the ayre, and so living in the open fields, occasioneth even the youngest amongst them to be very observant of those *Heavenly* Lights.

Mautáubon, chicháuquat wompan.	*It is day.*
Aumpatâuban.	*It is broad day.*
Tou wuttúttan?	*How high is the Sunne?* that is, *What is't a clocke?*
Páspisha.	*It is Sunne-rise.*
Nummáttaquaw.	*Fore-noone.*
Yáhen Páushaquaw.	*Allmost noone.*
Páweshaquaw.	*Noone.*
Quttúkquaquaw, Panicómpaw.	*After dinner.*
Nawwâuwquaw.	*After-noone.*
Yo wuttúttan.	*The Sunne thus high.*
Yáhen waiyàuw.	*Allmost Sun-set.*
Wayaàwi.	*The Sun is set.*
Wunnáuquit.	*Evening.*
Póppakunnetch, aucháugotch.	*Darke night.*
Túppaco, & Otematíppocat.	*Toward night.*
Nanashowatíppocat.	*Midnight.*
Chouoéatch.	*About Cockcrowing.*
Kitompanisha.	*Breake of day.*
Yò tàunt nippéean.	*The Sun thus high, I will come.*

Obs. They are punctuall in their promises of keeping time; and sometimes have charged mee with a lye for not punctually keeping time, though hindred.

Yo tàunt cuppeeyâumen.	*Come by the Sunne thus high.*
Anamakéesuck.	*This day.*
Saûop.	*To morrow.*
Wussâume tátsha.	*It is too late.*
Tiaquockaskéesakat.	*A short day.*
Quawquonikéesakat.	*A long day.*
Quawquonikeesaqutcheas.	*Long dayes.*
Nquittakeesiquóckat, Nquittakeespúmmishen.	*One dayes walke.*
Paukúnnum.	*Darke.*
Wequâi.	*Light.*
Wequáshim.	*Moon-light.*

The generall observation from their time of the day.

The *Sunne* and *Moone,* in the observation of all the *sonnes* of *men,* even the wildest, are the great *Directors* of the *day* and *night;* as it pleased *God* to appoint in the first *Creation.*

More particular.

1. *The* Indians *find the* Sun *so sweet,*
He is a God *they say;*
Giving them Light, *and* Heat, *and* Fruit,
And Guidance *all the day.*

2. *They have no helpe of* Clock *or* Watch,
And Sunne *they* overprize.

Having those artificiall helps, the Sun
We unthankfully despise.

[3.] God *is a* Sunne *and* Shield,
A thousand times more bright;
Indians, *or* English, *though they see,*
Yet how few prise his Light?

CHAP. X.

Of *the season of the Yeere.*

Nquittaqúnnegat.	*One day.*
Neesqúnnagat.	2 *dayes.*
Shuckqunóckat.	3 *dayes.*
Yowunnóckat, &c.	4 *dayes.*
Piuckaqúnnagat.	10 *dayes.*
Piuckaqúnnagat nabnaquìt.	11 *dayes.*
Piuckaqúnnagat nab neeze, *&c.*	12 *dayes.*
Neesneechektashuck qunnóckat.	20 *dayes.*
Neesneechektashuck qunnockat-nabnaquìt, &c.	21 *dayes.*
Séquan.	*The Spring.*
Aukeeteámitch.	*Spring,* or *Seed-time.*
Néepun, *&* Quaqúsquan.	*Summer.*
Taquònck.	*Fall of leafe* and *Autumne.*
Papòne.	*Winter.*
Saséquacup.	*This Spring last.*
Yo neepúnnacup.	*This Summer last.*
Yò taquónticup.	*This Harvest last.*
Papapôcup.	*Winter last.*
Yaûnedg.	*The last yeere.*
Nippaûus.	*The Sunne.*
Munnánnock, Nanepaûshat.	*The Moone.*
Nquitpawsuckenpaûus.	1 *Moneth.*
Neespausuckenpaûus.	2 *Moneths.*
Shwe pausuckenpaûus, &c.	3 *Moneths.*
Neesneáhettit.	2 *Moneths.*

Shwinneáhettit.	3 *Moneths.*
Yowinneáhettit, &c.	4 *Moneths.*

Obs. They have thirteen *Moneths* according to the severall *Moones;* and they give to each of them significant names: *as,*

Sequanakéeswush.	*Spring moneth.*
Neepunnakéeswush.	*Summer moneth.*
Taquontikéeswush.	*Harvest moneth.*
Paponakéeswush, &c.	*Winter moneth, &c.*
Nquittecautúmmo.	1 *Yeere.*
Tashecautúmmo?	*How many yeeres?*
Chashecautúmmo cuttáppemus?	*How many yeeres since you were borne?*
Neesecautúmmo.	2 *Yeere.*
Shwecautúmmo.	3 *Yeere.*
Yowecautúmmo.	4 *Yeere.*
Piukquecautúmmo.	10 *Yeere.*
Piuckquecautúmmo, nabnaquìt, &c.	11 *Yeere, &c.*

Obs. If the yeere proove drie, they have great and solemne meetings from all parts at one high place, to supplicate their gods, and to beg raine, and they will continue in this worship ten dayes, a fortnight; yea, three weekes, untill raine come.

Tashínash papónash?	*How many winters?*
Aháuqushapapòne.	*A sharpe winter.*
Kéesqush, Keesuckquâi.	*By day.*
Náukocks, nokannáwi.	*By night.*

Generall Observation *from their* Seasons *of the Yeere.*

The *Sunne* and *Moone,* and *Starres* and *seasons* of the yeere doe preach a *God* to all the sonnes of men, that they which know no letters, doe yet read an *eternall Power* and *God-head* in these:

More speciall.

1. *The* Sun *and* Moone *and* Stars *doe preach,*
The Dayes *and* Nights *sound out:*
Spring, Summer, Fall, *and* Winter *eke*
Each Moneth *and* Yeere *about.*

2. *So that the* wildest *sonnes of men*
Without excuse shall say,
Gods righteous *sentence past on us,*
(In dreadfull Judgement day.)

[3.] *If so, what doome is theirs that see,*
Not onely Natures *light;*
But Sun *of* Righteousnesse, *yet chose*
To live in darkest Night?

CHAP. XI.
Of *Travell.*

Máyi.	*A way.*
Mayúo?	*Is there a way?*
Mat mayanúnno.	*There is no way.*
Peemáyagat.	*A little way.*
Mishimmáyagat.	*A great path.*
Machípscat.	*A stone path.*

Obs. It is admirable to see, what paths their naked hardned feet have made in the wildernesse in most stony and rockie places.

Nnatotemúckaun.	*I will aske the way.*
Kunnatótemous.	*I will inquire of you.*
Kunnatotemì?	*Doe you aske me?*
Tou nishin méyi?	*Where lies the way?*
Kokotemíinnea méyi.	*Shew me the way.*
Yo áinshick méyi.	*There the way lies.*
Kukkakótemous.	*I will shew you.*
Yo cummittamáyon.	*There is the way you must goe.*
Yo chippachâusin.	*There the way divides.*
Maúchatea.	*A guide.*
Máuchase.	*Be my guide.*

Obs. The wildernesse being so vast, it is a mercy, that for a hire a man shall never want guides, who will carry provisions, and such as hire them over the Rivers and Brookes, and find out often times hunting-houses, or other lodgings at night.

Anóce wénawash.	*Hire him.*
Kuttánnoonsh.	*I will hire you.*

Kuttaúnckquittaunch.	*I will pay you.*
Kummuchickónckquatous.	*I will pay you well.*
Tocketaonckquittíinnea?	*What wil you give me?*
Cummáuchanish.	*I will conduct you.*
Yò aûnta.	*Let us goe that way.*
Yò cuttâunan.	*Goe that way.*
Yo mtúnnock.	*The right hand.*
Yo nmúnnatch.	*The left hand.*
Cowéchaush.	*I will goe with you.*
Wétash.	*Goe along.*
Cowéchaw ewò.	*He will goe with you.*
Cowechauatímmin.	*I will goe with you.*
Wechauatíttea.	*Let us accompany.*
Taûbot wétáyean.	*I thanke you for your company.*

Obs. I have heard of many *English* lost, and have oft been lost my selfe, and my selfe and others have often been found, and succoured by the *Indians.*

Pitchcowáwwon.	*You will lose your way.*
Meshnowáwwon.	*I lost my way.*
Nummauchèmin, Ntanniteímmin.	*I will be going.*
Mammauchêtuck.	*Let us be going.*
Ânakiteunck.	*He is gone.*
Memauchêwi ánittui, Memauchegushánnick, Anakugushánnick.	*They are gone.*
Tunnockuttòme, Tunnockkuttoyeâim?	*Whither goe you?*
Tunnockkuttínshem, Nnegónshem.	*I will goe before.*
Cuppompáish.	*I will stay for you.*
Negónshesh.	*Goe before.*
Mittummayaûcup.	*The way you went before.*

Cummáttanish.	*I will follow you.*
Cuppahímmin.	*Stay for me.*
Tawhich quaunqua quêan?	*Why doe you run so?*
Nowecóntum púmmishem.	*I have a mind to travell.*
Konkenuphshâuta.	*Let us goe apace.*
Konkenúppe.	*Goe apace.*
Michéme nquanunquaquêmin.	*I have run alwayes.*
Yo ntoyamâushem.	*I goe this pace.*

Obs. They are generally quick on foot, brought up from the breasts to running: their legs being also from the wombe stretcht and bound up in a strange way on their Cradle backward, as also annointed; yet have they some that excell: so that I have knowne many of them run betweene fourescoure or an hundred miles in a Summers day, and back within two dayes: they doe also practice running of *Races;* and commonly in the Summer, they delight to goe without shoes, although they have them hanging at their backs: they are so exquisitely skilled in all the body and bowels of the Countrey (by reason of their huntings) that I have often been guided twentie, thirtie, sometimes fortie miles through the woods, a streight course, out of any path.

Yò wuchê.	*From hence.*
Tounúckquaque yo wuchê?	*How far from hence?*
Yò anúckquaque.	*So farre.*
Yo anuckquaquêse.	*So little a way.*
Waunaquêse.	*A little way.*
Aukeewushaûog.	*They goe by land.*
Mìshoon hómwock.	*They goe* or *come by water.*
Naynayoûmewot.	*A Horse.*
Wunnìa, naynayoûmewot.	*He rides on Horse-back.*

Obs. Having no Horses, they covet them above other Cattell, rather preferring ease in riding, then their profit and belly, by milk and butter from Cowes and Goats, and they are loth to come to the *English* price for any.

Aspumméwi.	*He is not gone by.*
Aspumméwock.	*They are not gone by.*
Awánick payánchick?	*Who come there?*
Awanick negonsháchick?	*Who are these before us?*
Yo cuppummesicómmin.	*Crosse over into the way there.*
Cuppì-machàug.	*Thick wood: a Swamp.*

Obs. These thick Woods and Swamps (like the Boggs to the *Irish*) are the Refuges for Women and children in Warre, whil'st the men fight. As the Country is wondrous full of Brookes and Rivers, so doth it also abound with fresh ponds, some of many miles compasse.

Níps -nipsash.	*Pond: Ponds.*
Wèta: wétedg.	*The Woods on fire.*
Wussaumpatámmin.	*To view* or *looke about.*
Wussaum patámoonck.	*A Prospect.*
Wuttocékémin.	*To wade.*
Tocekétuck.	*Let us wade.*
Tou wuttáuqussin?	*How deepe?*
Yò ntaúqussin.	*Thus deep.*
Kunníish.	*I will carry you.*
Kuckqússuckqun.	*You are heavy.*
Kunnâukon.	*You are light.*
Pasúckquish.	*Rise.*
Anakish: maúchish.	*Goe.*
Quaquìsh.	*Runne.*
Nokus káuatees.	*Meet him.*
Nockuskauatítea.	*Let us meet.*
Neenmeshnóckuskaw.	*I did meet.*

Obs. They are joyfull in meeting of any in travell, and will strike fire either with stones or sticks, to take Tobacco, and discourse a little together.

Mesh Kunnockqus kauatímmin? — *Did you meet? &c.*
Yò Kuttauntapímmin. — *Let us rest here.*
Kussackquêtuck. — *Let us sit downe.*
Yo appíttuck. — *Let us sit here.*
Nissówanis, Nissowànishkaûmen. — *I am weary.*
Nickqússaqus. — *I am lame.*
Ntouagonnausinnúmmin. — *We are distrest undone,* or *in misery.*

Obs. They use this word properly in wandring toward Winter night, in which case I have been many a night with them, and many times also alone, yet alwayes mercifully preserved.

Teâno wonck nippéeam. — *I will be here by and by againe.*
Mat Kunníckansh. — *I will not leave you.*
Aquie Kunnickatshash. — *Doe not leave me.*
Tawhítch nickatshiêan? — *Why doe you forsake me?*
Wuttánho. — *A staffe.*
Yò íish Wuttánho. — *Use this staffe.*

Obs. Sometimes a man shall meet a lame man or an old man with a Staffe: but generally a Staffe is a rare sight in the hand of the eldest, their Constitution is so strong. I have upon occasion travelled many a score, yea many a hundreth mile amongst them, without need of stick or staffe, for any appearance of danger amongst them: yet it is a rule amongst them, that it is not good for a man to travell without a Weapon nor alone.

Taquáttin. — *Frost.*
Auke taquátsha. — *The ground is frozen.*
Séip taquáttin. — *The River is frozen.*
Now ánnesin. — *I have forgotten.*
Nippittakûnnamun. — *I must goe back.*

Obs. I once travalled with neere 200 who had word of neere 700. Enemies in the way, yet generally they all resolved that it was a shame to feare and goe back.

Nippanishkokómmin, Npussagokommìn.	*I have let fall something.*
Mattaâsu.	*A little way.*
Naûwot.	*A great way.*
Náwwatick.	*Farre of at Sea.*
Ntaquatchuwaûmen.	*I goe up hill.*
Taguatchòwash.	*Goe up hill.*
Wáumsu.	*Downe hill.*
Mauúnshesh.	*Goe slowly* or *gently.*
Mauanisháuta.	*Let us goe gently.*
Tawhìtch cheche qunnuwáyean?	*Why doe you rob me?*
Aquie chechequnnuwásh.	*Doe not rob me.*
Chechequnnuwáchick.	*Robbers.*
Chechequnníttin.	*There is a Robbery committed.*
Kemineantúock.	*They murder each other.*

Obs. If any Robbery fall out in Travell, between Persons of diverse States, the offended State sends for Justice; If no Justice bee granted and recompence made, they grant out a kind of Letter of Mart to take satisfaction themselves, yet they are carefull not to exceed in taking from others, beyond the Proportion of their owne losse.

Wúskont àwaùn nkemineíucqun.	*I feare some will murther mee.*

Obs. I could never heare that Murthers or Robberies are comparably so frequent, as in parts of *Europe* amongst the English, French, &c.

Cutchachewussímmin.	*You are almost there.*
Kiskecuppeeyáumen.	*You are a little short.*

Cuppeeyáumen.	*Now you are there.*
Muckquétu.	*Swift.*
Cummúmmuckquete.	*You are swift.*
Cussásaqus.	*You are slow.*
Sassaqushâuog.	*They are slow.*
Cuttinneapúmmishem?	*Will you passe by?*
Wuttineapummushâuta, Keeatshaûta.	*Let us passe by.*
Ntinneapeeyaûmen.	*I come for no busines.*
Acoûwe.	*In vaine* or *to no purpose.*
Ntackówwepeyaùn.	*I have lost my labour.*
Cummautússakou.	*You have mist him.*
Kihtummâyi-wussáuhumwi.	*He went just now forth.*
Pittúckish.	*Goe back.*
Pittuckétuck.	*Let us goe back.*
Pónewhush.	*Lay downe your burthen.*

Generall Observations of their Travell.

As the same Sun shines on the Wildernesse that doth on a Garden! so the same faithfull and all sufficient God, can comfort, feede and safely guide even through a desolate howling Wildernesse.

More particular.

1. *God makes a Path, provides a Guide,*
And feeds in Wildernesse!
His glorious Name while breath remaines,
O that I may confesse.

2. *Lost many a time, I have had no Guide,*
No House, but hollow Tree!
In stormy Winter night no Fire,
No Food, no Company:

3. *In him I have found a House, a Bed,*
A Table, Company:
No Cup so bitter, but's made sweet,
When God shall Sweet'ning be.

CHAP. XII.
Concerning the Heavens and Heavenly Lights.

Kéesuck.	*The Heavens.*
Keesucquíu.	*Heavenward.*
Aúke, Aukeeaseíu.	*Downwards.*
Nippâwus.	*The Sun.*
Keesuckquànd.	*A name of the Sun.*

(*Obs.*) By which they acknowledge the Sun, and adore for a God or divine power.

Munnánnock.	*A name of the Sun.*
Nanepaùshat, & Munnánnock.	*The Moone.*
Wequáshim.	*A light Moone.*
Pashpíshea.	*The Moone is up.*
Yo wuttútan.	*So high.*

Obs. And so they use the same rule, and words for the course of the Moone in the *Night,* as they use for the course of the Sun by *Day,* which wee mentioned in the Chapter of the Houre, or time of the Day concerning the Sunnes rising, course, or Sunne setting.

Yò Ockquitteunk.	*A new Moone.*
Paushésui.	*Halfe Moone.*
Yo wompanámmit.	*The Moone so old,*

Obs. which they measure by the setting of it, especially when it shines till *Wómpan,* or day.

Anóckqus: anócksuck.	*A Starre, Starres.*

Obs. By occasion of their frequent lying in the Fields and Woods, they much observe the Starres, and their very children can give Names to many of them, and observe their Motions, and they have the same words for their rising, courses, and setting, as for the Sun or Moone, as before.

Mosk or *Paukúnawaw* the great Beare, or *Charles Waine,* which words *Mosk,* or *Paukúnnawwáw* signifies a Beare, which is so much the more observable, because, in most Languages that signe or Constellation is called the Beare.

Shwishcuttowwáuog.	*The Golden Metewand.*
Mishánnock.	*The morning Starre.*
Chippápuock.	*The Brood-hen, &c.*

Generall Observations of the Heavenly Bodies.

The wildest sons of Men heare the preaching of the Heavens, the Sun, Moone, and Starres, yet not seeking after God the Maker are justly condemned, though they never have nor despise other preaching, as the civiliz'd World hath done.

More particular.

[1.] *When Sun doth rise the Starres doe set,*
Yet there's no need of Light,
God shines a Sunne *most glorious,*
When Creatures all are Night.

2. *The very* Indian *Boyes can give,*
To many Starres their *name,*
And know their Course, and therein doe
Excell the English tame.

3. English *and* Indians *none enquire,*
Whose hand these Candles hold:
Who gives these Stars *their Names, himself* *Job.* 35.
More bright ten thousand fold.

CHAP. XIII.
Of the Weather.

Tocke tussinnámmin kéesuck?	*What thinke you of the Weather?*
Wekineaûquat.	*Faire Weather.*
Wekinnàuquocks.	*When it is faire weather.*
Tahkì, *or* tátakki.	*Cold weather.*
Tahkeès.	*Cold.*

Obs. It may bee wondred why since *New-England* is about 12. degrees neerer to the Sun, yet some part of Winter it is there ordinarily more cold then here in *England*: the reason is plaine: All Ilands are warmer then maine Lands and Continents, *England* being an Iland, *Englands* winds are Sea winds, which are commonly more thick and vapoury, and warmer winds: The *Nor West* wind (which occasioneth *New-England* cold) comes over the cold frozen Land, and over many millions of Loads of Snow: and yet the pure wholsomnesse of the Aire is wonderfull, and the warmth of the Sunne, such in the sharpest weather, that I have often seen the Natives Children runne about starke naked in the coldest dayes, and the *Indians,* Men and Women, lye by a Fire, in the Woods in the coldest nights, and I have been often out my selfe such nights without fire, mercifully, and wonderfully preserved.

Taúkocks.	*Cold weather.*
Káusitteks.	*Hot weather.*
Kussúttah.	*It is hot.*
Núckqusquatch nnóonakom.	*I am a cold.*
Nickqussittâunum.	*I Sweat.*
Mattáuqus.	*A cloud.*

Máttaquat, Cúppaquat.	*It is over-cast.*
Sókenun, ánaquat.	*Raine.*
Anamakéesuck sókenun.	*It will raine to day.*
Sókenitch.	*When it raines.*
Sóchepo, *or* Cône.	*Snow.*
Animanâukock-Sóchepo.	*It will snow to night.*
Sóchepwutch.	*When it snowes.*
Mishúnnan.	*A great raine.*
Pâuqui, pâuquaquat.	*It holds up.*
Nnáppi.	*Drie.*
Nnáppaquat.	*Drie weather.*
Tópu.	*A frost.*
Missittópu.	*A great Frost.*
Capàt.	*Ice.*
Néechipog.	*The Deaw.*
Míchokat.	*A Thaw.*
Míchokatch.	*When it thawes.*
Missuppâugatch.	*When the rivers are open.*
Cutshâusha.	*The Lightning.*
Neimpâuog.	*Thunder.*
Neimpâuog peskhómwock.	*Thunderbolts are shot.*

Obs. From this the Natives conceiving a consimilitude between our Guns and Thunder, they call a Gunne *Péskunck,* and to discharge *Peskhómmin* that is to thunder.

Observation generall of the Weather.

That Judgement which the Lord Jesus pronounced against the Weather-wise (but ignorant of the God of the weather) will fall most justly upon those *Natives,* and all men who are wise in Naturall things, but willingly blind in spirituall.

[More particular.]

[1.] English *and* Indians *spie a Storme,*
And seeke a hiding place:
O hearts of stone that thinke and dreame,
Th'everlasting stormes t'out-face.

[2.] *Proud filthy* Sodome *saw the Sunne,*
Shine or'e her head most bright.
The very day that turn'd she was
To stincking heaps, 'fore night.

[3.] *How many millions now alive,*
Within few yeeres shall rot?
O blest that Soule, *whose portion is*
That Rocke *that changeth not.*

CHAP. XIV.

Of *the Winds.*

Waûpi.	*The Wind.*
Wâupanash.	*The Winds.*
Tashínash wáupanash?	*How many winds are there?*

Obs. Some of them account of seven, some eight, or nine; and in truth, they doe upon the matter reckon and observe not onely the foure but the eight Cardinall winds, although they come not to the accurate division of the 32. upon the 32. points of the compasse, as we doe.

Nanúmmatin, & Sunnâdin.	*The North wind.*
Chepewéssin.	*The North east.*
Sáchimoachepewéssin.	*Strong North east wind.*
Nopâtin.	*The East wind.*
Nanóckquittin.	*The South east wind.*
Touwúttin.	*South wind.*
Papônetin.	*West wind.*
Chékesu.	*The Northwest.*
Chékesitch.	*When the wind blowes Northwest.*
Tocketunnántum?	*What thinke you?*
Tou pìtch wuttìn?	*Where wil the wind be?*
Nqénouhìck wuttìn.	*I stay for a wind.*
Yo pìtch wuttìn Sâuop.	*Here the wind will be to morrow.*
Pìtch Sowwánishen.	*It will be Southwest.*

Obs. This is the pleasingest, warmest wind in the Climate, most desired of the *Indians,* making faire weather ordinarily; and therefore they have a *Tradition,* that to the

Southwest, which they call *Sowwaníu,* the gods chiefly dwell; and hither the soules of all their Great and Good men and women goe.

This Southwest wind is called by the *New-English,* the Sea turne, which comes from the Sunne in the morning, about nine or ten of the clock Southeast, and about South, and then strongest Southwest in the after-noone, and towards night, when it dies away.

It is rightly called the Sea turne, because the wind commonly all the Summer, comes off from the North and Northwest in the night, and then turnes againe about from the South in the day: as *Salomon* speaks of the vanitie of the Winds in their changes, *Eccles.* 1. 6.

Mishâupan.	*A great wind.*
Mishitáshin.	*A storme.*
Wunnágehan, *or,* Wunnêgin waúpi.	*Faire wind.*
Wunnêgitch wuttìn.	*When the wind is faire.*
Mattágehan.	*A crosse wind.*
Wunnágehatch.	*When the wind comes fair.*
Mattágehatch.	*When the wind is crosse.*
Cowunnagehúckamen.	*You have a faire wind.*
Cummattagehúckamen.	*The wind is against you.*
Nummattagehúckamen.	*The wind is against mee.*

Generall Observations *of the* Winds.

God is wonderfully glorious in bringing the *Winds* out of his Treasure, and riding upon the wings of those *Winds* in the eyes of all the sonnes of men in all Coasts of the world.

More particular:

1. English *and* Indian *both observe*
The various blasts of wind:
And both I have heard in dreadfull stormes
Cry out aloud, I have sinn'd.

[2.] *But when the stormes are turn'd to calmes,*
And seas grow smooth and still:
Both turne (like Swine) *to wallow in,*
The filth of former will.

[3.] *'Tis not a storme on sea, or shore,*
'Tis not the Word that can;
But 'tis the Spirit *or* Breath *of God*
That must renew the man.

CHAP. XV.
Of *Fowle*.

Npesháwog, Npussekesèsuck.	*Fowle.*
Ntauchâumen.	*I goe a fowling* or *hunting.*
Auchaûi.	*Hee is gone to hunt* or *fowle.*
Pepemôi.	*He is gone to fowle.*
Wómpissacuk.	*An Eagle.*
Wompsacuckquâuog.	*Eagles.*
Néyhom, mâuog.	*Turkies.*
Páupock, sûog.	*Partridges.*
Aunckuck, quâuog.	*Heath-cocks.*
Chógan, éuck.	*Black-bird, Black-birds.*

Obs. Of this sort there be millions, which are great devourers of the *Indian* corne as soon as it appeares out of the ground; Unto this sort of Birds, especially, may the mysticall Fowles, the Divells be well resembled (and so it pleaseth the Lord Jesus himselfe to observe, *Matth.* 13.) which mysticall Fowle follow the sowing of the Word, and picke it up from loose and carelesse hearers, as these Black-birds follow the materiall seed.

Against the Birds the *Indians* are very carefull, both to set their corne deep enough that it may have a strong root, not so apt to be pluckt up, (yet not too deep, lest they bury it, and it never come up:) as also they put up little watch-houses in the middle of their fields, in which they, or their biggest children lodge, and earely in the morning prevent the Birds, &c.

Kokókehom, Ohómous. *An Owle.*
Káukont -tuock. *Crow, Crowes.*

Obs. These Birds, although they doe the corne also some hurt, yet scarce will one *Native* amongst an hundred kil them, because they have a tradition, that the Crow brought them at first an *Indian* Graine of Corne in one Eare, and an *Indian* or *French* Beane in another, from the Great God *Kautántouwits* field in the Southwest, from whence they hold came all their Corne and Beanes.

Hònck, hónckock,
Wómpatuck -quâuog. *Goose, Geese.*
Wéquash -shâuog. *Swan, Swans.*
Munnùcks, munnùcksuck. *Brants,* or *Brantgeese.*
Quequécum -mâuog. *Ducks.*

Obs. The *Indians* having abundance of these sorts of Foule upon their waters, take great pains to kill any of them with their Bow and Arrowes; and are marvellous desirous of our *English* Guns, powder, and shot (though they are wisely and generally denied by the *English*) yet with those which they get from the *French,* and some others (*Dutch* and *English*) they kill abundance of Fowle, being naturally excellent marks-men; and also more hardened to endure the weather, and wading, lying, and creeping on the ground, &c.

I once saw an exercise of training of the *English,* when all the *English* had mist the mark set up to shoot at, an *Indian* with his owne Peece (desiring leave to shoot) onely hit it.

Kítsuog. *Cormorants.*

Obs. These they take in the night time, where they are asleepe on rocks, off at Sea, and bring in at break of day great store of them.

Yo aquéchinock. *There they swim.*
Nipponamouôog. *I lay nets for them.*

Ob. This they doe on shore, and catch many fowle upon the plaines, and feeding under *Okes* upon *Akrons,* as Geese, Turkies, Cranes, and others, &c.

Ptowéi.	*It is fled.*
Ptowewushánnick.	*They are fled.*
Wunnùp -pash.	*Wing, Wings.*
Wunnúppaníck ánawhone.	*Wing-shot.*
Wuhóckgock ânwhone.	*Body-shot.*
Wuskówhàn.	*A Pigeon.*
Wuskowhánannûaog.	*Pigeons.*
Wuskowhannanaûkit.	*Pigeon Countrie.*

Obs. In that place these Fowle breed abundantly, and by reason of their delicate Food (especially in Strawberrie time when they pick up whole large Fields of the old grounds of the *Natives*) they are a delicate fowle, and because of their abundance, and the facility of killing of them, they are and may be plentifully fed on.

Sachim: a little Bird about the bignesse of a swallow, or lesse, to which the *Indians* give that name, because of its *Sachim* or Princelike courage and Command over greater Birds, that a man shall often see this small Bird pursue and vanquish and put to flight the Crow, and other Birds farre bigger then it selfe.

Sowwánakitauwaw.	*They go to the South ward.*

That is the saying of the *Natives,* when the Geese and other Fowle at the approach of Winter betake themselves, in admirable Order and discerning their Course even all the night long.

Chepewâukitaûog.	*They fly Northward.*

That is when they returne in the Spring. There are abundance of singing Birds whose names I have little as yet inquired after, &c.

The *Indians* of *Martins* vineyard, at my late being

amongst them, report generally, and confidently of some Ilands, which lie off from them to Sea, from whence every morning early, certaine Fowles come and light amongst them, and returne at Night to lodging, which Iland or Ilands are not yet discovered, though probably, by other Reasons they give, there is Land, &c.

Taûnek -kaûog.	*Crane, Cranes.*
Wushówunan.	*The Hawke.*

Which the *Indians* keep tame about their houses to keepe the little Birds from their Corne.

The generall Observation of Fowle.

How sweetly doe all the severall sorts of Heavens Birds, in all Coasts of the World, preach unto Men the prayse of their Makers Wisedome, Power, and Goodnesse, who feedes them and their young ones Summer and Winter with their severall suitable sorts of Foode: although they neither sow nor reape, nor gather into Barnes?

More particularly:

[1.] *If Birds that neither sow nor reape*
Nor store up any food,
Constantly find to them and theirs
A maker kind and Good!

[2.] *If man provide eke for his Birds,*
In Yard, in Coops, in Cage.
And each Bird spends in songs and Tunes,
His little time and Age!

[3.] *What care will Man, what care will God,*
For's wife and Children take?
Millions of Birds and Worlds will God
Sooner then His forsake.

CHAP. XVI.

Of the Earth, and the Fruits thereof, &c.

Aûke, & Sanaukamuck.	*Earth* or *Land.*
Níttauke.	*My Land.*
Nissawnâwkamuck, Wuskáukamuck.	*New ground.*
Aquegunnítteash.	*Fields worne out.*
Mihtúck -quash.	*Trees.*
Pauchautaqun, -nêsash.	*Branch, Branches.*
Wunnèpog -guash.	*Leafe, leaves.*
Wattàp.	*A root of Tree.*
Séip.	*A River.*
Toyùsk.	*A bridge.*
Sepoêse.	*A little River.*
Sepoêmese.	*A little Rivulet.*
Takêkum.	*A Spring.*
Takekummûo?	*Is there a Spring?*
Sepûo?	*Is there a River?*
Toyusquanûo?	*Is there a Bridge?*

Obs. The *Natives* are very exact and punctuall in the bounds of their Lands, belonging to this or that Prince or People, (even to a River, Brooke &c.) And I have knowne them make bargaine and sale amongst themselves for a small piece, or quantity of Ground: notwithstanding a sinfull opinion amongst many that Christians have right to *Heathens* Lands: but of the delusion of that phrase, I have spoke in a discourse concerning the *Indians* Conversion.

Paugáutemisk.	*An Oake.*
Wómpimish.	*A Chesnut Tree.*
Wómpimineash.	*Chesnutts.*

Obs. The *Indians* have an Art of drying their Chesnuts, and so to preserve them in their barnes for a daintie all the yeare.

Anáuchemineash. *Akornes.*

These Akornes also they drie, and in case of want of Corne, by much boyling they make a good dish of them: yea sometimes in plentie of Corne doe they eate these Acornes for a Novelty.

Wússoquat. *A Wallnut Tree.*
Wusswaquatómineug. *Wallnuts.*

Of these Wallnuts they make an excellent Oyle good for many uses, but especially for their annoynting of their heads. And of the chips of the Walnut-Tree (the barke taken off) some *English* in the Countrey make excellent Beere both for Tast, strength, colour, and inoffensive opening operation.

Sasaunckapâmuck. *The* Sassafrasse *Tree.*
Mishquáwtuck. *The Cedar tree.*
Cówaw -ésuck. *Pine, young Pine.*
Wenomesíppaguash. *The Vine-Tree.*
Micúckaskeete. *A Medow.*
Tataggoskìtuash. *A fresh Medow.*
Maskituash. *Grasse* or *Hay.*
Wékinash -quash. *Reed, Reedes.*
Manisimmín. *To cut* or *mow.*
Qussuckomineânug. *The Cherry Tree.*
Wuttáhimneash. *Strawberries.*

Obs. This Berry is the wonder of all the Fruits growing naturally in those parts: It is of it selfe Excellent: so that one of the chiefest Doctors of *England* was wont to say, that God could have made, but God never did make a better Berry: In some parts where the *Natives* have planted, I have many times seen as many as would fill a good ship within few miles compasse: the *Indians* bruise them in a Morter, and mixe them with meale and make Strawberry bread.

Wuchípoquameneash.	*A kind of sharp Fruit like a Barbary in tast.*

Sasèmineash another sharp cooling Fruit growing in fresh Waters all the Winter, Excellent in conserve against Feavers.

Wenómeneash.	*Grapes.*
Wuttahimnasíppaguash.	*Strawberry leaves.*
Peshaûiuash.	*Violet leaves.*
Nummoúwinneem.	*I goe to gather.*
Mowinne -aûog.	*He* or *they gather.*
Atáuntowash.	*Clime the Tree.*
Ntáuntawem.	*I clime.*
Punnoûwash.	*Come downe.*
Npunnowaûmen.	*I come downe.*
Attitaash.	*Hurtle-berries.*

Of which there are divers sorts sweete like Currants, some opening, some of a binding nature.

Saútaash are these Currants dried by the *Natives,* and so preserved all the yeare, which they beat to powder, and mingle it with their parcht meale, and make a delicate dish which they cal *Sautáuthig;* which is as sweet to them as plum or spice cake to the *English.*

They also make great use of their Strawberries having such abundance of them, making Strawberry bread, and having no other Food for many dayes, but the *English* have exceeded, and make good Wine both of their Grapes and Strawberries also in some places, as I have often tasted.

Ewáchim -neash.	*Corne.*
Scannémeneash.	*Seed-Corne.*
Wompiscannémeneash.	*White seed-corne.*

Obs. There be diverse sorts of this Corne, and of the colours: yet all of it either boild in milke, or buttered. If the use of it were knowne and received in *England* (it is the opinion of some skillfull in physick) it might save many thousand lives in *England,* occasioned by the binding nature of *English* wheat, the *Indian* Corne keeping the body in a constant moderate loosenesse.

Aukeeteaûmen.	*To plant Corne.*
Quttáunemun.	*To plant Corne.*
Anakáusu.	*A Labourer.*
Anakáusichick.	*Labourers.*
Aukeeteaûmitch.	*Planting time.*
Aukeeteáhettit.	*When they set Corne.*
Nummautaukeeteaûmen.	*I have done planting.*
Anaskhómmin.	*To how* or *break up.*

Obs. The Women set or plant, weede, and hill, and gather and barne all the corne, and Fruites of the field: Yet sometimes the man himselfe, (either out of love to his Wife, or care for his Children, or being an old man) will help the Woman which (by the custome of the Countrey) they are not bound to.

When a field is to be broken up, they have a very loving sociable speedy way to dispatch it: All the neighbours men and Women forty, fifty, a hundred &c, joyne, and come in to help freely.

With friendly joyning they breake up their fields, build their Forts, hunt the Woods, stop and kill fish in the Rivers, it being true with them as in all the World in the Affaires of Earth or Heaven: By concord little things grow great, by discord the greatest come to nothing *Concordiâ parvæ res crescunt, Discordiâ magnæ dilabuntur.*

Anáskhig-anash.	*How, Howes.*
Anaskhómwock.	*They how.*
Anaskhommonteâmin.	*They break for me.*
Anaskhomwáutowwin.	*A breaking up How.*

The *Indian* Women to this day (notwithstanding our Howes) doe use their naturall Howes of shells and Wood.

Monaskúnnemun. *To weede.*
Monaskunnummaûtowwin. *A weeding* or *broad How.*
Petascúnnemun. *To hill the Corne.*
Kepenúmmin &
Wuttúnnemun. *To gather Corne.*
Núnnowwa. *Harvest time.*
Anoûant. *At harvest.*
Wuttúnnemitch-Ewáchim. *When harvest is in.*
Pausinnúmmin. *To dry the corne.*

Which they doe carefully upon heapes and Mats many dayes, before they barne it up, covering it up with Mats at night, and opening when the Sun is hot.

Sókenug. *A heap of corne.*

Obs. The woman of the family will commonly raise two or three heaps of twelve, fifteene, or twentie bushells a heap, which they drie in round broad heaps; and if she have helpe of her children or friends, much more.

Pockhómmin. *To beat* or *thrash out.*
Npockhómmin. *I am threshing.*
Cuppockhómmin? *Doe you thrash?*
Wuskokkamuckómeneash. *New ground Corne.*
Nquitawánnanash. *One basketfull.*
Munnòte -tash. *Basket, Baskets.*
Maûseck. *A great one.*
Peewâsick. *A little one.*
Wussaumepewâsick. *Too little.*
Pokowánnanash. *Halfe a basketfull.*
Neesowánnanash. *Two baskets full.*
Shóanash. *Three.*
Yowanánnash. *Foure, &c.*
Aníttash. *Rotten corne.*

Wawéekanash. — *Sweet corne.*
Tawhìtch quitche máuntamen? — *Why doe you smell to it?*
Auqúnnash. — *Barnes.*
Necawnaúquanash. — *Old barnes.*

Asqútasquash, their Vine aples, which the *English* from them call *Squashes* about the bignesse of Apples of severall colours, a sweet, light wholesome refreshing.

Uppakumíneash. — *The seed of them.*

The Observation *generall of the* Fruits *of the Earth.*

God hath not left himselfe without wit[ness] in all parts and coasts of the world; the raines and fruitfull seasons, the Earth, Trees, Plants, &c. filling mans heart with food and gladnesse, witnesseth against, and condemneth man for his unthankfulnesse and unfruitfulnesse towards his Maker.

More particular:

[1.] *Yeeres thousands since, God gave command*
(As we in Scripture find)
That Earth *and* Trees *&* Plants *should bring*
Forth fruits each in his kind.

[2.] *The Wildernesse remembers this,*
The wild and howling land
Answers the toyling labour of
The wildest Indians *hand.*

[3.] *But man forgets his* Maker, *who*
Fram'd him in Righteousnesse.
A paradise in Paradise, now worse
Then Indian *Wildernesse.*

CHAP. XVII.
Of *Beasts, &c.*

Penashímwock. *Beasts.*
Netasûog. *Cattell.*

Obs. This name the *Indians* give to tame Beasts, yea, and Birds also which they keepe tame about their houses.

Muckquashim -wock. *Wolves.*
Moattôqus. *A blacke Wolfe.*
Tummòck -quaûog,
Nóosup, } -paûog.
Súmhup. } *Beaver, Beavers.*

Obs. This is a Beast of wonder; for cutting and drawing with his teeth great pieces of trees, with which, and sticks and earth I have often seen, faire streames and rivers damm'd and stopt up by them: upon these streames thus damm'd up, he builds his house with stories, wherein he sits drie in his chambers, or goes into the water at his pleasure.

Mishquáshim. *A red Fox.*
Péquawus. *A gray Fox.*

Obs. The *Indians* say they have black Foxes, which they have often seene, but never could take any of them: they say they are *Manittóoes,* that is, Gods, Spirits or Divine powers, as they say of every thing which they cannot comprehend.

Aûsup-pánnog. *Racoone, Racoones.*
Nkèke, nkéquock. *Otter, Otters.*
Pussoûgh. *The wildcat.*

Ockqutchaun -nug. A wild beast of a reddish haire

about the bignesse of a *Pig,* and rooting like a *Pig;* from whence they give this name to all our *Swine.*

Mishánneke -quock.	*Squirrill, Squirrils.*
Anéqus, anéquussuck.	*A litle coloured Squirril.*
Waûtuckques.	*The Conie.*

Obs. They have a reverend esteeme of this Creature, and conceive there is some Deitie in it.

Attuck -quock, Nóonatch, noónatchaug.	*Deere.*
Moósquin.	*A Fawn.*
Wawwúnnes.	*A young Bucke.*
Kuttíomp & Paucottâuwaw.	*A great Bucke.*
Aunàn-quunèke.	*A Doe.*
Qunnequáwese.	*A little young Doe.*
Naynayoûmewot.	*A Horse.*
Côwsnuck.	*Cowes.*
Gôatesuck.	*Goats.*
Hógsuck, Pígsuck.	*Swine.*

Obs. This Termination *suck,* is common in their language; and therefore they adde it to our *English* Cattell, not else knowing what names to give them.

Anùm.	*A Dog.*

Yet the varietie of their Dialects and proper speech within thirtie or fortie miles each of other, is very great, as appeares in that word,

<table>
<tr><td>Anùm, The Cowweset
Ayím, The Narriganset
Arúm. The Qunnippiuck
Alùm. The Neepmuck</td><td>} Dialect.</td></tr>
</table>

So that although some pronounce not *L,* nor *R,* yet it is the most proper Dialect of other places, contrary to many reports.

Enewáshim. — *A Male.*
Squáshim. — *A Female.*
Moòs -sóog. — *The great Oxe,* or rather *a red Deere.*
Askùg. — *A Snake.*
Móaskug. — *Black Snake.*
Sések. — *Rattle Snake.*
Natúppwock. — *They feed.*
Téaqua natuphéttit? — *What shall they eat?*
Natuphéttitch yo sanáukamick. — *Let them feed on this ground.*

The generall Observation *of the Beasts.*

The Wildernesse is a cleere resemblance of the world, where greedie and furious men persecute and devoure the harmlesse and innocent as the wilde beasts pursue and devoure the Hinds and Roes.

More particular.

1. *The* Indians, *Wolves, yea, Dogs and Swine,*
I have knowne the Deere devoure;
Gods children are sweet prey to all,
But yet the end proves sowre.

2. *For though Gods children lose their lives,*
They shall not loose an haire;
But shall arise, and judge all those,
That now their Judges are.

3. New-England's *wilde beasts are not fierce,*
As other wild beasts are:
Some men are not so fierce, and yet
From mildnesse are they farre.

CHAP. XVIII.
Of *the Sea.*

Wechêkum, Kítthan. *The Sea.*

Paumpágussit. *The Sea-God*, or, that name which they give that Deitie or Godhead which they conceive to be in the Sea.

Mishoòn. *An* Indian *Boat,* or *Canow* made of a Pine or Oake, or Chesnut-tree.

Obs. I have seene a Native goe into the woods with his hatchet, carrying onely a Basket of Corn with him, & stones to strike fire when he had feld his tree (being a *chesnut*) he made him a little House or shed of the bark of it, he puts fire and followes the burning of it with fire, in the midst in many places: his corne he boyles and hath the Brook by him, and sometimes angles for a little fish: but so hee continues burning and hewing untill he hath within ten or twelve dayes (lying there at his worke alone) finished, and (getting hands,) lanched his Boate; with which afterward hee ventures out to fish in the Ocean.

Mishoonémese. *A little Canow.*

Some of them will not well carry above three or foure: but some of them twenty, thirty, forty men.

Wunnauanoûnuck. *A Shallop.*

Wunnauanounuckquèse. *A Skiffe.*

Obs. Although themselves have neither, yet they give them such names, which in their Language signifieth carrying Vessells.

Kitônuck.	*A Ship.*
Kitónuckquese.	*A little ship.*
Mishíttouwand.	*A great Canow.*
Peewàsu.	*A little one.*
Paugautemissaûnd.	*An Oake Canow.*
Kowawwaûnd.	*A pine Canow.*
Wompmissaûnd.	*A chesnut Canow.*
Ogwhan.	*A boat adrift.*
Wuskon-tógwhan.	*It will goe adrift.*
Cuttunnamíinnea.	*Help me to launch.*
Cuttunnummútta.	*Let us launch.*
Cuttúnnamoke.	*Launch.*
Cuttánnummous.	*I will help you.*
Wútkunck.	*A paddle* or *Oare.*
Namacóuhe cómishoon.	*Lend me your Boate.*
Paûtousnenótehunck.	*Bring hither my paddle.*
Comishóonhom?	*Goe you by water?*
Chémosh-chémeck.	*Paddle* or *row.*
Maumínikish & Maumanetepweéas.	*Pull up,* or *row lustily.*
Sepâkehig.	*A Sayle.*
Sepagehommaûta.	*Let us saile.*
Wunnâgehan.	*We have a faire wind.*

Obs. Their owne reason hath taught them, to pull of a Coat or two and set it up on a small pole, with which they will saile before a wind ten, or twenty mile, &c.

Wauaúpunish.	*Hoyse up.*
Wuttáutnish.	*Pull to you.*
Nókanish.	*Take it downe.*
Pakétenish.	*Let goe* or *let flie.*
Nikkoshkowwaúmen.	*We shall be drown'd.*
Nquawupshâwmen.	*We overset.*
Wussaûme pechepaûsha.	*The Sea comes in too fast upon us.*
Maumaneeteántass.	*Be of good courage.*

Obs. It is wonderfull to see how they will venture in those Canoes, and how (being oft overset as I have my selfe been with them) they will swim a mile, yea two or more safe to Land: I having been necessitated to passe waters diverse times with them, it hath pleased God to make them many times the instruments of my preservation; and when sometimes in great danger I have questioned safety, they have said to me: Feare not, if we be overset I will carry you safe to Land.

Paupaútuckquash.	*Hold water.*
Kínnequass.	*Steere.*
Tiáckomme kínniquass.	*Steere right.*
Kunnósnep.	*A Killick,* or *Anchor.*
Chowwophómmin.	*To cast over-boord.*
Chouwóphash.	*Cast over-board.*
Touwopskhómmke.	*Cast anchor.*
Mishittáshin.	*It is a storme.*
Awêpesha.	*It caulmes.*
Awêpu.	*A calme.*
Nanoúwashin.	*A great caulme.*
Tamóccon.	*Floud.*
Nanashowetamóccon.	*Halfe Floud.*
Keesaqúshin.	*High water.*
Taumacoks.	*Upon the Floud.*
Mishittommóckon.	*A great Floud.*
Maúchetan & skàt.	*Ebb.*
Mittâeskat.	*A low Ebb.*
Awánick Paûdhuck?	*Who comes there?*

Obs. I have knowne thirty or forty of their Canowes fill'd with men, and neere as many more of their enemies in a Sea-fight.

Caupaúshess.	*Goe ashoare.*
Caupaushâuta.	*Let us goe ashoare.*
Wusséheposh.	*Heave out the water.*

Askképunish.	*Make fast the Boat.*
Kspúnsh & Kspúnemoke.	*Tie it fast.*
Maumínikish.	*Tie it hard.*
Neene Cuthómwock.	*Now they goe off.*
Kekuthomwushánnick.	*They are gone already.*

Generall Observations *of the* Sea.

How unsearchable are the depth of the Wisedome and Power of God in separating from *Europe, Asia* and *Africa* such a mightie vast continent as *America* is? and that for so many ages? as also, by such a Westerne Ocean of about three thousand of *English* miles breadth in passage over?

More particular:

[1.] *They see Gods wonders that are call'd*
Through dreadfull Seas to passe,
In tearing winds and roaring seas,
And calmes as smooth as glasse.

[2.] *I have in* Europes *ships, oft been*
In King of terrours hand;
When all have cri'd, Now, now we sinck,
Yet God brought safe to land.

[3.] *Alone 'mongst* Indians *in Canoes,*
Sometime o're-turn'd, I have been
Halfe inch from death, in Ocean deepe,
Gods wonders I have seene.

CHAP. XIX.
Of *Fish* and *Fishing.*

Namaùs -suck.	*Fish, Fishes.*
Pauganaùt -tamwock.	*Cod,* Which is the first that comes a little before the Spring.
Qunnamáug -suck.	*Lampries,* The first that come in the Spring into the fresh Rivers.
Aumsûog, *&* Munnawhatteaûg.	*A Fish somewhat like a Herring.*
Missúckeke -kéquock.	*Basse.* The *Indians* (and the

English too) make a daintie dish of the *Uppaquóntup,* or head of this Fish; and well they may, the braines and fat of it being very much, and sweet as marrow.

Kaúposh -shaûog.	*Sturgeon.*

Obs. Divers parts of the Countrey abound with this Fish; yet the Natives for the goodnesse and greatnesse of it, much prize it, and will neither furnish the *English* with so many, nor so cheape, that any great trade is like to be made of it, untill the *English* themselves are fit to follow the fishing.

The Natives venture one or two in a Canow, and with an harping Iron, or such like Instrument sticke this fish, and so hale it into their Canow; sometimes they take them by their nets, which they make strong of Hemp.

Ashòp. *Their Nets.* Which they will set thwart some little River or Cove wherein they kil Basse (at the fall of the water) with their arrows, or sharp sticks, especially if headed with Iron, gotten from the *English,* &c.

Aucùp. — *A little Cove* or *Creeke.*
Aucppâwese. — *A very little one.*
Wawwhunnekesûog. — *Mackrell.*
Mishquammaúquock. — *Red fish, Salmon.*
Osacóntuck. — *A fat sweet fish,* something like a *Haddock.*

Mishcùp -paûog,
Sequanamâuquock. — *Breame.*

Obs. Of this fish there is abundance, which the Natives drie in the Sunne and smoake, and some *English* begin to salt; both wayes they keepe all the yeere; and it is hoped it may be as well accepted as Cod at a Market, and better, if once knowne.

Taut -aúog. — *Sheeps-heads.*
Neeshaúog,
Sassamaúquock,
Nquittéconnauog. — *Eeles.*
Tatackommâuog. — *Porpuses.*
Pótop -paúog. — *Whales:* Which in some places are often cast up; I have seene some of them, but not above sixtie foot long: The *Natives* cut them out in severall parcells, and give and send farre and neere for an acceptable present, or dish.

Missêsu. — *The whole.*
Poquêsu. — *The halfe.*
Waskèke. — *The Whalebone.*
Wussúckqun. — *A taile.*
Aumaúog. — *They are fishing.*
Ntaûmen. — *I am fishing.*
Kuttaúmen? — *Doe you fish?*
Nnattuckqunnúwem. — *I goe afishing.*
Aumáchick,
Natuckqunnuwâchick. — *Fishers.*
Aumaûi. — *He is gone to fish.*

Awácenick kukkattineanaûmen?	*What doe you fish for?*
Ashaúnt -teaúg.	*Lobsters.*
Opponenaúhock.	*Oysters.*
Sickìssuog.	*Clams.*

Obs. This is a sweet kind of shelfish, which all *Indians* generally over the Countrey, Winter and Summer delight in; and at low water the women dig for them: this fish, and the naturall liquor of it, they boile, and it makes their broth and their *Nasaúmp* (which is a kind of thickned broth) and their bread seasonable and savory, in stead of Salt: and for that the *English* Swine dig and root these Clams wheresoever they come, and watch the low water (as the *Indian* women do) therefore of all the *English* Cattell, the Swine (as also because of their filthy disposition) are most hatefull to all Natives, and they call them filthy cut throats &c.

Séqunnock, Poquaûhock.	*A Horse-fish.*

Obs. This the English call Hens, a little thick shel fish which the Indians wade deepe and dive for, and after they have eaten the meat there (in those which are good) they breake out of the shell, about halfe an inch of a blacke part of it, of which they make their *Suckaúhock,* or black money, which is to them pretious.

Meteaûhock. *The Periwinckle.* Of which they make their *Wómpam,* or white money, of halfe the value of their *Suckáwhock,* or blacke money, of which more in the Chapter of their Coyne.

Cumménakiss, Cummenakíssamen, Cummuchickinneanâwmen?	*Have you taken store?*
Numménakiss.	*I have taken store.*
Nummuchikineanâwmen.	*I have killed many.*

Machàge. *I have caught none.*
Aúmanep. *A fishing-line.*
Aumanápeash. *Lines.*

The Natives take exceeding great paines in their fishing, especially in watching their seasons by night; so that frequently they lay their naked bodies many a cold night on the cold shoare about a fire of two or three sticks, and oft in the night search their Nets; and sometimes goe in and stay longer in frozen water.

Hoquaùn -aûnash. *Hooke, hookes.*
Peewâsicks. *Little hookes.*
Maúmacocks. *Great hookes.*
Nponamouôog. *I set nets for them.*
Npunnouwaûmen. *I goe to search my nets.*
Mihtúckquashep. *An Eele-pot.*
Kunnagqunneûteg. *A greater sort.*
Onawangónnakaun. *A baite.*
Yo onawangónnatees. *Baite with this.*
Moamitteaúg. *A little sort of fish,* halfe as big as Sprats, plentifull in Winter.

Paponaumsúog. *A winter fish,* which comes up in the brookes and rivulets; some call them Frost fish, from their comming up from the Sea into fresh Brookes, in times of frost and snow.

Qunôsuog. *A fresh fish;* [for] which the *Indians* break the Ice in fresh ponds, when they take also many other sorts: for, to my knowledge the Country yeelds many sorts of other fish, which I mention not.

The generall Observation *of Fish.*

How many thousands of Millions of those under water, sea-Inhabitants, in all Coasts of the world, preach to the sonnes of men on shore, to adore their glorious Maker by presenting themselves to Him as themselves (in a manner) present their lives from the wild Ocean, to the very doores of men, their fellow creatures in *New England.*

More Particular.

[1.] *What* Habacuck *once spake, mine eyes*
Have often seene most true,
The greater fishes devoure the lesse,
And cruelly pursue.

[2.] *Forcing them through Coves and Creekes,*
To leape on driest sand,
To gaspe on earthie element, or die
By wildest Indians *hand.*

[3.] *Christs little ones must hunted be,*
Devour'd, yet rise as Hee.
And eate up those which now a while
Their fierce devourers be.

CHAP. XX.
Of *their nakednesse* and *clothing.*

Paúskesu. *Naked.*
Pauskesítchick. *Naked men and women.*
Nippóskiss. *I am naked.*

They have a two-fold nakednesse:

First ordinary and constant, when although they have a Beasts skin, or an English mantle on, yet that covers ordinarily but their hinder parts and all the foreparts from top to toe, (except their secret parts, covered with a little Apron, after the patterne of their and our first Parents) I say all else open and naked.

Their male children goe starke naked, and have no Apron untill they come to ten or twelve yeeres of age; their Female they, in a modest blush cover with a little Apron of an hand breadth from their very birth.

Their second nakednesse is when their men often abroad, and both men and women within doores, leave off their beasts skin, or English cloth, and so (excepting their little Apron) are wholly naked; yet but few of the women but will keepe their skin or cloth (though loose) neare to them ready to gather it up about them.

Custome hath used their minds and bodies to it, and in such a freedom from any wantonnesse, that I have never seen that wantonnesse amongst them, as, (with griefe) I have heard of in *Europe.*

Nippóskenitch. *I am rob'd of my coat.*
Nippóskenick ewò. *He takes away my Coat.*
Acòh. *Their Deere skin.*
Tummóckquashunck. *A Beavers coat.*
Nkéquashunck. *An Otters coat.*

Mohéwonck. *A Rakoone-skin coat.*
Natóquashunck. *A Wolves-skin coat.*
Mishannéquashunck. *A Squirrill-skin coat.*
Neyhommaûashunck. *A Coat* or *Mantle,* curiously made of the fairest feathers of their *Neyhommaúog,* or Turkies, which commonly their old men make; and is with them as Velvet with us.

Maúnek: nquittiashíagat. *An English Coat* or *Mantell.*
Cáudnish. *Put off.*
Ocquash. *Put on.*
Neesashíagat. *Two coats.*
Shwíshiagat. *Three coats.*
Piuckquashíagat. *Ten coats, &c.*

Obs. Within their skin or coat they creepe contentedly, by day or night, in house, or in the woods, and sleep soundly counting it a felicitie, (as indeed an earthly one it is) *Intra pelliculam quemque tenere suam,* That every man be content with his skin.

Squáus aúhaqut. *A Womans Mantle.*
Muckíis aúhaqut. *A childs Mantle.*
Pétacaus. *An English Wastecoat.*
Petacawsunnèse. *A little wastecoat.*
Aútah & aútawhun. *Their apron.*
Caukóanash. *Stockins.*
Nquittetiagáttash. *A paire of stockins.*
Mocússinass, & Mockussínchass. *Shooes.*

Obs. Both these, Shoes and Stockins they make of their Deere skin worne out, which yet being excellently tann'd by them, is excellent for to travell in wet and snow; for it is so well tempered with oyle, that the water cleane wrings out; and being hang'd up in their chimney, they presently drie without hurt, as my selfe hath often proved.

Noonacóminash.	*Too little.*
Taubacóminash.	*Big enough.*
Saunketíppo, *or,* Ashónaquo.	*A Hat* or *Cap.*
Moôse.	*The skin of a great Beast* as big as an Ox, some call it a red Deere.
Wussuckhósu.	*Painted.*

They also commonly paint these *Moose* and Deere-skins for their Summer wearing, with varietie of formes and colours.

Petouwássinug. *Their Tobacco-bag,* which hangs at their necke, or sticks at their girdle, which is to them in stead of an English pocket.

Obs. Our English clothes are so strange unto them, and their bodies inured so to indure the weather, that when (upon gift &c.) some of them have had *English* cloathes, yet in a showre of raine, I have seen them rather expose their skins to the wet then their cloaths, and therefore pull them off, and keep them drie.

Obs. While they are amongst the *English* they keep on the *English* apparell, but pull of all, as soone as they come againe into their owne Houses, and Company.

Generall Observations *of their Garments.*

How deep are the purposes and Councells, of God? what should bee the reason of this mighty difference of One mans children that all the Sonnes of men on this side the way (in *Europe, Asia* and *Africa*) should have such plenteous clothing for Body, for Soule! and the rest of *Adams* sonnes and Daughters on the other side, or *America* (some thinke as big as the other three,) should neither have nor desire clothing for their naked Soules, or Bodies.

More particular:

[1.] *O what a Tyrant's Custome long,*
How doe men make a tush,
At what's in use, though ne're so fowle:
Without once shame or blush?

[2.] *Many thousand proper Men and Women,*
I have seen met in one place:
Almost all naked, yet not one,
Thought want of clothes disgrace.

[3.] *Israell was naked, wearing cloathes!* } *Exod.* 32.
The best clad English-man,
Not cloth'd with Christ, more naked is:
Then naked Indian.

CHAP. XXI.

Of Religion, the soule, &c.

Manìt, manittówock. — *God, Gods.*

Obs. He that questions whether God made the World, the *Indians* will teach him. I must acknowledge I have received in my converse with them many Confirmations of those two great points, *Heb.* 11. 6. *viz:*

1. That God is.

2. That hee is a rewarder of all them that diligently seek him.

They will generally confesse that God made all: but then in speciall, although they deny not that *English-mans* God made *English* Men, and the Heavens and Earth there! yet their Gods made them, and the Heaven and Earth where they dwell.

Nummusquaunamúckqun manìt. — *God is angry with me.*

Obs. I have heard a poore *Indian* lamenting the losse of a child at break of day, call up his Wife and children, and all about him to Lamentation, and with abundance of teares cry out! O God thou hast taken away my child! thou art angry with me: O turne thine anger from me, and spare the rest of my children.

If they receive any good in hunting, fishing, Harvest &c. they acknowledge God in it.

Yea, if it be but an ordinary accident, a fall, &c. they will say God was angry and did it. *musquàntum manit* God is angry. But herein is their Misery.

First they branch their God-head into many Gods.

Secondly, attribute it to Creatures.

First, many Gods: they have given me the Names of thirty seven, which I have, all which in their solemne Worships they invocate: as

Kautántowwit the great *South-West* God, to whose House all soules goe, and from whom came their Corne, Beanes, as they say.

Wompanànd.	*The Easterne God.*
Chekesuwànd.	*The Westerne God.*
Wunnanaméanit.	*The Northerne God.*
Sowwanànd.	*The Southerne God.*
Wetuómanit.	*The house God.*

Even as the Papists have their He and Shee Saint Protectors as St. *George,* St. *Patrick,* St. *Denis,* Virgin *Mary,* &c.

Squáuanit.	*The Womans God.*
Muckquachuckquànd.	*The Childrens God.*

Obs. I was once with a *Native* dying of a wound, given him by some murtherous *English* (who rob'd him and run him through with a Rapier) from whom in the heat of his wound, he at present escaped—but dying of his wound, they suffered Death at new *Plymouth,* in *New-England*—this *Native* dying call'd much upon *Muckquachuckquànd,* who of other *Natives* I understood (as they believed) had appeared to the dying young man, many yeares before, and bid him when ever he was in distresse call upon him.

Secondly, as they have many of these fained Deities: so worship they the Creatures in whom they conceive doth rest some Deitie:

Keesuckquànd.	*The Sun God.*
Nanepaûshat.	*The Moone God.*
Paumpágussit.	*The Sea* [*God*].
Yotáanit.	*The Fire God,*

Supposing that Deities be in these, &c.

When I have argued with them about their Fire-God: can it, say they, be but this fire must be a God, or Divine power, that out of a stone will arise in a Sparke, and when a poore naked *Indian* is ready to starve with cold in the House, and especially in the Woods, often saves his life, doth dresse all our Food for us, and if it be angry will burne the House about us, yea if a spark fall into the drie wood, burnes up the Country? (though this burning of the Wood to them they count a Benefit, both for destroying of vermin, and keeping downe the Weeds and thickets).

Præsentem narrat quæ libet herba Deum.

Every little Grasse doth tell,
The sons of Men, there God doth dwell.

Besides there is a generall Custome amongst them, at the apprehension of any Excellency in Men, Women, Birds, Beasts, Fish, &c. to cry out *Manittóo,* that is, it is a God, as thus if they see one man excell others in Wisdome, Valour, strength, Activity &c. they cry out *Manittóo* A God: and therefore when they talke amongst themselves of the *English* ships, and great buildings, of the plowing of their Fields, and especially of Bookes and Letters, they will end thus: *Manittôwock* They are Gods: *Cummanittôo,* you are a God, &c. A strong Conviction naturall in the soule of man, that God is; filling all things, and places, and that all Excellencies dwell in God, and proceed from him, and that they only are blessed who have that Jehovah their portion.

Nickómmo. *A Feast* or *Dance.*

Of this Feast they have publike, and private, and that of two sorts.

First in sicknesse, or Drouth, or Warre, or Famine.

Secondly, After Harvest, after hunting, when they enjoy a caulme of Peace, Health, Plenty, Prosperity, then *Nickómmo* a Feast, especially in Winter, for then (as the Turke saith of the Christian, rather the Antichristian,) they run mad once a yeare in their kind of Christmas feasting.

Powwáw.	*A Priest.*
Powwaûog.	*Priests.*

Obs. These doe begin and order their service, and Invocation of their Gods, and all the people follow, and joyne interchangeably in a laborious bodily service, unto sweating, especially of the Priest, who spends himselfe in strange Antick Gestures, and Actions even unto fainting.

In sicknesse the Priest comes close to the sick person, and performes many strange Actions about him, and threaten and conjures out the sicknesse. They conceive that there are many Gods or divine Powers within the body of a man: In his pulse, his heart, his Lungs, &c.

I confesse to have most of these their customes by their owne Relation, for after once being in their Houses and beholding what their Worship was, I durst never bee an eye witnesse, Spectatour, or looker on, least I should have been partaker of Sathans Inventions and Worships, contrary to *Ephes.* 5. 11.

Nanouwétea.	*An over-Seer* and *Orderer of their Worship.*
Neen nanowwúnnemun.	*I will order* or *oversee.*

They have an exact forme of King, Priest, and Prophet, as was in Israel typicall of old in that holy Land of *Canaan,* and as the Lord *Jesus* ordained in his spirituall Land of *Canaan* his Church throughout the whole World: their Kings or Governours called *Sachimaüog,* Kings, and *Atauskowaúg,* Rulers, doe govern: Their Priests, performe and manage their Worship: Their wise men and old men (of which number the Priests are also,) whom they call *Taupowaüog* they make solemne speeches and Orations, or Lectures to them, concerning Religion, Peace, or Warre and all things.

Nowemaúsitteem.	*I give away at the Worship.*

He or she that makes this *Nickòmmo* Feast or Dance, besides the Feasting of sometimes twenty, fifty, an hundreth, yea I have seene neere a thousand persons at one of these Feasts, they give I say a great quantity of money, and all sort of their goods (according to and sometimes beyond their Estate) in severall small parcells of goods, or money, to the value of eighteen pence, two Shillings, or thereabouts to one person: and that person that receives this Gift, upon the receiving of it goes out, and hollowes thrice for the health and prosperity of the Party that gave it, the Mr. or Mistris of the Feast.

Nowemacaúnash.	*Ile give these things.*
Nitteaúguash.	*My money.*
Nummaumachíuwash.	*My goods.*

Obs. By this Feasting and Gifts, the Divell drives on their worships pleasantly (as he doth all false worships, by such plausible Earthly Arguments of uniformities, universalities, Antiquities, Immunities, Dignities, Rewards, unto submitters, and the contrary to Refusers) so that they run farre and neere and aske

Awaun. Nákommit?	*Who makes a Feast?*
Nkekinneawaûmen.	*I goe to the Feast.*
Kekineawaúi.	*He is gone to the Feast.*

They have a modest Religious perswasion not to disturb any man, either themselves *English, Dutch,* or any in their Conscience, and worship, and therefore say:

Aquiewopwaúwash, Aquiewopwaúwock.	*Peace, hold your peace.*
Peeyaúntam.	*He is at Prayer.*
Peeyaúntamwock.	*They are praying.*
Cowwéwonck.	*The Soule,*

Derived from *Cowwene* to sleep, because say they, it workes and operates when the body sleepes. *Míchachunck* the soule, in a higher notion, which is of affinity, with a word signifying a looking glasse, or cleere resemblance, so that it hath its name from a cleere sight or discerning, which indeed seemes very well to suit with the nature of it.

Wuhóck.	*The Body.*
Nohòck: cohòck.	*My body, your body.*
Awaunkeesitteoúwinco-hòck?	*Who made you?*
Tunna-awwa commítchich-unck-kitonckquèan?	*Whether goes your soule when you die?*
An. Sowánakitauwaw.	*It goes to the South-West.*

Obs. They beleive that the soules of Men and Women goe to the Sou-west, their great and good men and Women to *Cautàntouwit* his House, where they have hopes (as the Turkes have) of carnall Joyes: Murtherers thieves and Lyers, their Soules (say they) wander restlesse abroad.

Now because this Book (by Gods good providence) may come into the hand of many fearing God, who may also have many an opportunity of occasionall discourse with some of these their wild brethren and Sisters, and may speake a word for their and our glorious Maker, which may also prove some preparatory Mercy to their Soules: I shall propose some proper expressions concerning the Creation of the World, and mans Estate, and in particular theirs also, which from my selfe many hundreths of times, great numbers of them have heard with great delight, and great convictions: which who knowes (in Gods holy season) may rise to exalting of the Lord Jesus Christ in their conversion, and salvation?

Nétop Kunnatótemous.	*Friend, I will aske you a Question.*
Natótema.	*Speake on.*
Tocketunnántum?	*What thinke you?*
Awaun Keesiteoûwin Kéesuck?	*Who made the Heavens?*

Aûke Wechêkom?	*The Earth, the Sea?*
Míttauke.	*The World.*

Some will answer *Tattá* I cannot tell, some will answer *Manittôwock* the Gods.

Tasuóg Maníttowock?	*How many Gods bee there?*
Maunaúog Mishaúnawock.	*Many, great many.*
Nétop machàge.	*Friend, not so.*
Paúsuck naúnt manìt.	*There is onely one God.*
Cuppíssittone.	*You are mistaken.*
Cowauwaúnemun.	*You are out of the way.*

A phrase which much pleaseth them, being proper for their wandring in the woods, and similitudes greatly please them.

Kukkakótemous, wâchitquáshouwe.	*I will tell you, presently.*
Kuttaunchemókous.	*I will tell you newes.*
Paûsuck naúnt manít kéesittin keesuck, &c.	*One onely God made the Heavens, &c.*
Napannetashè mittannauge cautúmmo nab nshque.	*Five thousand yeers ago and upwards.*
Naúgom naúnt wukkesittínes wâme teâgun,	*He alone made all things,*
Wúche mateâg.	*Out of nothing.*
Quttatashuchuckqun-nacauskeesitínnes wâme.	*In six dayes he made all things.*
Nquittaqúnne, Wuckéesitin wequâi.	*The first day Hee made the Light.*
Néesqunne, Wuckéesitin Keésuck.	*The second day Hee made the Firmament.*
Shúckqunne wuckéesitin Aúke kà wechêkom.	*The third day hee made the Earth and Sea.*

Yóqunne wuckkéesitin Nippaúus kà Nanepaúshat,	*The fourth day he made* *the Sun and the Moon,*
Neenash-mamockiuwash wequanantíganash,	*Two great Lights,*
Kà wáme anócksuck.	*And all the Starres.*
Napannetashúckqunne Wuckéesittin pussuckseésuck wâme	*The fifth day hee made all* *the Fowle*
Keesuckquíuke,	*In the Ayre,* or *Heavens,*
Ka wáme namaúsuck Wechekommíuke.	*And all the Fish in* *the Sea.*
Quttatashúkqunne wuckkeésittin penashímwock wamè.	*The sixth day hee made all* *the Beasts of the Field.*
Wuttàke wuchè wuckeesittin pausuck Enìn, *or,* Eneskéetomp	*Last of all he made one* *Man*
Wuche mishquòck,	*Of red Earth,*
Ka wesuonckgonnakaûnes Adam, túppautea mishquòck.	*And call'd him Adam,* or *red Earth.*
Wuttàke wuchè, Câwit míshquock,	*Then afterward, while* *Adam,* or *red Earth slept,*
Wuckaudnúmmenes manìt peetaúgon wuchè Adam,	*God tooke a rib from Adam,* or *red Earth,*
Kà wuchè peteaúgon Wukkeesitínnes pausuck squàw,	*And of that rib he made* *One woman,*
Kà pawtouwúnnes Adâmuck.	*And brought her to Adam.*
Nawônt Adam wuttúnnawaun nuppeteâgon ewò.	*When Adam saw her, he* *said, This is my bone.*
Enadatashúckqunne, aquêi,	*The seventh day hee rested,*

Nagaû wuchè quttatashúckqune anacaúsuock Englishmánuck.	*And therefore Englishmen worke six dayes.*
Enadatashuckqunnóckat taubataúmwock.	*On the seventh day they praise God.*

Obs. At this Relation they are much satisfied, with a reason why (as they observe) the *English* and *Dutch,* &c. labour six dayes, and rest and worship the seventh.

Besides, they will say, Wee never heard of this before: and then will relate how they have it from their Fathers, that *Kautántowwit* made one man and woman of a stone, which disliking, he broke them in pieces, and made another man and woman of a Tree, which were the Fountaines of all mankind.

They apprehending a vast difference of Knowledge betweene the *English* and themselves, are very observant of the *English* lives: I have heard them say to an Englishman (who being hindred, broke a promise to them) You know God, Will you lie Englishman?

Nétop kíhkita.	*Hearken to mee.*
Englishmánnuck,	*English-men,*
Dutchmánnuck, kéenouwin kà wamè mittaukêuk-kitonckquéhettit,	*Dutch men, and you and all the world, when they die,*
Mattùx swowánnakit aúog, Michichónckquock.	*Their soules goe not to the Southwest.*
Wàme, ewò pâwsuck Manìt wawóntakick,	*All that know that one God,*
Ewò manìt waumaûsachick kà uckqushanchick,	*That love and feare Him,*
Keésaqut aùog.	*They goe up to Heaven.*
Michéme weeteantámwock,	*They ever live in joy,*
Naûgom manìt wêkick.	*In Gods owne House.*

Ewo manìt mat wauóntakick,	*They that know not this God,*
Matwaumaûsachick	*That love*
Màt ewò uckqushánchick,	*And feare him not,*
Kamóotakick,	*Thieves,*
Pupannouwâchick,	*Lyers,*
Nochisquauónchick,	*Uncleane persons,*
Nanompaníssichick,	*Idle persons,*
Kemineíachick,	*Murtherers,*
Mammaúsachick,	*Adulterers,*
Nanisquégachick,	*Oppressors or fierce,*
Wame naûmakiaûog.	*They goe to Hell* or *the Deepe.*
Micheme maûog.	*They shall ever lament.*
Awaun kukkakotemógwunnes?	*Who told you so?*
Manittóo wússuckwheke.	*Gods Booke* or *Writing.*

Obs. After I had (as farre as my language would reach) discoursed (upon a time) before the chiefe *Sachim* or *Prince* of the Countrey, with his *Archpriests,* and many others in a full Assembly; and being night, wearied with travell and discourse, I lay downe to rest; and before I slept, I heard this passage:

A *Qunníhticut* Indian (who had heard our discourse) told the *Sachim Miantunnómu,* that soules went [not] up to Heaven, or downe to Hell; For, saith he, Our fathers have told us, that our soules goe to the *Southwest.*

The *Sachim* answered, But how doe you know your selfe, that your soules goe to the *Southwest;* did you ever see a soule goe thither?

The Native replyed; when did he (naming my selfe) see a soule goe to Heaven or Hell?

The *Sachim* againe replied: He hath books and writings, and one which God himselfe made, concerning mens soules, and therefore may well know more then wee that have none, but take all upon trust from our forefathers.

The said *Sachim,* and the chiefe of his people, discoursed by themselves, of keeping the Englishmans day of worship, which I could easily have brought the Countrey to, but that I was perswaded, and am, that Gods way is first to turne a soule from it's Idolls, both of heart, worship, and conversation, before it is capable of worship, to the true and living God, according to I *Thes.* 1. 9. You turned to God from Idolls to serve or worship the living and true God. As also, that the two first Principles and Foundations of true Religion or worship of the true God in Christ, are Repentance from dead workes, and Faith towards God, before the Doctrine of Baptisme or washing and the laying on of hands, which containe the Ordinances and Practises of worship; the want of which, I conceive, is the bane of million of soules in England, and all other Nations professing to be Christian Nations, who are brought by publique authority to Baptisme and fellowship with God in Ordinances of worship, before the saving worke of Repentance, and a true turning to God, *Heb.* 6. 2.

Nétop, kitonckquêan kunnúppamin michéme.	*Friend, when you die you perish everlastingly.*
Michéme cuppauqua neímmin.	*You are everlastingly undone.*
Cummusquaunamúckqun manìt.	*God is angry with you.*
Cuppauquanúckqun	*He will destroy you*
Wuchè cummanittówock manâuog.	*For your many Gods.*
Wáme pìtch chíckauta mittaùke.	*The whole world shall ere long be burnt.*

Obs. Upon the relating that God hath once destroyed the world by water; and that He will visit it the second time with consuming fire: I have been asked this profitable question of some of them, What then will become of us? Where then shall we be?

Manìt ánawat,	*God commandth,*
Cuppittakúnnamun wèpe wáme.	*That all men now repent.*

The generall Observation *of* Religion, *&c.*

The wandring Generations of *Adams* lost posteritie, having lost the true and living God their Maker, have created out of the nothing of their owne inventions many false and fained Gods and Creators.

More particular:

[1.] *Two sorts of men shall naked stand*
Before the burning ire 2 Thes. 1.8
Of him that shortly shall appeare,
In dreadfull flaming fire.

[2.] *First, millions know not God, nor for*
His *knowledge care to seeke:*
Millions have knowledge store, but in
Obedience are not meeke.

[3.] *If woe to* Indians, *Where shall* Turk,
Where shall appeare the Jew?
O, where shall stand the Christian false?
O blessed then the True.

CHAP. XXII.

Of *their Government* and *Justice.*

Sâchim -maûog.	*King, Kings.*
Sachimaûonck.	*A Kingdome* or *Monarchie.*

Obs. Their Government is Monarchicall, yet at present the chiefest government in the Countrey is divided betweene a younger *Sachim,* Miantunnômu, and an elder *Sachim,* Caunoúnicus, of about fourescore yeeres old, this young mans Uncle; and their agreement in the Government is remarkable:

The old *Sachim* will not be offended at what the young *Sachim* doth; and the young *Sachim* will not doe what hee conceives will displease his Uncle.

Saunks.	*The Queen,* or *Sachims Wife.*
Sauncksquûaog.	*Queenes.*
Otân -nash.	*The towne, townes.*
Otânick.	*To the towne.*

Sachimmaacómmock. *A Princes house,* which according to their condition, is farre different from the other house, both in capacity or receit; and also the finenesse and quality of their Mats.

Ataúskawaw -wáuog.	*Lord, Lords.*
Wauôntam.	*A Wise man* or *Counsellour.*
Wauóntakick.	*Wise men.*
Enàtch *or* eàtch Keèn anawáyean.	*Your will shall be law.*
Enàtch neèn ánowa.	*Let my word stand.*
Ntínnume.	*He is my man.*

Ntacquêtunck ewò.	*He is my subject.*
Kuttackquêtous.	*I will [be] subject to you.*

Obs. Beside their generall subjection to the highest *Sachims,* to whom they carry presents: They have also particular Protectors, under *Sachims,* to whom they also carry presents, and upon any injury received, and complaint made, these Protectors will revenge it.

Ntannôtam.	*I will revenge it.*
Kuttannótous.	*I will revenge you.*
Miâwene.	*A Court* or *meeting.*
Wèpe cummiâwene.	*Come to the meeting.*
Miawêtuck.	*Let us meet.*
Wauwháutowash.	*Call a meeting.*
Miawêmucks.	*At a meeting.*
Miawéhettit.	*When they meet.*

Obs. The *Sachims,* although they have an absolute Monarchie over the people; yet they will not conclude of ought that concernes all, either Lawes, or Subsides, or warres, unto which the people are averse, and by gentle perswasion cannot be brought.

Peyaùtch naûgum.	*Let himselfe come here.*
Pétiteatch.	*Let him come.*
Mishaúntowash.	*Speake out.*
Nanántowash.	*Speake plaine.*
Kunnadsíttamen wèpe.	*You must inquire after this.*
Wunnadsittamútta.	*Let us search into it.*
Neen pitch-nnadsíttamen.	*I will inquire into it.*
Machíssu ewò.	*He is naught.*
Cuttiantacompàwwem.	*You are a lying fellow.*
Cuttiantakiskquáwquaw.	*You are a lying woman.*
Wèpe cukkúmmoot.	*You have stole.*
Mat méshnawmônash.	*I did not see those things.*
Mat mèsh nummám menash.	*I did not take them.*

Wèpe kunnishquêko cummiskissâwwaw.	*You are fierce and quarrelsome.*

Obs. I could never discerne that excesse of scandalous sins amongst them, which *Europe* aboundeth with. Drunkennesse and gluttony, generally they know not what sinnes they be; and although they have not so much to restraine them (both in respect of knowledge of God and Lawes of men) as the *English* have, yet a man shall never heare of such crimes amongst them of robberies, murthers, adulteries, &c. as amongst the *English:* I conceive that the glorious Sunne of so much truth as shines in *England,* hardens our *English* hearts; for what the Sunne softeneth not, it hardens.

Tawhìtch yò enêan?	*Why doe you so?*
Tawhìtch cummootóan?	*Why doe you steale?*
Tawhìtch nanompanieân?	*Why are you thus idle* or *base?*
Wewhepapúnnoke.	*Bind him.*
Wèpe kunnishaûmis.	*You kild him.*
Wèpe kukkemineantín.	*You are the murtherer.*
Sasaumitaúwhitch.	*Let him be whipt.*
Upponckquittaúwhitch.	*Let him be imprisoned.*
Nìppitch ewò.	*Let him die.*
Níphéttitch.	*Let them die.*
Nìss-Nìssoke.	*Kill him.*
Púm-púmmoke.	*Shoot him.*

Obs. The most usuall Custome amongst them in executing punishments, is for the *Sachim* either to beat, or whip, or put to death with his owne hand, to which the common sort most quietly submit: though sometimes the *Sachim* sends a secret Executioner, one of his chiefest Warriours to fetch of a head, by some sudden unexpected blow of a Hatchet, when they have feared Mutiny by publike execution.

Kukkeechequaûbenitch.	*You shall be hanged.*
Níppansínnea.	*I am innocent.*

Uppansìnea-ewo. *He is innocent.*
Matmeshnowaûwon. *I knew nothing of it.*
Nnowaûntum. *I am sorry.*
Nummachiemè. *I have done ill.*
Aumaúnemoke. *Let it passe,* or *take away this accusation.*

Konkeeteatch Ewo. *Let him live.*
Konkeeteáhetti. *Let them live.*

Observation Generall, of their Government.

The wildest of the sonnes of Men have ever found a necessity, (for preservation of themselves, their Families and Properties) to cast themselves into some Mould or forme of Government.

More particular:

1. *Adulteries, Murthers, Robberies, Thefts,*
Wild Indians *punish these!*
And hold the Scales of Justice so,
That no man farthing leese.

2. *When* Indians *heare the horrid filths,*
Of Irish, English *Men,*
The horrid Oaths and Murthers late,
Thus say these Indians *then:*

[3.] *We weare no Cloaths, have many Gods,*
And yet our sinnes are lesse:
You are Barbarians, Pagans wild,
Your Land's the Wildernesse.

CHAP. XXI[II].
Of Marriage.

Wuskéne.	*A young man.*
Keegsquaw.	*A Virgin* or *Maide.*
Segaûo.	*A Widdower.*
Segoúsquaw.	*A Widdow.*
Wussénetam.	*He goes a wooing.*
Nosénemuck.	*He is my sonne in Law.*
Wussenetûock, Awetawátuock.	*They make a match.*

Obs. Single fornication they count no sin, but after Mariage (which they solemnize by consent of Parents and publique approbation publiquely) then they count it hainous for either of them to be false.

Mammaûsu.	*An adulterer.*
Nummam mógwun ewò.	*He hath wronged my bed.*
Pallè nochisquaûaw.	*He* or *She hath committed adultery.*

Obs. In this case the wronged party may put away or keepe the party offending: commonly, if the Woman be false, the offended Husband will be solemnly revenged upon the offendor, before many witnesses, by many blowes and wounds, and if it be to Death, yet the guilty resists not, nor is his Death revenged.

Nquittócaw.	*He hath one Wife.*
Neesócaw.	*He hath two Wives.*
Sshócowaw.	*He hath three.*
Yócowaw.	*Foure Wives, &c.*

Their Number is not stinted, yet the chief Nation in the Country, the Narrigansets (generally) have but one Wife.

Two causes they generally alledge for their many Wives.

First desire of Riches, because the Women bring in all the increase of the Field, &c. the Husband onely fisheth, hunteth, &c.

Secondly, their long sequestring themselves from their wives after conception, untill the child be weaned, which with some is long after a yeare old, generally they keep their children long at the breast:

Commíttamus, Cowéewo.	*Your Wife.*
Tahanawátu ta shin-commaúgemus?	*How much gave you for her?*
Napannetashom paûgatash.	*Five fathome of their Money.*
Quttá, enada shoasuck ta shompaúgatash.	*Six,* or *seven,* or *eight Fathome.*

If some great mans Daughter *Piuckquompaúgatash,* ten fathome.

Obs. Generally the Husband gives these payments for a Dowrie, (as it was in *Israell*) to the Father or Mother, or guardian of the Maide. To this purpose if the man be poore, his Friends and neighbours doe *pummenúmmin teàuguash,* that is contribute Money toward the Dowrie.

Nummíttamus, Nullógana.	*My Wife.*
Waumaûsu.	*Loving.*
Wunnêkesu.	*Proper.*
Maânsu.	*Sober and chast.*
Muchickéhea.	*Fruitfull.*
Cutchashekeâmis?	*How many children have you had?*
Nquittékea.	*I have had one.*
Neesékea.	*Two, &c.*

Obs. They commonly abound with Children, and increase mightily; except the plauge fall amongst them, or other lesser sicknesses, and then having no meanes of recovery, they perish wonderfully.

Katoû eneéchaw.	*She is falling into Travell.*
Néechaw.	*She is in Travell.*
Paugcótche nechaúwaw.	*She is already delivered.*
Kitummâyi-mes-néchaw.	*She was just now delivered.*

Obs. It hath pleased God in wonderfull manner to moderate that curse of the sorrowes of Child-bearing to these poore Indian Women: So that ordinarily they have a wonderfull more speedy and easie Travell, and delivery then the Women of *Europe*: not that I thinke God is more gracious to them above other Women, but that it followes, First from the hardnesse of their constitution, in which respect they beare their sorrowes the easier.

Secondly from their extraordinary great labour (even above the labour of men) as in the Field, they sustaine the labour of it, in carrying of mighty Burthens, in digging clammes and getting other Shelfish from the Sea, in beating all their corne in Morters: &c. Most of them count it a shame for a Woman in Travell to make complaint, and many of them are scarcely heard to groane. I have often knowne in one Quarter of an houre a Woman merry in the House, and delivered and merry again: and within two dayes abroad, and after foure or five dayes at worke, &c.

Noosâwwaw.	*A Nurse.*
Noònsu Nonánnis.	*A sucking Child.*
Wunnunògan.	*A Breast.*
Wunnunnóganash.	*Breasts.*

Munnúnnug.	*Milke.*
Aumaúnemun.	*To take from the breast,* or *Weane.*

Obs. They put away (as in Israell) frequently for other occasions beside Adultery, yet I know many Couples that have lived twenty, thirty, forty yeares together.

Npakétam.	*I will put her away.*
Npakénaqun.	*I am put away.*
Aquie pakétash.	*Doe not put away.*
Aquie pokesháttous Awetawátuonck.	*Doe not break the knot of Marriage.*
Tackquiúwock.	*Twins.*
Towiû-ûwock.	*Orphans.*
Ntouwiú.	*I am an Orphane.*
Wáuchaúnat.	*A Guardian.*
Wauchaúamachick.	*Guardians.*
Nullóquaso.	*My charge* or *Pupill,* or *Ward.*
Peewaúqun.	*Looke well to him &c.*

Generall Observations *of their Mariage.*

God hath planted in the Hearts of the Wildest of the sonnes of Men, an High and Honourable esteeme of the Mariage bed, insomuch that they universally submit unto it, and hold the Violation of that Bed, Abominable, and accordingly reape the Fruit thereof in the abundant increase of posterity.

More Particular.

[1.] *When Indians heare that some there are,*
(That Men the Papists call)
Forbidding Mariage Bed and yet,
To thousand Whoredomes fall:

[2.] *They aske if such doe goe in Cloaths,*
And whether God they know?
And when they heare they're richly clad,
Know God, yet practice so.

[3.] *No sure they're Beasts not men (say they,)*
Mens shame and foule disgrace,
Or men have mixt with Beasts and so,
Brought forth that monstrous Race.

CHAP. XXIV.

Concerning their Coyne.

The *Indians* are ignorant of *Europes* Coyne; yet they have given a name to ours, and call it *Moneash* from the *English* Money.

Their owne is of two sorts; one white, which they make of the stem or stocke of the *Periwincle,* which they call Meteaûhock, when all the shell is broken off: and of this sort six of their small Beads (which they make with holes to string the bracelets) are currant with the *English* for a peny.

The second is black, inclining to blew, which is made of the shell of a fish, which some *English* call *Hens,* Poquaûhock, and of this sort three make an *English* peny.

They that live upon the Sea side, generally make of it, and as many make as will.

The *Indians* bring downe all their sorts of Furs, which they take in the Countrey, both to the *Indians* and to the *English* for this *Indian* Money: this Money the *English, French* and *Dutch,* trade to the *Indians,* six hundred miles in severall parts (North and South from *New-England*) for their Furres, and whatsoever they stand in need of from them: as Corne, Venison, &c.

Nquittómpscat.	1 *peny.*
Neesaúmscat.	2 *pence.*
Shwaúmscat.	3 *pence.*
Yowómscat.	4 *pence.*
Napannetashaúmscat.	5 *pence.*
Quttatashaúmscat, *or,* quttáuátu.	6 *pence.*
Enadatashaúmscat.	7 *pence.*

Shwoasuck tashaúmscat.	8 *pence.*
Paskugittashaúmscat.	9 *pence.*
Piuckquaúmscat.	10 *pence.*
Piuckquaúmscat nab naqùit.	11 *pence.*
Piuckquaúmscat nab nèes, &c.	12 *pence.*

Obs. This they call *Neèn,* which is two of their *Quttáuatues,* or six pence.

Piukquaúmscat nab nashoasuck, *which they call* Shwìn.	18$^{d.}$ 3 quttáuatues.
Neesneecheckaúmscat nab yòh, *or,* yowin.	2$^{s.}$ 4 quttáuatues.
Shwinchékaúmscat, *or* napannetashin.	2$^{s.}$ 6$^{d.}$ 5 quttáuatues.
Shwinchekaúmscat.	2$^{s.}$ 6$^{d.}$ 6 quttáuatues.
Yowinnchekaúmscat nab neèse.	3$^{s.}$ 6$^{d.}$ 7 quttáuatues.
Yowinncheckaúmscat nabnashòasuck.	4$^{s.}$ 8 quttáuatues.
Napannetashwincheckáumscat nab yòh.	4$^{s.}$ 6$^{d.}$ 9 quttáuatues.
Quttatashincheck aumscat, *or, more commonly used* Piúckquat.	5$^{s.}$ 10 quttaúatues, *or,* 10 six pences.

Obs. This *Piúckquat* being sixtie pence, they call *Nquittómpeg,* or *nquitnishcáusu,* that is, one fathom, 5 shillings.

This one fathom of this their stringed money, now worth of the English but five shillings (sometimes more) some few yeeres since was worth nine, and sometimes ten shillings *per* Fathome: the fall is occasioned by the fall of Beaver in *England:* the Natives are very impatient, when for English commodities they pay so much more of their money, and not understanding the cause of it; and many say the English cheat and deceive them, though I have laboured to make them understand the reason of it.

Neesaumpaúgatuck.	10 shil. 2 Fathom.
Shwaumpáugatuck.	15 shil. 3 Fathom.
Yowompáugatuck, &c.	20 shil. 4 Fathom.
Piuckquampáugatuck *or* Nquit pâusck.	50 shil. 10 Fathome.
Neespausuckquompáugatuck.	5 lib' 20 Fathome.
Shwepaûsuck.	30 Fathome.
Yowe paûsuck, &c.	40 Fathome, *or,* 10. pounds.
Nquittemittannauganompáugatuck.	[1000 Fathome, *or,* 250. pounds.]
Neesemittannug, &c.	[2000 Fathome, *or,* 500. pounds.]
Tashincheckompáugatuck?	*How many* Fathom?

Obs. Their white they call *Wompam* (which signifies white): their black *Suckáuhock* (*Súcki* signifying blacke.)

Both amongst themselves; as also the English and Dutch, the blacke peny is two pence white; the blacke fathom double, or, two fathom of white.

Wepe kuttassawompatímmin.	*Change my money.*
Suckaúhock, nausakésachick.	*The blacke money.*
Wauômpeg, *or* Wauompésichick-mêsim.	*Give me white.*
Assawompatíttea.	*Come, let us change.*
Anâwsuck.	*Shells.*
Meteaûhock.	*The Periwinckle.*
Suckauanaûsuck.	*The blacke shells.*

Suckauaskéesaquash. *The blacke eyes,* or that part of the shel-fish called *Poquaúhock* (or Hens) broken out neere the eyes, of which they make the blacke.

Puckwhéganash &
Múcksuck. *Awle blades.*
Papuckakíuash. *Britle,* or *breaking,* which they desire to be hardened to a britle temper.

Obs. Before ever they had *Awle blades* from *Europe,* they made shift to bore this their shell money with stone, and so fell their trees with stone set in a wooden staff, and used woden *howes:* which some old & poore women (fearfull to leave the old tradition) use to this day.

Natouwómpitea. *A Coyner* or *Minter.*
Nnanatouwómpiteem. *I cannot coyne.*
Natouwómpitees. *Make money* or *Coyne.*
Puckhùmmin. *To bore through.*
Puckwhegonnaûtick. *The Awle blade sticks.*
Tutteputch anâwsin. *To smooth them,* which they doe on stones.
Qussùck -anash. *Stone, Stones.*
Cauómpsk. *A Whetstone.*
Nickáutick. *A kinde of wooden Pincers* or *Vice.*
Enomphómmin. *To thread* or *string.*
Aconaqunnaûog. *Thread the Beads.*
Enomphómmin. *Thread,* or *string these.*
Enomphósachick. *Strung ones.*
Sawhóog &
Sawhósachick. *Loose Beads.*
Naumpacoûin. *To hang about the necke.*

Obs. They hang these strings of money about their necks and wrists; as also upon the necks and wrists of their wives and children.

Máchequoce. *A Girdle:* Which they make curiously of one two, three, foure, and five inches thicknesse and more, of this money which (sometimes to the value of ten pounds and more) they weare about their middle and as a scarfe about their shoulders and breasts.

Yea the Princes make rich Caps and Aprons (or small breeches) of these Beads thus curiously strung into many formes and figures: their blacke and white finely mixt together.

Observations *generall of their* Coyne.

The Sonnes of men having lost their Maker, the true and onely Treasure, dig downe to the bowels of the earth for gold and silver; yea, to the botome of the Sea, for shells of fishes, to make up a Treasure, which can never truly inrich nor satisfie.

More particular:

1. *The* Indians *prize not* English *gold,*
Nor English Indians *shell:*
Each in his place will passe for ought,
What ere men buy or sell.

[2.] English *and* Indians *all passe hence,*
To an eternall place,
Where shels nor finest gold's worth ought,
Where nought's worth ought but Grace.

[3.] *This Coyne the* Indians *know not of,*
Who knowes how soon they may?
The English *knowing, prize it not,*
But fling't like drosse away.

CHAP. XXV.

Of buying and selling.

Anaqushaúog, *or* Anaqushánchick.	*Traders.*
Anaqushénto.	*Let us trade.*
Cúttasha? Cowachaúnum?	*Have you this* or *that?*
Nítasha, Nowachaúnum.	*I have.*
Nquénowhick.	*I want this, &c.*
Nowèkineam.	*I like this.*
Nummachinámmin.	*I doe not like.*
Máunetash nquénowhick.	*I want many things.*
Cuttattaúamish.	*I will buy this of you.*
Nummouanaquish.	*I come to buy.*
Mouanaqushaúog, Mouanaqushánchick.	*Chapmen.*

Obs. Amongst themselves they trade their Corne, skins, Coates, Venison, Fish, &c. and sometimes come ten or twenty in a Company to trade amongst the *English.*

They have some who follow onely making of Bowes, some Arrowes, some Dishes, and (the Women make all their earthen Vessells) some follow fishing, some hunting: most on the Sea-side make Money, and store up shells in Summer against Winter whereof to make their money.

Nummautanaqúsh.	*I have bought.*
Cummanóhamin?	*Have you bought?*
Cummanohamoùsh.	*I will buy of you.*
Nummautanóhamin.	*I have bought.*
Kunnauntatáuamish.	*I come to buy this.*
Comaunekunnúo?	*Have you any Cloth?*
Koppócki.	*Thick cloth.*
Wassáppi.	*Thin.*

Súckinuit.	*Black,* or *blackish.*
Míshquinuit.	*Red Cloth.*
Wómpinuit.	*White Cloath.*

Obs. They all generally prize a Mantle of *English* or *Dutch* Cloth before their owne wearing of Skins and Furres, because they are warme enough and Lighter.

Wompequáyi.	*Cloth inclining to white,*

Which they like not, but desire to have a sad coulour without any whitish haires, suiting with their owne naturall Temper, which inclines to sadnesse.

Etouwawâyi.	*Wollie on both sides.*
Muckúcki.	*Bare without Wool.*
Chechéke maútsha.	*Long lasting.*
Qúnnascat.	*Of a great breadth.*
Tióckquscat.	*Of little breadth.*
Wùss.	*The Edge* or *list.*
Aumpácunnish.	*Open it.*
Tuttepácunnish.	*Fold it up.*
Mat Weshegganúnno.	*There is no Wool on it.*
Tanógganish.	*Shake it.*
Wúskinuit.	*New Cloth.*
Tanócki, tanócksha.	*It is torne* or *rent.*
Eatawûs.	*It is Old.*
Quttaûnch.	*Feele it.*
Audtà.	*A paire of small breeches* or *Apron.*

Cuppáimish I will pay you, which is a word newly made from the *English* word pay.

Tahenaúatu?	*What price?*
Tummòck cumméinsh.	*I will pay you Beaver.*

Teaúguock Cumméinsh.	*I will give you Money.*
Wauwunnégachick.	*Very good.*

Obs. They have great difference of their Coyne, as the *English* have: some that will not passe without Allowance, and some again made of a Counterfeit shell, and their very black counterfeited by a Stone and other Materialls: yet I never knew any of them much deceived, for their danger of being deceived (in these things of Earth) makes them cautelous.

Cosaúmawem.	*You aske too much.*
Kuttíackqussaûwaw.	*You are very hard.*
Aquie iackqussaúme.	*Be not so hard.*
Aquie Wussaúmowash.	*Doe not aske so much.*
Tashin Commésim?	*How much shall I give you?*
Kutteaûg Comméinsh.	*I will give you your Money.*
Nkèke Comméinsh.	*I will give you an Otter.*
Coanombúqusse Kuttassokakómme.	*You have deceived me.*

Obs. Who ever deale or trade with them, had need of Wisedome, Patience, and Faithfulnesse in dealing: for they frequently say *Cuppànnawem,* you lye, *Cuttassokakómme,* you deceive me.

Misquésu Kunúkkeke.	*Your Otter is reddish.*
Yò aúwusse Wunnêgin.	*This is better.*
Yo chippaúatu.	*This is of another price.*
Augausaúatu.	*It is Cheap.*
Muchickaúatu.	*It is deare.*
Wuttunnaúatu.	*It is worth it.*
Wunishaúnto.	*Let us agree.*
Aquie neesquttónck qussish	*Doe not make adoe*
Wuchè nquíttompscat.	*About a penny.*

They are marvailous subtle in their Bargaines to save a penny: And very suspicious that *English* men labour to deceive them: Therefore they will beate all markets and try all places, and runne twenty thirty, yea forty mile, and more, and lodge in the Woods, to save six pence.

Cummámmenash nitteaúguash?	*Will you have my Money?*
Nonânum, Nóonshem.	*I cannot.*
Tawhitch nonanumêan?	*Why can you not?*
Machâge nkòckie.	*I get nothing.*
Tashaumskussayi commêsim?	*How many spans will you give me?*
Neesaumsqussáyi.	*Two spans.*
Shwaumscussayi.	*Three spans.*
Yowompscussáyi.	*Foure Spans.*
Napannetashaumscussâyi.	*Five spans.*
Quttatashaumskus Sáyi.	*Six spans.*
Endatashaumscussâyi.	*Seven spans.*
Enadatashaumskuttonâyi.	*Seven spans.*
Cowénaweke.	*You are a rich man.*

Obs. They will often confesse for their own ends, that the English are richer and wiser, and valianter then themselves; yet it is for their owne ends, and therefore they adde *Nanoúe,* give me this or that, a disease which they are generally infected with: some more ingenuous, scorne it; but I have often seene an *Indian* with great quant[it]ies of money about him, beg a Knife of an English man, who haply hath had never a peny of money.

Akêtash-tamòke.	*Tell my money.*
Nowannakese.	*I have mis-told.*
Cosaúmakese.	*You have told too much.*
Cunnoónakese.	*You have told too little.*
Shoo kekíneass.	*Looke here.*
Wunêtu nitteaûg.	*My money is very good.*
Mamattissuôg kutteauqùock.	*Your Beads are naught.*
Tashin mesh commaûg?	*How much have you given?*

Chichêgin.	*A Hatchet.*
Anáskunck.	*A Howe.*
Maumichémanege.	*A Needle.*
Cuttatuppaúnamum.	*Take a measure.*
Tatuppauntúhommin.	*To weigh with scales.*
Tatuppauntúock.	*They are aweighing.*
Netâtup.	*It is all one.*
Kaukakíneamuck, Pebenochichauquânick.	*A Looking Glasse.*

Obs. It may be wondred what they do with Glasses, having no beautie but a swarfish colour, and no dressing but nakednesse; but pride appeares in any colour, and the meanest dresse: and besides generally the women paint their faces with all sorts of colours.

Cummanohamógunna.	*They will buy it of you.*
Cuppittakúnnemous.	*Take your cloth againe.*
Cuppittakunnamì?	*Will you serve me so?*
Cosaumpeekúnnemun.	*You have tore me off too little cloth.*
Cummachetannakúnnamous.	*I have torn it off for you.*
Tawhìtch cuppittakunamiêan?	*Why doe you turne it upon my hand?*
Kutchichêginash, kaukinne pokéshaas.	*Your Hatchets will be soone broken.*
Teâno wáskishaas.	*Soone gapt.*
Natouashóckquittea.	*A Smith.*
Kuttattaúamish aûke.	*I would buy land of you.*
Tou núckquaque?	*How much?*
Wuche wuttotânick.	*For a Towne,* or, *Plantation.*
Nissékineam.	*I have no mind to sell.*
Indiánsuck sekineámwock.	*The Indians are not willing.*
Noonapúock naûgum.	*They want roome themselves.*

Cowetompátimmin. *We are friends.*
Cummaugakéamish. *I will give you land.*
Aquìe chenawaûsish. *Be not churlish.*

Generall Observation *of* Trade.

O the infinite wisedome of the most holy wise *God,* who hath so advanced *Europe,* above *America,* that there is not a sorry *Howe, Hatchet, Knife,* nor a rag of cloth in all *America,* but what comes over the dreadfull *Atlantick* Ocean from *Europe:* and yet that *Europe* be not proud, nor *America* discouraged. What treasures are hid in some parts of *America,* and in our *New-English* parts, how have foule hands (in smoakie houses) the first handling of those Furres which are after worne upon the hands of Queens and heads of Princes?

More particular:

1. *Oft have I heard these* Indians *say,*
These English *will deceive us.*
Of all that's ours, our lands and lives,
In th'end they will bereave us.

2. *So say they, whatsoever they buy,*
(Though small) which shewes they're shie
Of strangers, fearefull to be catcht
By fraud, deceipt, or lie.

3. Indians *and* English *feare deceits,*
Yet willing both to be
Deceiv'd and couzen'd of precious soule,
Of heaven, Eternitie.

CHAP. XXVI.

Of *Debts and Trusting.*

Noónat.	*I have not money enough.*
Noonamautuckquàwhe.	*Trust me.*
Kunnoonamaútuckquaush.	*I will owe it you.*

Obs. They are very desirous to come into debt, but then he that trusts them, must sustaine a twofold losse:

First, of his Commoditie.

Secondly, of his custome, as I have found by deare experience: Some are ingenuous, plaine hearted and honest; but the most never pay, unlesse a man follow them to their severall abodes, townes and houses, as I my selfe have been forc'd to doe, which hardship and travells it hath yet pleased God to sweeten with some experiences and some little gaine of Language.

Nonamautuckquahéginash.	*Debts.*
Nosaumautackquáwhe.	*I am much in debt.*
Pitch nippáutowin.	*I will bring it you.*
Chenock naquómbeg cuppauútiin nitteaûguash?	*When will you bring mee my money?*
Kunnaúmpatous, Kukkeéskwhush.	*I will pay you.*
Keéskwhim teaug mésin.	*Pay me my money.*
Tawhítch peyáuyean?	*Why doe you come?*
Nnádgecom.	*I come for debts.*
Machêtu.	*A poore man.*
Nummácheke.	*I am a poore man.*
Mesh nummaúchnem.	*I have been sicke.*
Nowemacaûnash nitteaùquash.	*I was faine to spend my money in my sicknesse.*

Obs. This is a common, and (as they think) most satisfying answer, that they have been sick: for in those times they give largely to the Priests, who then sometimes heales them by conjurations; and also they keepe open house for all to come to helpe to pray with them, unto whom also they give money.

Mat noteaûgo.	*I have no money.*
Kekíneash nippêtunck.	*Looke here in my bag.*
Nummâche maúganash.	*I have already paid.*
Mat coanaumwaûmis.	*You have not kept your word.*
Kûnnampatowin keénowwin.	*You must pay it.*
Machàge wuttamaûntam.	*He minds it not.*
Machàge wuttammauntammôock.	*They take no care about paying.*
Michéme notammaûntam.	*I doe alwayes mind it.*
Mat nickowêmen naûkocks.	*I cannot sleep in the night for it.*

Generall Observations *of their debts.*

It is an universall Disease of folly in men to desire to enter into not onely necessary, but unnecessary and tormenting debts, contrary to the command of the only wise God: Owe no thing to any man, but that you love each other.

More particular:

[1.] *I have heard ingenuous* Indians *say,*
In debts, they could not sleepe.
How far worse are such English *then,*
Who love in debts to keepe?

[2.] *If debts of pounds cause restlesse nights*
In trade with man and man,

How hard's that heart that millions owes
To God, and yet sleepe can?

[3.] *Debts paid, sleep's sweet, sins paid, death's sweet,*
Death's night then's turn'd to light;
Who dies in sinnes unpaid, that soule
His light's eternall night.

CHAP. XXVII.
Of *their Hunting*, &c.

Wee shall not name over the severall sorts of Beasts which we named in the Chapter of Beasts.

The Natives hunt two wayes:

First, when they pursue their game (especially Deere, which is the generall and wonderfull plenteous hunting in the Countrey:) I say, they pursue in twentie, fortie, fiftie, yea, two or three hundred in a company, (as I have seene) when they drive the woods before them.

Secondly, They hunt by Traps of severall sorts, to which purpose, after they have observed in Spring-time and Summer the haunt of the Deere, then about Harvest, they goe ten or twentie together, and sometimes more, and withall (if it be not too farre) wives and children also, where they build up little hunting houses of Barks and Rushes (not comparable to their dwelling houses) and so each man takes his bounds of two, three, or foure miles, where hee sets thirty, forty, or fiftie Traps, and baits his Traps with that food the Deere loves, and once in two dayes he walks his round to view his Traps.

Ntauchaûmen.	*I goe to hunt.*
Ncáttiteam weeyoùs.	*I long for Venison.*
Auchaûtuck.	*Let us hunt.*
Nowetauchaûmen.	*I will hunt with you.*
Anúmwock.	*Dogs.*
Kemehétteas.	*Creepe.*
Pìtch nkemehétteem.	*I will creepe.*
Pumm púmmoke.	*Shoote.*
Uppetetoûa.	*A man shot accidentally.*

Ntaumpauchaûmen.	*I come from hunting.*
Cutchashineánna?	*How many have you kild?*
Nneesnneánna.	*I have kild two.*
Shwinneánna.	*Three.*
Nyowinneánna.	*Foure.*
Npiuckwinneánna.	*Ten, &c.*
Nneesneechecttashín-neánna.	*Twentie.*
Nummouashâwmen.	*I goe to set Traps.*
Apè -hana.	*Trap, Traps.*
Asháppock.	*Hempe.*
Masaûnock.	*Flaxe.*
Wuskapéhana.	*New Traps.*
Eataúbana.	*Old Traps.*

Obs. They are very tender of their Traps where they lie, and what comes at them; for they say, the Deere (whom they conceive have a Divine power in them) will soone smell and be gone.

Npunowwáumen.	*I must goe to my Traps.*
Nummíshkommin.	*I have found a Deere;*

Which sometimes they doe, taking a Wolfe in the very act of his greedy prey, when sometimes (the Wolfe being greedy of his prey) they kill him: sometimes the Wolfe having glutted himselfe with the one halfe, leaves the other for his next bait; but the glad *Indian* finding of it, prevents him.

And that wee may see how true it is, that all wild creatures, and many tame, prey upon the poore Deere (which are there in a right Embleme of Gods persecuted, that is, hunted people, as I observed in the Chapter of Beasts according to the old and true saying:

Imbelles Damæ quid nisi præda sumus?

To harmlesse *Roes* and *Does,*
Both wilde and tame are foes.)

I remember how a poore Deere was long hunted and chased by a Wolfe, at last (as their manner is) after the chase of ten, it may be more miles running, the stout Wolfe tired out the nimble Deere, and seasing upon it, kill'd: In the act of devouring his prey, two *English* Swine, big with Pig, past by, assaulted the Wolfe, drove him from his prey, and devoured so much of that poore Deere, as they both surfeted and dyed that night.

The Wolfe is an Embleme of a fierce bloodsucking persecutor.

The Swine of a covetous rooting worldling, both make a prey of the Lord Jesus in his poore servants.

Ncummóotamúckqun natóqus.	*The Wolfe hath rob'd me.*

Obs. When a Deere is caught by the leg in the Trap, sometimes there it lies a day together before the Indian come, and so lies a pray to the ranging Wolfe, and other wild Beasts (most commonly the Wolfe) who seaseth upon the Deere and robs the Indian (at his first devouring) of neere halfe his prey, and if the Indian come not the sooner, hee makes a second greedie Meale, and leaves him nothing but the bones, and the torne Deere-skins, especially if he call some of his greedy Companions to his bloody banquet.

Upon this the *Indian* makes a falling trap called *Sunnúckhig,* (with a great weight of stones) and so sometimes knocks the Wolfe on the head, with a gainefull Revenge, especially if it bee a blacke Wolfe, whose Skins they greatly prize.

Nanówwussu.	*It is leane.*
Wauwunnockôo.	*It is fat.*
Weékan.	*It is sweet.*
Machemóqut.	*It smells ill.*
Anìt.	*It is putrified.*
Poquêsu.	*Halfe a Deere.*

WHOLESALERS TO LIBRARIES
ESTABLISHED 1875

CAROL COX BOOK COMPANY

20 BOOKER STREET, WESTWOOD, NEW JERSEY 07675 P. O. BOX 717

• P.O. # Date C.S. # 13012-95 C.A. # 1640216

Code Seminole G-424

• Author Williams, Roger Quantity 1 Publisher Wayne State

• Title A KEY INTO THE LANGUAGE OF AMERICA

Year Ed. Vol. ◯ SO

14.95

FOR OFFICE USE ONLY: List

☐ J ☐ SJ ☐ CCC ☐ CPS ☐ NP L

☐ RO ☐ Cover ☐ Westbind ☐ SR

☐ 3mo. ☐ 6mo. ☐ SP ☐ CR S N

LC #

☐ N/C RPL. Reason: ____________

REPORT! Availability Date ____________

And Check Appropriate Boxes Please

☐ OP ☐ OSI ☐ NYP ☐ OS ☐ NOP

OEA	OEA	OEA		
☐ Paper	☐ Cloth	☐ LB	☐ Clarity	☐ PUBL. P.P.

Poskáttuck & Missêsu.	*A whole Deere.*
Kuttíomp, Paucottaúwat.	*A Buck.*
Wawúnnes.	*A young Buck.*
Qunnèke.	*A Doe.*
Aunàn, Moósqin.	*A Fawne.*
Yo asipaúgon.	*Thus thick of fat.*
Noónatch, *or,* attuck ntíyu.	*I hunt Venison.*
Mishánneke ntíyu.	*I hunt a Squirrill.*
Paukunnawaw ntío.	*I hunt a Beare, &c.*
Wusséke.	*The hinder part of the Deere.*
Apome -ichàsh.	*Thigh: Thighes.*
Uppèke -quòck.	*Shoulder, shoulders.*
Wuskàn.	*A bone.*
Wussúckqun.	*A taile.*
Awemanìttin.	*Their Rutting time.*
Paushinùmmin.	*To divide.*
Paushinummauatíttea.	*Let us divide.*

This they doe when a Controversie falls out, whose the Deere should bee.

Caúskashunck.	*The Deere skin.*
Púmpom.	*A tribute Skin.*

Obs. When a Deere (hunted by the Indians, or Wolves) is kild in the water. This skin is carried to the *Sachim* or Prince, within whose territory the Deere was slaine.

Ntaúmpowwushaûmen.	*I come from hunting.*

Generall Observation *of their hunting.*

There is a blessing upon endeavour, even to the wildest *Indians;* the sluggard rosts not that which he tooke in hunting, but the substance of the diligent (either in earthly or heavenly affaires) is precious, *Prov.* 25.

More particular:

[1.] *Great pains in hunting th'*Indians *Wild,*
And eke the English *tame,*
Both take, in woods and forrests thicke,
To get their precious game.

[2.] *Pleasure and Profit, Honour false,*
(The world's great Trinitie)
Drive all men through all wayes, all times,
All weathers, wet and drie.

[3.] *Pleasure and Profits, Honour sweet,*
Eternall, sure and true,
Laid up in God, with equall paines;
Who seekes, who doth pursue?

CHAP. XXVIII.
Of *their* Gaming, *&c.*

Their *Games,* (like the *English*) are of two sorts; private and publike:

Private, and sometimes publike; A *Game* like unto the *English* Cards; yet, in stead of Cards they play with strong *Rushes.*

Secondly, they have a kinde of Dice which are Plumb stones painted, which they cast in a Tray, with a mighty noyse and sweating: Their publique *Games* are solemnized with the meeting of hundreds; sometimes thousands, and consist of many vanities, none of which I durst ever be present at, that I might not countenance and partake of their folly, after I once saw the evill of them.

Ahânu.	*Hee laughes.*
Tawhitch ahánean?	*Why doe you laugh?*
Ahánuock.	*They are merry.*
Nippauochâumen.	*We are dancing.*
Pauochaûog.	*They are playing* or *dancing.*
Pauochaútowwin.	*A Bauble to play with.*
Akésuog.	*They are at Cards,* or *telling of Rushes.*
Pissinnéganash.	*Their playing Rushes.*
Ntakésemin.	*I am at telling,* or *counting;*

for their play is a kind of Arithmatick.

Obs. The chiefe Gamesters amongst them much desire to make their Gods side with them in their Games (as our *English* Gamesters so farre also acknowledge God) therefore I have seene them keepe as a precious stone a piece of Thunderbolt, which is like unto a Chrystall, which they dig out of the ground under some tree, Thunder-smitten, and from this stone they have an opinion of successe, and I have not heard any of these prove losers, which I conceive may be *Satans* policie, and Gods holy Justice to harden them for their not rising higher from the Thunderbolt, to the God that send or shoots it.

Ntaquìe akésamen.	*I will leave play.*
Nchikossimúnnash.	*I will burne my Rushes.*
Wunnaugonhómmin.	*To play at dice in their Tray.*
Asaúanash.	*The painted Plumbstones which they throw.*
Puttuckquapúonck.	*A Playing Arbour.*

Obs. This Arbour or Play-house is made of long poles set in the earth, foure square, sixteen or twentie foot high, on which they hang great store of their stringed money, have great stakings, towne against towne, and two chosen out of the rest by course to play the *Game* at this kinde of Dice in the midst of all their Abettors, with great shouting and solemnity: beside, they have great meetings of foot-ball playing, onely in Summer, towne against towne, upon some broad sandy shoare, free from stones, or upon some soft heathie plot, because of their naked feet, at which they have great stakings, but seldome quarrell.

Pasuckquakohowaûog.	*They meet to foot-ball.*
Cukkúmmote wèpe.	*You steale;* As I have often

told them in their gamings, and in their great losings (when they have staked and lost their money, clothes, house, corne, and themselves, if single persons) they will confesse it, being weary of their lives, and ready to make away themselves, like many an *English* man: an Embleme of the horrour of conscience, which all poore sinners walk in at last, when they see what wofull games they have played in their life, and now find themselves eternall Beggars.

Keesaqúnnamun, Another kinde of solemne publike meeting, wherein they lie under the trees, in a kinde of Religious observation, and have a mixture of Devotions and sports: But their chiefest Idoll of all for sport and game, is (if their land be at peace) toward Harvest, when they set up a long house called *Qunnèkamuck.* Which signifies *Long house,* sometimes an hundred, somtimes two hundred foot long upon a plaine neer the Court (which they call *Kitteickaúick*) where many thousands, men and women meet, where he that goes in danceth in the sight of all the rest; and is prepared with money, coats, small breeches, knifes, or what hee is able to reach to, and gives these things away to the poore, who yet must particularly beg and say, *Cowequetúmmous,* that is, *I beseech you:* which word (although there is not one common beggar amongst them) yet they will often use when their richest amongst them would fain obtain ought by gift.

Generall Observations *of their* Sports.

This life is a short minute, eternitie followes. On the improvement or dis-improvement of this short minute, depends a joyfull or dreadfull eternity; yet (which I tremble to thinke of) how cheape is this invaluable Jewell, and how many vaine inventions and foolish pastimes have the sonnes of men in all parts of the world found out, to passe time & post over this short minute of life, untill like some pleasant River they have past into *mare mortuum,* the dead sea of eternall lamentation.

More particular:

1. *Our* English *Gamesters scorne to stake*
Their clothes as Indians *do,*
Nor yet themselves, alas, yet both
Stake soules and lose them to.

2\. *O fearfull Games! the divell stakes*
But Strawes and Toyes and Trash,
(For what is All, compar'd with Christ,
*But *Dogs meat and Swines wash?)* *Phil. 3. 8.
σχύδαία

3\. *Man stakes his Jewell-darling soule,*
(His owne most wretched foe)
Ventures, and loseth all in sport
At one most dreadfull throw.

CHAP. XXIX.
Of *their* Warre, *&c.*

Aquène.	*Peace.*
Nanoúeshin, & Awêpu.	*A peaceable calme;* for *Awépu* signifies a calme.
Chépewess, & Mishittâshin.	*A Northern storme of warre,*

as they wittily speake, and which *England* now wofully feeles, untill the Lord Jesus chide the winds, and rebuke the raging seas.

Nummusquântum.	*I am angry.*
Tawhìtch musquawnaméan?	*Why are you angry?*
Aquie musquántash.	*Cease from anger.*
Chachépissu, nishqûetu.	*Fierce.*
Tawhìtch chachepiséttit nishquéhettit?	*Why are they fierce?*
Cummusquáunamuck.	*He is angry with you.*
Matwaûog.	*Souldiers.*
Matwaûonck.	*A Battle.*
Cummusquaúnamish.	*I am angry with you.*
Cummusquawnamè?	*Are you angry with me?*
Miskisaûwaw.	*A quarrelsome fellow.*
Tawhítch niskqúekean?	*Why are you so fierce?*
Ntatakcómmuckqun ewò.	*He strucke mee.*
Nummokókunitch, Ncheckéqunnitch.	*I am robbed.*
Mecaûtea.	*A fighter.*
Mecauntítea.	*Let us fight.*
Mecaúnteass.	*Fight with him.*
Wepè cummécautch.	*You are a quarreller.*
Jûhettítea.	*Let us fight.*

Jûhetteke. *Fight,* Which is the word of incouragement which they use when they animate each other in warre; for they use their tongues in stead of drummes and trumpets.

Awaùn necáwni aum píasha?	*Who drew the first bow,* or *shot the first shot?*
Nippakétatunck.	*He shot first at me.*
Nummeshannántam, Nummayaôntam.	*I scorne,* or *take it* [*in*] *indignation.*

Obs. This is a common word, not only in warre, but in peace also (their spirits in naked bodies being as high and proud as men more gallant) from which sparkes of the lusts of pride and passion, begin the flame of their warres.

Whauwháutowaw ánowat.	*There is an Alarum.*
Wopwawnónckquat.	*An hubbub.*
Amaúmuwaw paúdsha.	*A Messenger is come.*
Keénomp / Múckquomp } paûog.	*Captaines,* or *Valiant men.*
Negonshâchick.	*Leaders.*
Kúttowonck.	*A Trumpet.*
Popowuttáhig.	*A Drumme.*

Obs. Not that they have such of their owne making; yet such they have from the *French:* and I have knowne a good Drumme made amongst them in imitation of the *English.*

Quaquawtatatteâug.	*They traine.*
Machíppog.	*A Quiver.*
Caúquat -tash.	*Arrow, Arrowes.*
Onúttug.	*An halfe Moone in war.*
Péskcunck.	*A Gunne.*
Saûpuck.	*Powder.*
Mátit.	*Unloden.*
Méchimu.	*Loden.*
Mechimúash.	*Lode it.*

Shóttash. *Shot;* A made word from us, though their Gunnes they have from the *French,* and often sell many a score to the *English,* when they are a little out of frame or Kelter.

Pummenúmmin teáuquash. *To contribute to the warres.*
Askwhítteass. *Keep watch.*
Askwhitteâchick. *The Guard.*
Askwhitteaûg. *It is the Guard.*

Obs. I once travelled (in a place conceived dangerous) with a great Prince, and his Queene and Children in company, with a Guard of neere two hundred; twentie, or thirtie fires were made every night for the Guard (the Prince and Queene in the midst) and Sentinells by course, as exact as in *Europe;* and when we travelled through a place where ambushes were suspected to lie, a speciall Guard, like unto a Life-guard, compassed (some neerer, some farther of) the King and Queen, my selfe and some *English* with me.

They are very copious and patheticall in Orations to the people, to kindle a flame of wrath, Valour or revenge from all the Common places which Commanders use to insist on.

Wesássu. *Afraid.*
Cowésass? *Are you afraid?*
Tawhitch wesásean? *Why feare you?*
Manowêsass. *I feare none.*
Kukkúshickquock. *They feare you.*
Nosemitteúnckquock. *They fly from us.*
Onamatta cowaûta. *Let us pursue.*
Núckqusha. *I feare him.*
Wussémo -wock. *He flies, they flie.*
Npauchíppowem. *I flie for succour.*
Keesaúname. *Save me.*
Npúmmuck. *I am shot.*
Chenawaúsu. *Churlish.*
Waumaûsu. *Loving.*

Tawhìtch chenawaûsean?	*Why are you churlish?*
Aumánsk, Waukaunòsint.	*A Fort.*
Cupshitteaûg.	*They lie in the way.*
Aumanskitteaúg.	*They fortifie.*
Kekaúmwaw.	*A scorner* or *mocker.*
Nkekaúmuck ewò.	*He scornes me.*
Aquie kekaúmowash.	*Doe not scorne.*

Obs. This mocking (between their great ones) is a great kindling of Warres amongst them: yet I have known some of their chiefest say, what should I hazard the lives of my precious Subjects, them and theirs, to kindle a Fire, which no man knowes how farre, and how long it will burne, for the barking of a Dog?

Sékineam.	*I have no mind to it.*
Nissékineug.	*He likes not me.*
Nummánneug.	*He hates me.*
Sekinneauhettúock, Maninnewahettúock.	*They hate each other.*
Nowetompátimmin.	*We are Friends.*
Wetompâchick.	*Friends.*
Nowepinnátimin.	*We joyne together.*
Nowepinnâchick.	*My Companions in War,* or *Associats.*
Nowechusettímmin.	*We are Confederates.*
Nechusé ewò.	*This is my Associate.*
Wechusittûock.	*They joyne together.*
Nwéche kokkêwem.	*I will be mad*[*e one*] *with him.*
Chickaúta wêtu.	*An house fired.*

Once lodging in an Indian house full of people, the whole Company (Women especially) cryed out in apprehension that the Enemy had fired the House, being about midnight: The house was fired but not by an Enemy: the men ran up on the house top, and with their naked hands beat out the Fire: One scorcht his leg, and suddenly after they came into the house againe, undauntedly cut his leg with a knife to let out the burnt blood.

Yo ánawhone.	*There I am wounded.*
Missínnege.	*A Captive.*
Nummissinnàm ewo.	*This is my Captive.*
Waskeiûhettímmitch.	*At beginning of the fight.*
Nickqueintónckquock.	*They come against us.*
Nickqueintouôog.	*I will make Warre upon them.*
Nippauquanaúog.	*I will destroy them.*
Queintauatíttea.	*Let us goe against them.*
Kunnauntatáuhuckqun.	*He comes to kill you.*
Paúquana.	*There is a slaughter.*
Pequttôog paúquanan.	*The Pequts are slaine.*
Awaun Wuttúnnene?	*Who have the Victory?*
Tashittáwho?	*How many are slaine?*
Neestáwho.	*Two are slaine.*
Piuckunneánna.	*Ten are slaine.*

Obs. Their Warres are farre lesse bloudy and devouring then the cruell Warres of *Europe;* and seldome twenty slaine in a pitcht field: partly because when they fight in a wood every Tree is a Bucklar.

When they fight in a plaine, they fight with leaping and dancing, that seldome an Arrow hits, and when a man is wounded, unlesse he that shot followes upon the wounded, they soone retire and save the wounded: and yet having no Swords, nor Guns, all that are slaine are commonly slain with great Valour and Courage: for the Conquerour ventures into the thickest, and brings away the Head of his Enemy.

Niss-níssoke.	*Kill kill.*
Kúnnish.	*I will kill you.*
Kunnìshickqun ewò.	*He will kill you.*
Kunníshickquock.	*They will kill you.*

Siuckissûog.	*They are stout men.*
Nickummissúog.	*They are Weake.*
Nnickummaunamaûog.	*I shall easily vanquish them.*
Neene núppamen.	*I am dying.*
Cowaúnckamish.	*Quarter, quarter.*
Kunnanaumpasúmmish.	*Mercy, Mercy.*
Kekuttokaúnta.	*Let us parley.*
Aquétuck.	*Let us cease Armes.*
Wunnishaúnta.	*Let us agree.*
Cowammáunsh.	*I love you.*
Wunnêtu ntá.	*My heart is true.*
Tuppaûntash.	*Consider what I say.*
Tuppaúntamoke.	*Doe you all consider.*
Cummequaùnum cummíttamussussuck ka cummuckiaûg.	*Remember your Wives, and Children.*
Eatch kèen anawâyean.	*Let all be as you say.*
Cowawwunnaûwem.	*You speake truly.*
Cowauôntam.	*You are a wise man.*
Wetompátitea.	*Let us make Friends.*

Generall Observations *of their Warres.*

How dreadfull and yet how righteous is it with the most righteous Judge of the whole World, that all the generations of Men being turn'd Enemies against, and fighting against Him who gives them breath and Being, and all things, (whom yet they cannot reach) should stab, kill, burne, murther and devoure each other?

More Particular.

1. *The Indians count of Men as Dogs,*
It is no Wonder then:
They teare out one anothers throats!
But now that English *Men,*

2. *(That boast themselves Gods Children, and*
Members of Christ to be,)
That they should thus break out in flames,
Sure 'tis a Mystery!

[3.] *The second seal'd Mystery or red* Horse,
Whose Rider hath power and will,
To take away Peace from Earthly Men,
They must Each *other* kill.
} *Rev.* 2. 6.

CHAP. XXX.
Of their paintings.

1. They paint their Garments, &c.
2. The men paint their Faces in Warre.
3. Both Men and Women for pride, &c.

Wómpi.	*White.*
Mówi-súcki.	*Black.*
Msqùi.	*Red.*
Wesaûi.	*Yellow.*
Askáski.	*Greene.*
Peshaúi.	*Blew, &c.*

Obs. Wunnàm their red painting which they most delight in, and is both the Barke of the Pine, as also a red Earth.

Míshquock.	*Red Earth.*
Métewis.	*Black Earth.*

From this *Métewis* is an Indian Towne a day and a halfes Journey, or lesse (*West,* from the *Massachusets*) called *Metewémesick.*

Wussuckhòsu.	*A painted Coat.*

Of this and *Wússuckwheke,* (the English Letters, which comes neerest to their painting) I spake before in the Chapter of their clothing.

Aunakêsu.	*He is painted.*
Aunakéuck.	*They are painted.*
Tawhìtch aunakéan?	*Why doe you paint your selfe?*
Chéskhosh.	*Wipe off.*

Cummachiteoûwunash kuskeésuckquash.	*You spoile your Face.*
Mat pitch cowáhick Manìt keesiteónckqus.	*The God that made you will not know you.*

Generall Observations of their paintings.

It hath been the foolish Custome of all barbarous Nations to paint and figure their Faces and Bodies (as it hath been to our shame and griefe, wee may remember it of some of our Fore-Fathers in this Nation.) How much then are we bound to our most holy Maker for so much knowledge of himselfe revealed in so much Civility and Piety? and how should we also long and endeavour that *America* may partake of our mercy:

More particular:

[1.] *Truth is a Native, naked Beauty; but*
Lying Inventions are but Indian Paints;
Dissembling hearts their Beautie's but a Lye.
Truth is the proper Beauty of Gods Saints.

2. *Fowle are the* Indians *Haire and painted Faces,*
More foule such Haire, such Face in Israel.
England *so calls her selfe, yet there's*
Absoloms *foule Haire and Face of* Jesabell.

[3.] *Paints will not bide Christs washing Flames of fire,*
Fained Inventions will not bide such stormes:
O that we may prevent him, that betimes,
Repentance Teares may wash of all such Formes.

CHAP. XXXI.

Of Sicknesse.

Nummaúchnem.	*I am sick.*
Mauchinaúi.	*He is sick.*
Yo Wuttunsín.	*He keepes his Bed.*
Achie nummauchnem.	*I am very sick.*
Nóonshem metesímmin.	*I cannot eate.*
Machage nummetesímmin.	*I eat nothing.*
Tocketussinámmin?	*What think you?*
Pitch nkéeteem?	*Shall I recover?*
Niskéesaqush máuchinaash.	*My eyes faile me.*
Ncussawóntapam.	*My head akes.*
Npummaúmpiteunck.	*My Teeth ake.*
Nchesammáttam, Nchésammam.	*I am in paine.*

Obs. In these cases their Misery appeares, that they have not (but what sometimes they get from the *English*) a raisin or currant or any physick, Fruit or spice, or any Comfort more than their Corne and Water, &c. In which bleeding case wanting all Meanes of recovery, or present refreshing I have been constrained to and beyond my power to refresh them, and I beleeve to save many of them from Death, who I am confident perish many Millions of them (in that mighty continent) for want of Meanes.

Nupaqqóntup Kúspissem.	*Bind my head.*
Wauaúpunish Nippaquóntup.	*Lift up my head.*
Nchésamam nséte.	*My Foot is sore.*
Machàge nickowêmen.	*I sleep not.*
Nnanótissu.	*I have a Feaver.*

Wàme kussópita nohóck.	*My body burnes.*
Ntátupe nòte *or* chíckot.	*I am all on fire.*
Yo ntéatchin.	*I shake for Cold.*
Ntátuppe wunnêpog.	*I shake as a leafe.*
Puttuckhúmma.	*Cover me.*
Paútous nototámmin.	*Reach me the drinke.*

Obs. Which is onely in all their extremities, a little boild water, without the addition of crum or drop of other comfort: O *Englands* mercies, &c.

Tahaspunâyi?	*What ayles he?*
Tocketúspanem?	*What aile you?*
Tocketuspunnaúmaqun?	*What hurt hath he done to you?*
Chassaqúnsin?	*How long hath he been sick?*
Nnanowwêteem.	*I am going to visit.*

Obs. This is all their refreshing, the Visit of Friends, and Neighbours, a poore empty visit and presence, and yet indeed this is very solemne, unlesse it be in infectious diseases, and then all forsake them and flie, that I have often seene a poore House left alone in the wild Woods, all being fled, the living not able to bury the dead: so terrible is the apprehension of an infectious disease, that not only persons, but the Houses and the whole Towne takes flight.

Nummòckquese.	*I have a swelling.*
Mocquêsui.	*He is swelled.*
Wàme wuhòck-Mockquêsui.	*All his body is swelled.*
Mamaskishaûi.	*He hath the Pox.*
Mamaskishaûonck.	*The Pox.*
Mamaskishaûmitch.	*The last pox.*
Wesauashaûi.	*He hath the plague.*
Wesauashaûonck.	*The plague.*
Wesauashaûmitch.	*The great plague.*

Obs. Were it not that they live in sweet Aire, and remove persons and Houses from the infected, in ordinary course of subordinate Causes, would few or any be left alive, and surviving.

Nmunnádtommin.	*I vomit.*
Nqúnnuckquus.	*I am lame.*
Ncúpsa.	*I am deafe.*
Npókunnum.	*I am blind.*
Npockquanámmen.	*My disease is I know not what.*
Pésuponck.	*An Hot-house.*
Npesuppaûmen.	*I goe to sweate.*
Pesuppaûog.	*They are sweating.*

Obs. This Hot-house is a kind of little Cell or Cave, six or eight foot over, round, made on the side of a hill (commonly by some Rivulet or Brooke) into this frequently the men enter after they have exceedingly heated it with store of wood, laid upon an heape of stones in the midle. When they have taken out the fire, the stones keepe still a great heat: Ten, twelve, twenty, more or lesse, enter at once starke naked, leaving their coats, small breeches (or aprons) at the doore, with one to keepe all: here doe they sit round these hot stones an houre or more, taking *Tobacco,* discoursing, and sweating together; which sweating they use for two ends: First, to cleanse their skin: Secondly, to purge their bodies, which doubtlesse is a great meanes of preserving them, and recovering them from diseases, especially from the *French* disease, which by sweating and some potions, they perfectly and speedily cure: when they come forth (which is matter of admiration) I have seene them runne (Summer and Winter) into the Brooks to coole them, without the least hurt.

Misquineash.	*The vaines.*
Msqui, neépuck.	*Blood.*
Nsauapaushaûmen.	*I have the bloody Flixe.*

Matux puckquátchick aúwaw. — *He cannot goe to stool.*
Powwâw. — *Their Priest.*
Maunêtu. — *A Conjurer.*
Powwâw nippétea. — *The priest is curing him.*
Yo Wutteántawaw. — *He is acting his Cure.*

Obs. These Priests and Conjurers (like *Simon Magus*) doe bewitch the people, and not onely take their Money, but doe most certainly (by the help of the Divell) worke great Cures, though most certaine it is that the greatest part of their Priests doe meerly abuse them, and get their Money, in the times of their sicknesse, and to my knowledge, long for sick times; and to that end the poore people store up Money, and spend both Money and goods on the *Powwâws,* or Priests in these times; the poore people commonly dye under their hands, for alas, they administer nothing, but howle and roare, and hollow over them, and begin the song to the rest of the People about them, who all joyne (like a Quire) in Prayer to their Gods for them.

Máskit ponamíin. — *Give me a Plaister.*
Máskit Cotatámhea. — *Give me some physicke Drinke.*

Both which they earnestly desire of the *English,* and doe frequently send to my selfe, and others for, having experimentally found some Mercy of that kind (through Gods blessing) from us.

Nickeétem. — *I am recovered.*
Kitummâyi nickêekon. — *I am just now recovered.*

Generall Observation *of their sicknesse.*

It pleaseth the most righteous, and yet patient God to warne and summon, to try and arraigne the universall race of *Adams* sonnes (commonly) upon Beds of sicknesse before he proceed to execution of Death and Judgement: Blessed those soules which prevent Judgement, Death and sicknesse to, and before the evill dayes come, Arraigne, and Judge themselves, and being sick for Love to Christ, find him or seek him in his Ordinances below, and get unfained Assurance of Eternall enjoyment of Him, when they are here no more.

More particular:

1. *One step twix't Me and Death,* (*twas* Davids *speech,*)
And true of sick Folks all:
Mans Leafe it fades, his Clay house cracks,
Before it's dreadfull Fall.

2. *Like Grashopper the* Indian *leapes,*
Till blasts of sicknesse rise:
Nor soule nor Body Physick hath,
Then Soule and Body dies.

[3.] *O happy* English *who for both,*
Have precious physicks store:
How should (*when Christ hath both refresh't*)
Thy Love and zeale be more?

CHAP. XXXII.
Of Death *and* Buriall, &c.

As Pummíssin.	*He is not yet departed.*
Neenè.	*He is drawing on.*
Paúsawut kitonckquêwa.	*He cannot live long.*
Chachéwunnea.	*He is neere dead.*
Kitonckquêi.	*Hee is dead.*
Nipwì mâw.	*He is gone.*
Kakitonckquêban.	*They are dead and gone.*
Sequttôi.	*He is in blacke;* That is, He

hath some dead in his house (whether wife or child *&c.*) for although at the first being sicke, all the Women and Maides blacke their faces with soote and other blackings; yet upon the death of the sicke, the father, or husband, and all his neighbours, the Men also (as the *English* weare blacke mourning clothes) weare blacke *Faces,* and lay on soote very thicke, which I have often seene clotted with their teares.

This blacking and lamenting they observe in most dolefull manner, divers weekes and moneths; yea, a yeere, if the person be great and publike.

Séqut.	*Soote.*
Michemeshâwi.	*He is gone for ever.*
Mat wònck kunnawmòne.	*You shall never see him more.*
Wunnowaúntam Wullóasin.	*Grieved and in bitternesse.*
Nnowántam, nlôasin.	*I am grieved for you.*

Obs. As they abound in lamentations for the dead, so they abound in consolation to the living, and visit them frequently, using this word *Kutchímmoke, Kutchímmoke,* Be of good cheere, which they expresse by stroaking the cheeke and head of the father or mother, husband, or wife of the dead.

Chepassôtam.	*The dead Sachim.*
Mauchaúhom.	*The dead man.*
Mauchaúhomwock, Chépeck.	*The dead.*
Chepasquâw.	*A dead woman.*
Yo ápapan.	*He that was here.*
Sachimaûpan.	*He that was Prince here.*

Obs. These expressions they use, because, they abhorre to mention the dead by name, and therefore, if any man beare the name of the dead he changeth his name; and if any stranger accidentally name him, he is checkt, and if any wilfully name him he is fined; and amongst States, the naming of their dead *Sachims,* is one ground of their warres; so terrible is the King of Terrors, Death, to all naturall men.

Aquie míshash, aquie mishómmoke.	*Doe not name.*
Cowewênaki.	*You wrong mee,* to wit, *in naming my dead.*
Posakúnnamun.	*To bury.*
Aukùck pónamun.	*To lay in the earth.*

Wesquáubenan. *To wrap up,* in winding mats or coats, as we say, winding sheets.

Mockuttásuit, One of chiefest esteeme, who winds up and buries the dead, commonly some wise, grave, and well descended man hath that office.

When they come to the Grave, they lay the dead by the Grave's mouth, and then all sit downe and lament, that I have seen teares run downe the cheekes of stoutest Captaines, as well as little children in abundance: and after the dead is laid in Grave, and sometimes (in some parts) some goods cast in with them, They have then a second great lamentation, and upon the Grave is spread the Mat that the party died on, the Dish he eat in; and sometimes a faire Coat of skin hung upon the next tree to the Grave, which none will touch, but suffer it there to rot with the dead: Yea, I saw with mine owne eyes that at my late comming forth of the Countrey, the chiefe and most aged peaceable Father of the Countrey, *Caunoúnicus,* having buried his sonne, he burn'd his owne Palace, and all his goods in it, (amongst them to a great value) in a sollemne remembrance of his sonne, and in a kind of humble Expiation to the Gods, who (as they believe) had taken his sonne from him.

The generall Observation *of their* Dead.

O, how terrible is the looke, the speedy and serious thought of death to all the sons of men? Thrice happy those who are dead and risen with the Sonne of God, for they are past from death to life, and shall not see death (a heavenly sweet Paradox or Ridle) as the Son of God hath promised them.

More particular:

[1.] *The* Indians *say their bodies die,*
Their soules they doe not die;
Worse are then Indians *such, as hold*
The soules mortalitie.

[2.] *Our hopelesse Bodie rots, say they,*
Is gone eternally,
English *hope better, yet some's hope*
Proves endlesse miserie.

[3.] *Two Worlds of men shall rise and stand*
'Fore Christs most dreadfull barre;
Indians, *and* English *naked too,*
That now most gallant are.

[4.] *True Christ most Glorious then shall make*
New Earth, *and Heavens New;*
False Christs, false Christians then shall quake,
O blessed then the True.

Now, to the most High and most Holy, Immortall, Invisible, and onely Wise God, who alone is *Alpha* and *Omega,* the *Beginning* and the *Ending,* the *First* and the *Last,* who *Was* and *Is,* and is to *Come;* from *Whom,* by *Whom,* and to *Whom* are all things; by *Whose* gracious assistance and wonderfull supportment in so many varieties of hardship and outward miseries, I have had such converse with Barbarous Nations, and have been mercifully assisted, to frame this poore KEY, which may, (through His Blessing in His owne holy season) open a Doore; yea, Doors of unknowne Mercies to Us and Them, be Honour, Glory, Power, Riches, Wisdome, Goodnesse and Dominion ascribed by all His in Jesus Christ to Eternity, *Amen.*

FINIS.

The TABLE.

I have further treated of these *Natives* of *New-England*, and that great point of their *Conversion* in a little additionall *Discourse* apart from this.

Facsimile of Table of Contents. (*By courtesy of the John Carter Brown Library, Brown University.*)

Textual Notes

Sigla

O —Octavo, 1643.
MHS—*Collections of the Massachusetts Historical Society,* Vols. 3 and 5. First series, 1794, 1798.
RIHS—*Collections of the Rhode-Island Historical Society,* Vol. 1, 1827.
TR —*A Key into the Language of America.* In *The Complete Writings of Roger Williams,* edited by J. Hammond Trumbull. Vol. 1. The Narragansett Club Publications, 1866. Reprint New York: Russell and Russell, 1963.
CH —*A Key into the Language of America,* Providence, 1936. With an introduction by Howard Chapin.

Symbols used in the textual notes

The textual notes are keyed to the text by page and line numbers, and identified by catchwords or phrases. The catchword is separated from the rest of the note by a right-closing bracket. When the reading adopted is that of O, the bracket is immediately followed by the variant reading(s) or previous textual emendations rejected by the present editors. An example:

85.13. *Wellhead*] well head RIHS; *wellhead* CH.

When the reading adopted is from a subsequent editor rather than from O, that edition is immediately identified; other readings, beginning with O, follow in chronological order. An example:

95.6–7. *from the*] RIHS; from the O; *the* MHS, which omits "from."

When the textual note has to do with a matter of punctuation, punctuation is included in the catchphrase, otherwise not. An example:

83.26 this I] this Key I MHS.

but,

85.5–6. *Indians, Natives*] MHS±; $\sim_{\wedge}\sim$O.

Three dots are meant to indicate omissions where no period is omitted, even if the material omitted runs to more than one line (the line numbers in the lemma will tell the reader how many lines are missing); if the omission begins in the middle of a line, to avoid confusion we list the word beginning the omission and follow it with three dots and the final word. Four dots are used to indicate omissions in which one or more periods are omitted. Thus, in the vocabulary sections, even though only one line is omitted, because the Indian word or phrase is followed by a period or other terminal punctuation mark, four dots are used before the last word of the omission.

In order to keep our textual notes as simple as possible we have kept the number of editorial symbols used to a minimum. They are five in number, and are as follows:

the caret ($_{\wedge}$) is used to indicate omissions. See the last example above.

the similar sign ($\sim$) is used in matters of punctuation to indicate that in instances of punctuation change associated words or phrases do not change. See the last example above.

+ is used to indicate that all subsequent editions follow the reading of the edition cited. An example:

94.21. *do*] MHS; *doth* O+.

± is used to indicate instances in which a reading is followed only by some subsequent editors, others following the earlier reading or substituting one of their own which will so be noted. An example:

83.2. Countrey-men] MHS±; Counrey-men O.

– is used to indicate that no subsequent editor follows the reading of the edition cited. An example:

104.31. *And*] RIHS–; *and* O.

In all cases the ordering of the material within individual textual notes is chronological.

83.2. Countrey-men] MHS±; Counrey-men O.
83.20. *friends,* of all sorts.] $\sim_{\wedge}\sim_{\wedge}$MHS; $\sim$, $\sim_{\wedge}$RIHS.
83.21. MHS does not paragraph.
83.23. specially] MHS±; spe-/ally O.
83.24–25. A . . . *Keyes*] MHS omits.
83.26. this I] this Key I MHS.
84.3. *mis-takes*] mis-takes CH.

84.14. those] these MHS.
85.1–2. *Nations* ‸ of] MHS±; ∼, ∼ O.
85.5–6. *Indians, Natives*] MHS±; ∼‸∼ O.
85.12. MHS does not paragraph.
85.13. parts] MHS±; pars O.
85.13. *Wellhead*] well head RIHS; *wellhead* CH.
85.18. *Wildernesse*] *wildernesse* CH.
85.19. say‸that] ∼, ∼ MHS.
85.23. *English* men] Englishmen RIHS.
85.25. heare ‸ that] hear, ∼ MHS.
85.30. discoursed,] ∼‸ RIHS.
85.32. ship,] ∼‸ MHS.
86.8. Thirdly] MHS±; Thirdy O.
86.12. seperate] separate TR.
86.16. me‸] ∼, MHS.
86.19. O assigns "2." to the following sentence, but clearly the division between Hebrew and Greek affinities occurs here. MHS paragraphs.

MHS follows O in positioning the numbers, but for "2." and "3." prints "1." and "2."

86.22. Waine) the *Beare,* ‸] ∼‸∼,) O; wain, the Bear, MHS.
86.26. *waters*] sea MHS.
86.28. *Sowaniu*] *Sowwaniu* MHS.
86.34. And] and TR.
87.5. MHS paragraphs, O+ do not.
87.6. 32.] thirty two MHS.
87.8–11. and . . . *America*] MHS omits.
87.12–13. *Conversion*] Conversion CH.
87.19. Sea;] ∼, O; ∼. MHS.
87.25. *preparation*] preparations RIHS.
87.32. Christ,] MHS; ∼‸ O.
88.1. mine] my MHS.
88.2. others.)] RIHS; ∼. ‸ O.
88.3. *Qunnihticut*] *Qunníbticut CH.*
88.4. (whom] ‸ whom O.
88.12. yeare] years MHS.
88.12. before,] MHS; ∼‸ O.
88.15. *All things*] *Allthings* CH.
88.15. and of his] and ‸ his MHS.
88.17. *your*] your O.
88.26. meeting.] ∼: CH.
88.27.–89.12. . . . . WILLIAMS] MHS omits.

88.34. *Indies;*] RIHS; ~, O.
89.5. perswade ‸] RIHS; ~, O.
89.8. (in *Europe*)] RIHS; ‸ ~(~) O.
89.9. Gentiles .‸] ~.) O.
90.1.–91.5. MHS omits the entire section.
90.5. *hope* ‸] ~, RIHS.
90.15. O begins a new line at "turne."
90.20. *Language*)] ~, O.
90.20–21. *Circumflexes;*] ~) O.
90.21. *leafe*] Leafe RIHS.
90.24. *leafe,*] *leafe*‸ O.
90.29. *the*] the O.
91.3. Cowáunckamish] Cowáuncakmish RIHS.
93.16. *them.*] MHS±; ~, O, CH.
94.12. reverently] MHS omits.
94.21. *do*] MHS, *doth* O+.
94.30. *Wêtu. An House*] MHS moves to precede 95.15.
95.2. Narigánset Countrey] Naroganset coutnty MHS.
95.6. Acawmenoakit,] ~‸ O.
95.6. *England*] They call Old England Acawmenoakit MHS.
95.6–7. *from the*] RIHS; from the O; *the* MHS, which omits "*from.*"
95.8. mile] miles MHS, which omits "or thereabouts."
95.21. Sorrowes] sorrow MHS.
96.2. nippompitámmen] nippompitam-men RIHS, preserving the line-break of O.
96.10–12. *Nullius* . . . named, *&c*] MHS omits.
96.16. Hope.)] ~. ‸MHS.
96.16. say,] ~) MHS.
96.17. who . . . names] MHS omits.
96.20. Which . . . them] MHS omits, and changes "being" to "is."
96.22. Ewò,] ~‸ O.
96.29. Nonànum] TR; Non ànum O+.
97.1. Maìsh,] TR; ~ – O+.
97.8. Tawhitch] Tawhich O+.
97.12. In this respect] MHS omits.
97.13. in] into their houses MHS.
97.13. any] they MHS.
97.30. again] against CH.
97.31.–98.3. hence . . . &c] MHS omits.
98.7. Cowâutam? *Understand you?*] ~, ~, RIHS.

98.11. Cowannántam] CH omits accent, and at 98.12.

98.16. *alone?*] ∼. RIHS.

98.18. Naneeshâumo] Naneeshûumo RIHS.

98.29. *language*] *Language* RIHS.

98.32. Nummaúchenèm.] MHS±; ∼? O.

99.6. Mauchéi] Mauchié RIHS.

99.9. *gone.*] ∼? RIHS.

99.11. *Do,*] ∼ ‸ RIHS, CH.

99.16. MHS omits "From" to the end of the chapter, and continues the pattern, omitting the general observations and poems throughout.

99.16. generall:] ∼; RIHS.

99.17. savour] favour CH.

99.28. *Nature*] *nature* RIHS.

99.29. *Natures*] *natures* RIHS.

100.15. middle,] ∼ ‸ TR, CH.

100.17. With] MHS does not paragraph.

100.22. *parc'd*] *parch'd* RIHS. The three variant spellings in this passage may very well be Williams's own.

101.8. *loves*] loaves MHS.

101.26. *something.*] ∼: O.

101.28. kusópita] kusópira CH.

102.3–10. A . . . *Natives*] MHS moves ahead to follow "refreshing" at 104.16.

102.10–11. and . . . subdue] MHS omits.

102.14. *hath*] *had* MHS.

102.15. maúchepwut] múchepwut RIHS.

102.21. Machíppoquat] Machíppiquat CH.

102.27. Waûmet,] TR; ∼‸O.

102.29. *Eenough*] Enough MHS, CH.

103.1–6. They . . . water] MHS moves back to follow "bodies" at 101.5.

103.9. Tabacco] Tobacco MHS, RIHS.

103.24. *Raysins*] Rapsins RIHS.

103.27. *Provision*] Provisions RIHS.

103.28. *snapsacke*] knapsack MHS.

103.31. . . . . *meale*] MHS omits.

104.2–5. Mohowaúgsuck. . . . *us*] MHS moves back to follow "*Natives*" at 102.9–10.

104.7–16. Whomsoever. . . . refreshing] MHS moves back to follow "water" at 103.6.

104.12. If] MHS does not paragraph.

104.19. *truth,*] ~‸ TR.

104.27. wine] Wine RIHS.

104.30. *in,*] ~‸ RIHS.

104.31. *And*] RIHS—; *and* O.

106.2. *Concerning*] Of O pageheadings.

106.5. Kukkowetoùs] MHS; Kukkovetoùs O.

106.8. . . . . *here*] MHS omits.

106.11. Which . . . doe] They will sleep without the doors contentedly MHS.

106.12–13. have been] are MHS.

106.15. In] MHS does not paragraph.

106.27. Wawhautowâwog] MHS; Wawhautowâvog O.

106.29. breake] brake MHS.

106.31. them,] ~‸ TR.

107.1. of] to MHS.

107.4. *finer . . . sleep*] fine, Sleep RIHS.

107.6. Maskítuash] Mask tuash CH.

107.7. Wudtúckqunash‸] TR; Wuddtúckqunash‸ O; ~, RIHS.

107.8. This . . . plentifully] They plentifully lay on wood MHS.

107.12. Fire,] ~‸ CH.

107.18. Tókish,] ~‸ CH.

107.18. *Wake, wake.*] MHS; ~‸~‸O.

107.25–27. So . . . &c] MHS omits.

107.32. wékick] TR; wéick O.

108.4. Breast,] ~‸ RIHS, TR, CH.

108.10. understandings,] ~‸ CH.

108.14. Creation:] ~‸MHS.

108.25. *On*] *on* O+.

108.27. *Sometimes*] *sometimes* O+.

108.29. *To*] *to* O+.

109.2. *Though*] *though* O+.

109.4. *Who*] *who* O+.

110.1. IV] IIII O±.

110.2. *Numbers*] MHS; *Names* O.

110.9. Énada] MHS; énada O.

110.14.–111.34. O prints commas after each number, "12" through "20," and tens, "50" through "90," and all numbers, "400" through "40000."

110.16–21. Piucknab . . . . 19] MHS omits, and abridges the list throughout.

110.23. 21, *&c*] 21, O.
110.24. 30.] 30, *&c.* O.
111.7. Shwoasuck] Swoasuck RIHS, which follows the printing error at 111.6.
111.19. Shoasucktashe] Shoasucktache RIHS.
111.25. Napannetashe] Napannetaihe CH, misreading a broken ligature long s.
112.4. mittánnug] mittánnuck O.
112.5. Shoasuck] Shoashuck RIHS.
112.16. Skeetomp] Sketomp RIHS.
112.20–25. . . . . nabnaquìt] MHS omits.
112.32. Quttatashínash] MHS omits to end of chapter.
112.33. Enadatashínash] Enadtashínash O.
114.19. *An*] *a* MHS.
114.27. *father*] MHS, CH; *fathee* O, TR.
115.11. commited] committed MHS, RIHS, TR.
115.22. Nullóquaso] Nullóquasso RIHS.
115.26. their haire] the hair MHS.
116.1. stob'd] stob d O; stabbed MHS.
116.5. I] MHS omits to end of chapter.
116.10. the] th*e* CH.
116.11. throw] threw O+.
116.15. *ruines*] *minds* RIHS.
116.18. 1.] Throughout we have normalized the numerical designations of the stanzas, as established by the preceding poems.
117.2–3. . . . *House*] *Of the Family businesses* O page headings.
117.4. *An*] *a* MHS.
117.9. *home*] RIHS omits.
117.10. Which] MHS omits.
117.13–14. confessing . . . homes] MHS omits.
117.16. Puttuckakâunese] MHS, RIHS; Puttcukakâunese O.
117.21. house] MHS adds "The Indians have houses with one, two, or three fires."
117.22. *longer*] long RIHS.
117.25. Abockquósinash] Abockqúosiuash RIHS.
118.9. *Burching*] burchen MHS.
118.24. Pawacómwushesh] Powacomwushesh MHS.
118.31. *Light a fire*] TR; *A light fire* O±.
119.8. keémat] heémat RIHS.
119.13. *All, some*] MHS±; *All-some* O.

119.14. *come*] *came* CH.

119.20. And then] MHS omits.

120.30. *doore*] the door MHS.

121.7. In steed] Instead MHS; Insteed RIHS.

121.11. Wéskhunck] Wéskunck RIHS.

121.24. Tunnatì? *Where?*] $\sim_\wedge\sim_\wedge$ O+.

122.17. nétop? *you?*] $\sim_\wedge\sim_\wedge$ O+.

122.25. at the] at a MHS.

122.27. called] MHS omits.

122.28. Wunnauchicómock] CH omits accent.

122.31. . . . . *me*] MHS omits.

123.5. Náumatuck] Náumtuck RIHS.

123.6. *Let goe*] let us go MHS.

123.8. Keesuckqíu] Keesuckgíu CH.

123.14. They] The women MHS.

123.29. *broke*] broken MHS.

124.3. . . . . *foole*] RIHS moves back to follow "*here*" at 122.32.

124.4. also] MHS omits.

124.10. Qushenáwsui] CH omits accent.

124.16. . . . . *this*] O+ two separate lines and repeats "*Mend this.*"

124.23. . . . . *doores*] MHS omits.

124.33. rich;] $\sim_\wedge$ CH.

125.4. Apíssumma] CH omits accent.

125.8. Napònsh] RIHS omits accent.

125.26. evening,] $\sim_\wedge$ CH.

125.26. night$_\wedge$they] $\sim$. They MHS.

125.30. In] MHS does not paragraph.

126.9. *snach*] *snatch* MHS, RIHS.

126.15. Máuks,] TR; $\sim_\wedge$ O±.

126.24. *it*] *is* O.

126.29. *as*] TR.

126.33. Tobaco] Tobacco MHS, RIHS.

126.35. *Obs*. . . . for] MHS omits.

127.2–3. sometimes] MHS paragraphs.

127.4. two] too RIHS.

127.7. three . . . us] MHS omits.

127.15. . . . . *Pipe*] O+ two lines and repeats "*A Pipe.*"

127.17. have] had MHS.

127.29. augwháttous] $\sim$? RIHS.

128.6. from . . . field] MHS omits.

128.23. there] RIHS omits.

128.27. up,] ∼‸ CH.

128.27. *Mats* and] MHS omits.

129.13. *Set*] Sets RIHS.

130.3. Uppaquóntup] Uppaquontop MHS.

130.4. Nuppaquóntup] Nuppaquontop MHS.

130.9. Yet] MHS omits.

130.24. hundred] RIHS.

130.23–24. that . . . us] MHS omits.

130.27. knowes‸] ∼) RIHS.

131.4. Wuttówwog] MHS; Wuttóvwog O±.

131.4. -guàsh] quash RIHS.

131.9. Which] The tooth ake MHS.

131.13. childbirth] child birth RIHS.

131.13–14. of . . . *Marriage*] MHS omits.

131.16. this paine] the tooth ake MHS.

131.20. Qúttuck] CH omits accent.

131.21. which] MHS omits.

131.22. to doe] in cutting off the heads of their enemies MHS.

131.23. enemie,] ∼‸ CH.

131.24. they] MHS omits.

131.34. fetcht] fecht TR.

132.2–3. appeares] appear MHS.

132.4. Mapànnog] Napànnog RIHS.

132.16. Wunnickégannash] Wunniskégannash RIHS.

132.19–21. Riches . . . these] MHS omits.

132.28. Tou nùckquaque] Tonnùckquaque RIHS.

132.31. Hence] MHS omits.

133.8. *are*] The inverted word order seems to result from a printer's error, his duplication of "*Weake*" and his mending of the line to arrive at the meaning "*You are weake*" compare 133.5).

133.10. Qunnauqussítchick] Qunnauqssítchick TR.

133.21. *blood,*] blood‸RIHS.

134.12. and . . . lesse] MHS omits.

134.14. *Manittóo* Manittóo CH.

134.23–24. round, double or treble] ∼‸∼‸TR, CH.

134.28. give] given RIHS.

134.29. consultation,] ∼‸ CH.

135.3. nippánnawem] nippánnawen RIHS.

135.11–12. *Obs.* . . . to] MHS omits.

135.15. *understand*] MHS; *understand* O±.

135.18. Coanâumwem] Coanâumwen RIHS.

135.19. *Obs.* . . . next] These MHS.

135.20. each to other] to each other MHS.

135.27. nippannawâutam] nippauna wâut am RIHS.

135.28. *Obs.* . . . me] One of the Indians MHS.

135.29. creation,] ∼‸RIHS.

136.10. ntúnnawem] ntúnnawen RIHS.

136.15. Enapwáuwwaw] Enapwauwwan MHS.

136.21. *say*] *says* MHS.

136.22. high] MHS omits.

136.27. Wunnaumwáyean] Wunnaunewáyean RIHS.

137.6. Tocketunáname] Pocketunáname RIHS, and so at 137.7.

137.18. obeying,] ∼‸CH.

137.23. This] The MHS.

137.23. comprise] MHS+; comp ise O, where the "r" has fallen into the Narragansett word below.

137.25. Awaunaguss] MHS±; Awaunagrs O, which seems to contain the "r" of "comprise" above; Awaunagress RIHS.

138.17. Páudsha] Páuosha RIHS; Páuasha CH.

138.25. where by] MHS—; whereby O.

138.30. Wussuckwhómmin] Wussuck-whómmen RIHS.

138.32–33. . . . . *Letter*] MHS omits.

140.1. That] MHS omits, and after "me" inserts "to write letters for them."

140.13. *eares,*] RIHS±; ∼. O.

140.13–14. . . . *feares*] CH lineates as prose.

141.4. *Starres;*] stars; MHS—; ∼, O.

141.5. ayre,] air, MHS—; ∼; O.

141.6. amongst] of MHS.

141.8. Mautáubon] Mautàbon RIHS.

141.30. tàunt] Tàunt RIHS.

142.1. keeping] Keeping RIHS.

142.8. Wussâume] Wuisaume MHS.

142.10. . . . . *day*] MHS omits.

142.20. wildest,] RIHS—; ∼‸O.

143.1. Sun‸] RIHS—; ∼, O.

143.4. . . . *bright*] O ranges this line right, opposite 143.2. and 143.3; RIHS positions it correctly, but without terminal punctuation, following O.

143.5. *see,*] ∼. O±; see ‸RIHS.

144.4.	Neesqúnnagat] Neesquunnegat MHS, to agree with 144.3.
144.5–14.	. . . . *dayes*] MHS omits.
144.15.	*The*] MHS omits.
144.16.	*Spring,* or] MHS omits.
144.18.	*Fall* . . . and] MHS omits.
144.25–27.	. . . . *Moone*] MHS omits.
144.30.	. . . . *Moneths*] MHS omits.
145.1–2.	. . . . *Moneths*] MHS omits.
145.5.	*as*] MHS omits.
145.8.	*moneth*] moneth &c. RIHS.
145.14–19.	. . . . *&c*] MHS omits.
146.5.	*sound*] *found* CH.
147.3.	*A way*] MHS—; *Away* O.
147.7.	Mishimmáyagat] CH omits accent.
147.17.	*the way lies*] *lies the way* MHS.
147.27.	hunting-houses] ∼‸∼MHS, RIHS.
147.29.	Anóce] Anòce CH.
148.12.	. . . . *you*] MHS omits.
148.16.	oft] often MHS.
148.27.	*They are gone*] O duplicates, ranging the first opposite "Memauchegushánnick."
149.26.	*a way*] *away* TR.
149.30–31.	. . . . *back*] MHS omits.
149.33.–150.1.	and belly] MHS omits.
150.5.	Awánick] Awânick TR; RIHS, CH omit accent.
150.11.	Refuges] refuge MHS.
150.12.	men] Men RIHS.
150.12.	wondrous] wonderous MHS.
151.3.	Yò] all editors omit accent.
151.9.	-min] mni RIHS.
151.10–13.	. . . . preserved] MHS omits.
151.9.	alone,] ∼‸CH.
151.17.	*me.*] me? RIHS.
151.19.	íish] úsh RIHS, TR.
151.22.	strong.] MHS, CH; ∼, O.
151.23.	hundreth mile] hundred miles MHS.
151.26.	man] Man RIHS.
151.28.	Taquáttin] Paquáttin RIHS.
152.11.	Wáumsu] RIHS, TR omit accent.
152.21–22.	Persons] MHS, RIHS; Person O.
152.22.	Justice;] RIHS; ∼, O±; ∼. MHS.

152.24. out] MHS omits.

153.9. Ntinneapeeyaûmen] MHS, TR; Ntinneapreyaûmen O±.

153.17. *burthen*] burthens RIHS.

153.21. comfort, feede] RIHS; ~=/~O, CH; ~=~TR.

154.3. *but's*] buts' RIHS.

154.4. *God*] *Go'd* O±; God RIHS.

154.4. *Sweet'ning*] Sweetning O±; sweetning RIHS.

155.2–3. *Concerning . . . Lights*] *Of the heavenly Lights* MHS.

155.3. *Lights.*] ~, O±.

155.9. the Sun] it MHS.

155.9–10. adore . . . power] adore it for a God MHS.

155.17.–156.3. . . . . before] MHS abridges the three Observations drastically, without altering the sense.

155.25. *The . . . old*] MHS—; O prints immediately following "*Obs.*" at 155.26.

156.2–3. rising, courses,] MHS; ~, ~‸RIHS; ~=~‸O±.

156.5. signifies] signify MHS.

156.25. *Course, and therein doe* ‸] ~‸~, O+.

156.29. *Names, himself*] names‸himself RIHS; ~‸~TR; O, followed by CH, ranges "*himself*" to the right of "*fold*" at 156.30.

157.9. *Cold.*] Cold. RIHS; ~, O±.

157.12. *England*] *Englands* CH.

157.15. winds,] ~‸TR.

157.16. *Nor‸West*] northwest MHS; Nor-West RIHS; ~=~ TR.

157.22–23. *Indians,* Men and Women,] ~‸~‸O±; Indian‸men and women‸MHS.

157.29. *a cold*] MHS, TR omit "*a*."

157.30. *Sweat*] *sweat* TR.

158.3. *to-day*] ~=~CH.

158.6. Animanâukock-Sóchepo] Animanâukocksóshepo RIHS.

158.9. Pâuqui,] ~‸RIHS, TR.

158.14. Capàt] Capát CH.

158.17. Míchokatch] MHS; Míchokateh O±.

159.2. *Storme,*] storme‸RIHS.

159.3. *And*] *and* O±; And RIHS.

159.6. *Sunne,*] Sunne‸RIHS.

159.7. *or'e*] ore RIHS.

159.9. *stincking*] Stincking RIHS.

159.12. *is*‸] is‸RIHS; ~, O±.

160.7. account of seven] account seven winds MHS.

160.9. winds,] ~‸RIHS.

160.10–11. 32. upon] ~:~ RIHS.

160.17. *South*] *the south* MHS.

160.18. *West*] *the west* MHS.

160.24. wuttìn] RIHS reverses the order of 160.23, 24 and prints "wouttín."

160.28. This] The southwest MHS.

161.1. *Sowwaníu*] *Sowwainíu* RIHS.

161.1. gods] Gods MHS.

161.12–13. as . . . 6] MHS omits.

161.13. 1. 6.] 1–6. CH.

161.24. Cowunnagehúckamen] Cowunnogehúckamen RIHS.

161.29. Winds] *Wind* RIHS.

162.2. *observe*‸] Observe‸RIHS; ~, O±.

162.6. *calmes,*] calmes‸RIHS.

162.7. *still:*] still; RIHS.

162.13. *man*] Man RIHS.

163.10. *An*] *the* MHS.

163.11. *Eagles*] *Eagle* O±; *eagles* MHS.

163.14. *Heath-cocks*] Heath‸cocks RIHS.

163.16. are] be MHS.

163.17. appeares] appears CH.

163.18–22. Unto . . . seed] MHS omits.

163.22. seed] feed CH.

163.23. Against] MHS does not paragraph.

163.23. the Birds] these MHS.

163.25. root,] ~‸RIHS.

163.25. yet] RIHS omits.

163.29. &c] from devouring the corn MHS.

164.1. Ohómous] Ohemous MHS.

164.1. *An*] *the* MHS.

164.4–5. hundred kil] hundred wil kil O±; hundred kill MHS.

164.7. Eare,] ~‸RIHS.

164.8. Southwest,] ~‸RIHS+.

164.12. *Swan*] Swan RIHS; *Swans* O±; MHS omits the plural form in both languages.

164.24. training of the] training the RIHS.

164.28. Kítsuog] Kitssuog RIHS.

164.31. them.] MHS; ~: O±.

164.32. aquéchinock] aquéchmock CH.

165.1. This they doe] They lay nets MHS.

165.1. fowle] fowls MHS.

165.2. *Akrons*] acorns MHS.

165.5. Ptowewushánnick] Ptowewunshánnick CH.

165.9. *A*] *the* MHS, which omits the plural at 165.10.

165.15. *Natives*)] ~, O±.

165.16. killing of them] killing them RIHS.

165.22. Crow,] ~‸RIHS.

165.26. themselves,] ~‸RIHS.

165.33.–166.6. . . . &c] MHS omits.

166.12. Heavens] Heaven CH.

166.19. *reape*] RIHS; ~. O±.

166.27. *God,*] God‸RIHS.

166.29. *God*‸] RIHS; ~. O±.

166.30. *then His*‸*forsake*] than his, forsake RIHS.

167.12. *of Tree*] *of a tree* MHS.

167.16. *Rivulet*] *Rivelet* MHS, following variant text.

167.18. *Spring?*] *spring?* MHS; ~. O±.

167.19. *River?*] *river*. MHS; River. RIHS.

167.20. *Bridge?*] ~. O±; *bridge?* MHS; Bridge. RIHS.

167.23. Brooke &c.] Brooke) &c. O±; brook, &c. MHS; Brooke, &c. RIHS.

167.27–28. but . . . Conversion] MHS omits.

167.29. *An*] *the* MHS, and moves ahead to precede 168.4.

167.30. *A*] *the* MHS.

168.7. sometimes] some times TR.

168.9. *A*] *the* MHS.

168.10. *Wallnuts*] *Wallnut* O±; *walnuts* MHS.

168.12. their] the MHS.

168.15. inoffensive] MHS; in offensive O±.

168.23. or *Hay*] MHS omits.

169.14. Mowinne] Mowinnee RIHS.

169.19. *Hurtle-berries*] *whortleberries* MHS.

169.31. also] MHS omits.

170.2. buttered. If] ~, if O+.

170.6. of *English*] of the English RIHS.

170.9. . . . . *Corne*] MHS omits.

170.15. . . . . *up*] MHS moves ahead to follow 170.32.

170.31. *magnæ*] *maximǣ* MHS.

170.34. *break for*] *break up for* MHS.

171.2. Howes‸] ~, O+.

171.12. Pausinnúmmin] RIHS, CH omit accent.

171.13. . . . carefully] They carefully dry the corn MHS.

171.17. woman] women MHS, RIHS to agree with "they" at 171.19 but clearly the agreement should be with "she" at 171.19.

171.20. friends,] ∼‸RIHS.

171.22. *threshing*] *thrashing* MHS.

171.23. *thrash*] trash RIHS.

171.25. *basketfull*] *basket full* MHS±.

171.27. *one*] *basket* MHS, and at 171.28.

171.30. *basketfull*] *basket full* MHS±.

171.31. Neesowánnanash] CH omits accent.

171.31–32. . . . . *Three*] MHS omits.

171.33. Yowanánnash] TR, CH omit accent.

172.6. aples] apple MHS.

172.9. *them*] *the squash* MHS.

172.12. witness] wit-/in O±; wit in RIHS; wit-in TR.

172.15. against,] ∼‸RIHS.

172.20. *As*] *as* O±; As RIHS.

172.22. *fruits*] fruit RIHS.

172.23. *this,*] this‸RIHS.

172.25. *of*‸] ∼, O±; of, RIHS.

172.27. *who*‸] ∼, O±; who, RIHS.

172.30. *Wildernesse*] *wildernesse* TR.

173.11. with . . . trees] of great pieces of trees with his teeth O+.

173.13. by them] MHS omits in an effort to restore the sense of 173.11.

173.18. Foxes,] ∼‸RIHS.

173.20. Gods,] MHS±; ∼‸O.

173.23. pánnog] pánuog RIHS.

174.3. *Squirrill*] Squirrell RIHS.

174.3. *Squirrils*] *quirrils* O±.

174.4. *litle*] *little* TR.

174.5. Waútuckques] Waûtuiiques RIHS, which prints "Conck" for "*Conie.*"

174.15. . . . . *Horse*] MHS omits.

174.16. Côwsnuck] Cowsuck MHS.

174.17. Gôatesuck] Goatsuck MHS.

174.17. *Goats*] Goates RIHS.

174.18. Pígsuck] MHS omits.

174.19. This Termination] This plural termination MHS.

174.19–20. language;] ∼‸RIHS.

174.24. each of other] of each other MHS.

174.30.	*R,*] ~. RIHS, CH.
175.6.	*Black*] *the black* MHS.
175.7.	*Rattle*] *the rattle* MHS.
175.13.	Wildernesse$_{\wedge}$] ~, RIHS.
175.14.	greedie] gredie RIHS.
175.18.	*Swine,*] Swine$_{\wedge}$RIHS.
175.19.	*devoure;*] ~, O±; devoure, RIHS.
175.20.	*all,*] ~; O±; all; RIHS.
175.26.	*fierce,*] fierce$_{\wedge}$ RIHS.
176.7–9.	. . . . Chesnut-tree] O, followed by all editors, prints this segment of the vocabulary as the beginning of "*Obs.*" 176.10. In amending, we have italicized consistent with our style.
176.8.	a] MHS omits.
176.9.	Chesnut] Chestnut CH.
176.11.	hatchet,] ~$_{\wedge}$RIHS.
176.12.	fire$_{\wedge}$when] ~. When MHS.
176.13.	him] MHS omits.
176.19.	lanched] launched MHS.
176.21.	. . . . *Canow*] MHS moves ahead to follow 177.3.
176.26.	themselves] the Indians MHS.
177.4.	*one*] *canoe* MHS.
177.10.	*launch*] Launch RIHS.
177.15.	Namacóuhe] Namacóuche RIHS.
177.21.	Sepâkehig] Sepãkehig TR.
177.26.	a wind] the wind MHS.
177.26.	mile, &c] miles$_{\wedge}$MHS.
177.27.	*Hoyse*] *hoist* MHS.
178.5.	times$_{\wedge}$] ~: RIHS.
178.14.	*boord*] *board* MHS±.
178.17.	Mishittáshin] RIHS, CH omit accent.
178.26.	Maúchetan] Maũchetan TR.
178.33.	*ashoare*] *ashore* TR.
179.22.	*o're-turn'd*] o'return'd RIHS.
180.8–9.	into the fresh] into fresh MHS.
180.10–11.	*a Herring*] herrings MHS.
180.12.	*Basse*] *the bass* MHS.
180.13.	*Uppaquóntup,*] MHS omits.
180.16.	*Sturgeon*] *the sturgeon* MHS.
180.17.	parts] MHS; part O±.
180.19.	prize it,] ~$_{\wedge}$CH.
180.22.	The] MHS does not paragraph.

180.22. venture one] venture out one MHS.
180.24. hale] haul MHS.
180.25. *Their*] MHS omits.
180.26. Which] MHS omits.
180.27. set thwart] set their nets thwart MHS.
180.29–30. *English*] TR; *Engish* O±; English MHS, RIHS.
181.1. Aucùp] CH omits accent.
181.4. Mishquammaúquock] CH omits accent.
181.8. *Breame*] *the bream* MHS.
181.9. abundance,] ~‸CH.
181.10. smoake,] ~; O+.
181.11. salt;] ~, O+.
181.12. a] MHS omits.
181.14. aúog] CH omits accent.
181.16. Sassamaúquock] CH omits accent.
181.19. *Whales*] *the whale* MHS.
181.19. Which] MHS omits.
181.20. places are] places whales are MHS.
181.21. foot] feet MHS.
181.21. out] MHS omits.
181.22. send farre] send them far MHS.
181.24. Missêsu] Miseêsu TR.
181.33. *Fishers*] TR; *Fishes* O±.
182.2. *for?*] for. RIHS.
182.5. Sickìssuog] Sickishuog MHS.
182.9. liquor] liquors RIHS.
182.17. *Horse-fish*] Horse‸fish RIHS.
182.22. black money] blackmoney RIHS.
182.25. *Wómpam*] *Wòmpans* CH.
182.26–27. of which . . . Coyne] MHS omits.
182.29. Cummenakíssamen] Cummenak ssamen CH.
183.2. *fishing-line*] fishing‸line RIHS.
183.3. Aumanápeash] RIHS omits accent.
183.16. Kunnagqunneûteg] Kunnagqunneúteg TR.
183.19. *sort of*] MHS omits.
183.25. times] time TR.
183.26. for] MHS.
183.27. take also] also take MHS.
183.32. sea-Inhabitants] sea‸inhabitants RIHS.
183.32. world,] ~‸ CH.
184.10. *through*] TR; *though* O±; through RIHS.
184.14. *be,*] ~‸O+.

184.15. *Devour'd,*] $\sim$; O+.

185.10. except] MHS, RIHS; excep O±.

185.11. after . . . else] MHS omits.

185.12. open] are open MHS.

185.17–18. often abroad] often go abroad MHS.

185.18. abroad,] $\sim_{\wedge}$ RIHS, TR.

185.19. skin] skins MHS.

185.19. cloth,] $\sim_{\wedge}$ RIHS, CH.

185.21. cloth (though loose)] cloth, loose MHS.

185.21. neare] or neare O+.

186.2. *Wolves-skin*] *wolf*$_{\wedge}$*skin* MHS.

186.6. men] Men RIHS.

186.7. Velvet] velvet RIHS.

186.17. is)] $\sim$; O±; $\sim$, MHS; $\sim$;) RIHS.

186.18. *quemque tenere suam*] *quen, que teneresuam* CH.

186.18. That . . . skin] MHS omits.

186.20. *A*] RIHS; *a* O±. From 186.20 to 187.4 the printer apparently found himself short of uppercase italic A's, and set lowercase italic except at 186.21 where he began the series by substituting a roman uppercase A. We have made consistent throughout.

186.22. Pétacaus] Petacus MHS.

186.23. . . . . *wastecoat*] MHS omits.

186.31. them,] $\sim_{\wedge}$ CH.

186.33. hang'd] hung MHS.

186.34. hurt,] MHS; $\sim_{\wedge}$ O±.

187.1. Noonacóminash] RIHS omits accent.

187.8. . . . . *Painted*] MHS omits.

187.9. also] MHS omits.

187.14. in stead] instead MHS, RIHS.

187.17. (upon gift &c.)] MHS omits.

187.17. yet] MHS omits.

187.19. pull] they pull MHS.

187.25. Councells,] $\sim_{\wedge}$RIHS.

187.28. *Africa*)] $\sim$, O±; Africa,) RIHS; $\sim_{\wedge}$ CH.

187.29. Body,] $\sim_{\wedge}$ CH.

187.29. Soule] soule RIHS.

188.3. *tush*] push RIHS.

188.12. *is:*] is $_{\wedge}$ RIHS.

189.2. . . . *&c*] *Of their Religion* MHS, to correspond with page headings.

189.3. manittówock] manittó-/wock O±; manittó./wock CH.

189.7. 11.] RIHS; II. O±; xi. MHS.

189.14. them, and the Heaven$_\wedge$] MHS; ~$_\wedge$~, O±; ~, ~, RIHS.

189.16. *me.*] MHS, RIHS; ~? O±.

189.18. have] RIHS omits.

189.29. First$_\wedge$] ~, MHS, RIHS.

190.2. seven,] ~$_\wedge$ CH.

190.2. which I have] MHS omits.

190.3. as] MHS omits.

190.4. *South-West*] South$_\wedge$West RIHS.

190.5–6. Corne, Beanes] corn and beans MHS.

190.7. Wompanànd] CH omits accent.

190.12–13. . . . &c] MHS omits.

190.13. *Denis*] Dennis RIHS.

190.17. some murtherous] some of the murtherous RIHS.

190.18. Rapier)] ~, O±; rapier, MHS; ~,) RIHS.

190.19. escaped] escaped from them O+.

190.19–21. —but . . . *England*—] We have substituted the abnormal dash for O's commas in order clearly to isolate the confusing aside. MHS uses colons.

190.22. who] which O+.

190.24. ever] MHS omits.

190.33. . . . &c] MHS omits.

191.2. can it, say they, be$_\wedge$] MHS; ~$_\wedge$~$_\wedge$~, O±; ~$_\wedge$~$_\wedge$~$_\wedge$ CH.

191.8. Country?] ~, O±; country?" MHS.

191.8. of the Wood] of wood MHS.

191.9. Benefit,] RIHS; ~$_\wedge$ O±; benefit, MHS. O prints as catchword "benefit,."

191.10. thickets).] MHS; ~?) O±.

191.11. *Præsentem*] *Presentem* CH.

191.12–13. . . . *dwell*] MHS omits.

191.23. is;] ~$_\wedge$ MHS, RIHS.

191.26. Jehovah their] Jehovah for their MHS.

191.28. private,] ~$_\wedge$ RIHS±.

191.32–33. then *Nickómmo*] then they have Nickommo MHS.

191.33.–192.2. for . . . feasting] MHS omits

192.1. saith] faith CH.

192.2. yeare$_\wedge$] RIHS—; ~) O.

192.3. Powwáw] CH omits accent.

192.7. sweating] sweatings CH.

192.11. threaten] threatens MHS, RIHS.

192.13. body of a man] Body of a Man RIHS.
192.17. durst never] never durst MHS.
192.19–20. contrary . . . 11] MHS omits.
192.20. 11] 14 O+.
192.25–27. as . . . World] MHS omits.
192.28–29. called . . . Rulers] MHS omits.
192.28. *Atauskowaúg,* Rulers,] $\sim_{\wedge}\sim_{\wedge}$ O+.
192.30. wise men and] wise and MHS.
192.30. men (of] RIHS; $\sim_{\wedge}\sim$ O±; ~, ~ MHS.
192.31. whom . . . they] MHS omits.
192.34. Nowemaúsitteem] Nowemasúitteem RIHS.
192.34. *away*] way RIHS.
193.1. makes] maketh MHS.
193.2. hundredth,] $\sim_{\wedge}$ RIHS.
193.4. Feasts,] ~) O±; feasts, MHS; ~: RIHS.
193.4. they give I say] give MHS.
193.9. of it] MHS omits "of".
193.10. Mr.] master MHS.
193.12. *Ile*] *I will* MHS.
193.21. *Nákommit*] Nickommit MHS.
193.23. Kekineawaúi] Kekineawùi RIHS.
193.25. man,] $\sim_{\wedge}$ MHS.
193.26. . . . say] MHS omits.
194.1. notion,] $\sim_{\wedge}$ RIHS, CH.
194.11 *An.*] $\text{Anan}_{\wedge}$ RIHS.
194.12. beleive] believe MHS, RIHS, CH.
194.12–13. Women goe] Women men goe RIHS.
194.14. *Cautàntouwit* his House] Cautantowwit's house MHS.
194.15. have)] $\sim_{\wedge}$O±; ~, MHS.
194.15. Joyes:] ~): O±; joys. MHS.
194.17.–197.11. . . . . will] MHS omits.
194.20. brethren] Brethren RIHS.
194.24. Estate,] $\sim_{\wedge}$ RIHS.
194.25. hundreths] hundredths RIHS.
194.31. Natótema] Nntótema RIHS.
194.32. Tocketunnántum] Tocketunnântum CH.
195.23. *all things*] *allthings* CH.
196.11. Ka wáme namaúsuck] Kawámeaúmausuck RIHS.
196.16–17. wuchè wuckeesittin] wuckèwuckeesittin RIHS.
196.24. *afterward*] TR; *afteward* O±; afterward RIHS.
197.4. *six dayes*] TR; *sixdayes* O±; six days RIHS.
197.11. relate] They relate MHS.

197.21.–198.4. . . . . *not*] MHS omits.
197.22. *English-men*] Englishmen RIHS; *English‸men* CH.
197.24–25. mittaukêuk-kitonckquéhettit] mittaukê/kukitonck quehettit RIHS.
198.12–17. . . . . *Writing*] MHS omits.
198.14. Micheme] Michem RIHS.
198.20. others] MHS—; other O.
198.22. and before] before MHS.
198.25. not] TR; other editors follow O.
199.9–10. You . . . God] MHS omits.
199.15–20. the want . . . God] MHS omits.
199.16. conceive,] ∼‸ RIHS.
199.17. Nations,] ∼‸ TR.
199.22.–200.24. . . . . *True*] MHS omits.
200.13. *stand‸*] ∼. O±; stand, RIHS.
200.14. *Before*] CH; *Befote* O, TR; Before RIHS.
200.15. *him‸*] him, RIHS.
200.18. *knowledge‸*] ∼, O±; knowledge‸ RIHS.
200.19. *but‸*] but, RIHS.
200.20. *Obedience‸*] Obedience, RIHS.
201.3–4. . . . . *Monarchie*] MHS omits.
201.4. *Kingdome*] kingdome RIHS.
201.6. Countrey] Counrey O±; country MHS; countrey RIHS.
201.9. mans] Mans RIHS.
201.14. *The Queen,* or] MHS omits.
201.16. *Queenes*] *the wives of sachims* MHS.
201.16–17. . . . . *towne*] MHS omits.
201.21. house] houses MHS.
201.21. or receit] MHS omits.
202.2. *be*] MHS; other editors follow O.
202.4. *Sachims,*] Sachims‸ RIHS.
202.5. under‸*Sachims*] Under-Sachims MHS.
202.6. presents,] ∼‸ RIHS.
202.17. people;] ∼: RIHS.
202.26. *search*] MHS; *seach* O±; search RIHS.
202.29. . . . . *fellow*] MHS omits.
202.31. *stole*] *stolen* MHS.
203.10–12. I . . . hardens] MHS omits.
203.24. Nìssoke] Nìssòke CH.
203.30. Executioner,] executioner‸ RIHS.
204.2. *knew*] *know* MHS.

204.20. *Men,*] Men$_\wedge$ RIHS.

204.22. *then:*] ∼. O±; then, RIHS.

204.26. *Wildernesse*] wildernesse RIHS.

205.3. . . . . *man*] MHS omits.

205.7. Wussénetam] Wusséntam RIHS.

205.13. then] MHS omits.

205.15. *adulterer*] Adulterer RIHS.

205.18. Pallè] Patte MHS.

205.20. In this case] In case a man or woman commit adultery MHS.

205.29. . . . . *&c*] MHS omits.

206.1. Number is] number of wives is MHS.

206.12. Tahanawátu$_\wedge$ta] MHS; ∼? ∼ O±.

206.13. commaúgemus?] ∼. O±; ∼$_\wedge$MHS.

206.14–15. *fathome of their Money*] *fathoms of money* MHS.

206.16–17. . . . . *Fathome*] MHS omits.

206.18. Daughter] daughter RIHS.

206.18. Daughter *Piuckquompaúgatash*] daughter they give Piuckquom paugatash MHS.

206.20. Generally] MHS omits.

206.20–21. these . . . *Israell*] from five to ten fathom of their money for his wife MHS.

206.22. To this purpose] MHS omits.

206.23–24. doe . . . is] MHS omits.

207.1. They] The women MHS.

207.16–17. not . . . it] MHS omits.

207.17. followes] This follows MHS.

207.18. hardnesse] hardiness MHS.

207.20. Secondly] MHS does not paragraph.

208.2. Aumaúnemun] Aumaúneman RIHS.

208.4. They] The men MHS; they RIHS.

208.4. (as in Israell)] MHS omits.

208.10. Aquie] Aquèi RIHS.

208.11. Awetawátuonck] MHS omits.

208.20. Observations] *Observation* RIHS.

208.20. *Mariage*] *Marriage* RIHS, and at 208.22.

208.25. abundant increase] abundance. RIHS.

209.4. *Know*] *know* O±; Know RIHS.

209.6. *foule*] *soule* CH.

209.8. *Brought*] *brought* O±; Brought RIHS.

210.1. XXIV] XXVI O–.

210.2. *Concerning their* Coyne] *Of their Coin* MHS.

210.8. which . . . Meteaûhock] MHS omits.

210.12. inclining] MHS±; incling O.

210.26–28. . . . . *pence*] MHS omits.

210.31.–211.4. . . . . *pence*] MHS omits.

211.7–8. *Quttáuatues*] Quáttautues RIHS.

211.8. or six pence] MHS omits.

211.11. $18^{d.}$] MHS omits, and at 211.13, 211.15, 211.24, 212.4, 212.8.

211.16–22. . . . . quttáuatues] MHS omits.

211.24–25. *or,* 10 six pences] MHS omits.

211.26. being sixtie pence] worth five shillings English money MHS.

211.27–28. 5 shillings] MHS omits.

211.29. This] MHS omits.

211.29–30. now worth of the English but] is worth MHS, which then omits the rest of the paragraph.

212.5–6. . . . . Fathom] MHS omits.

212.9–13. . . . . pounds] MHS omits.

212.14–17. Insertions are made following TR.

212.19. white] white money MHS

212.20. *Súcki*] Sácki RIHS.

212.26. . . . . *money*] MHS omits.

213.1. Puckwhéganash] Puchwhéganash RIHS.

213.3–4. which . . . temper] MHS omits.

213.5. ever] MHS omits.

213.5. *Europe,*] $\sim_{\wedge}$ CH.

213.6. this] MHS omits.

213.6. stone,] stones, RIHS; $\sim_{\wedge}$ CH.

213.7. and so fell] They also felled MHS; and to fell RIHS.

213.8–9. fearfull] fearing MHS.

213.24. Enomphómmin] Enomphommees MHS.

213.25. *ones*] *beads* MHS.

213.29. these] MHS omits.

214.15. English$_{\wedge}$] $\sim$, RIHS.

214.16. *will*] shall RIHS.

214.17. *men*] Men RIHS.

214.24. *knowing,*] $\sim_{\wedge}$ TR.

215.2. *Of buying*] *Of their buying* RIHS.

215.19. of] MHS omits.

215.20. $_{\wedge}$and] (and RIHS.

215.22. Sea-side] Sea$_{\wedge}$side RIHS.

215.29. *Have*] *Hove* O±.

216.10. haires,] ~‸ RIHS.
216.20. *Wool*] work RIHS.
216.23. Wúskinuit] Wúskanuit RIHS.
216.29. *Cuppáimish*] Cuppàmirh RIHS.
216.31. Tahenaúatu] Tahenautu RIHS.
217.8–9. cautelous] cautious MHS.
217.15. *Money.*] money? RIHS.
217.18. *me*] RIHS omits.
217.19. deale or trade] deals or trades MHS.
217.19. them,] ~‸ RIHS.
217.21. *Cuppànnawem*] Cuppánnawen RIHS; *Cuppànnauem* CH.
217.22. me] RIHS omits.
217.23. Kunúkkeke] kunnukke MHS.
217.26. Augausaúaru] Aagausaúatu RIHS.
218.11–15. . . . . *spans*] MHS omits.
218.12. *Three*] Three RIHS.
218.15. Quttatashaumskus] Quttatashaumíkus CH.
218.16. . . . *.spans*] MHS omits.
218.18. *man*] Man RIHS.
218.20. wiser,] ~‸ CH.
218.24. often] MHS omits.
218.25. haply] MHS; happily O±.
219.6. *aweighing*] *weighing* MHS, RIHS.
219.7. *all one*] *allone* CH.
219.10–14. . . . . colours] MHS omits.
219.13. women] Women RIHS.
219.15. Cummanohamógunna] Cuminanohamógunna CH.
219.18. Cosaumpeekúnnemun] Cosaumpeekúnneman RIHS.
219.18. *tore*] *torn* MHS.
219.32. *sell*] TR; *seeke* O±.
220.5. the infinite] theinfinite RIHS.
220.6. *Europe,*] Europe, RIHS; ~‸ TR, CH.
220.11. *New-English*] New English RIHS; *New English* TR; CH.
220.17. *lives,*] lives‸ RIHS.
220.21. *strangers*] Strangers RIHS.
220.22. *fraud*] Fraud RIHS.
220.25. *soule,*] soule‸ RIHS.
220.26. *heaven*] Heaven RIHS.
221.7. them,] ~‸ RIHS.
221.11. pay,] ~‸ RIHS, TR.

221.13–15. which . . . Language] MHS omits.
221.26. *for debts*] *for my debts* MHS.
222.1. This] It MHS.
222.1. (as they think] RIHS; ‸∼ (∼ O±.
222.3. heales] heal MHS.
222.23. debts,] ∼‸ CH.
222.24. no thing] nothing RIHS.
222.27. *sleepe.*] sleepe; RIHS.
222.29. *debts*] debt RIHS.
222.30. *debts*] Debts RIHS.
223.3. *death's sweet*] Death's Sweet RIHS.
224.8. I say] MHS omits.
224.23. Ncáttiteam] Ncattitean MHS; Ncáattiteam TR.
225.4–5. . . . . *Foure*] MHS omits.
225.6. *Ten*] *I have killed ten* MHS.
225.7–8. . . . . *Twentie*] MHS omits.
225.21.–226.12. . . . . servants.] MHS omits.
225.25. it,] ∼‸ RIHS.
225.27. tame,] ∼‸ CH.
225.28. is,] ∼‸ CH.
226.4. it,] ∼‸ RIHS.
226.26. knocks] Knocks RIHS.
227.2–4. . . . . *Doe*] MHS omits.
227.6. asipaúgon] CH omits accent.
227.12. . . . . *Thighes*] MHS omits.
227.19–20. . . . bee] MHS omits.
227.22. O prints this part of the vocabulary following "*Obs.*" at 227.23, and is followed by all editors. We have italized 227.21 and 227.22 consistent with our style.
227.25. or Prince] MHS omits.
227.29–30. hunting,] ∼‸ CH.
228.3. *tame,*] ∼; O±; tame, RIHS.
228.8. *all‸times*] ∼, ∼ O±; all‸times RIHS.
228.10. *Profits, Honour sweet*] ∼‸∼, ∼ O±; Profits, Honour sweet RIHS.
229.3. (like the *English*)] MHS omits.
229.5. . . . publike] RIHS omits.
229.21. *Bauble*] MHS±; *Bable* O.
229.25. *am at telling*] *am atelling* O±; *am telling* MHS; am a telling RIHS; *am a telling* TR.
229.28–29. (as . . . God)] MHS omits.
230.3. losers] loosers RIHS.

230.4. policie,] ∼‸ CH.

230.5. send] sends MHS±.

230.14. Play-house] ∼‸∼ RIHS, CH.

230.17. stakings,] staking‸ RIHS.

230.23. plot,] ∼‸ RIHS±.

230.23. feet,] ∼‸ RIHS, CH.

230.26–27. As . . . them] MHS omits.

230.27–28. and . . . lost] they will sometimes stake and lose MHS.

230.29. they . . . being] They then become MHS.

230.29. it,] ∼‸ O+.

230.31. man] Man RIHS.

230.31–34. an . . . Beggars] MHS omits.

231.7. hundred,] ∼‸ RIHS.

231.8–9. (. . . Kitteickaúick)] MHS omits.

231.8–9. *Kitteickaúick*] Kittcickaũick CH.

231.11. knifes] Knives RIHS.

231.13. poore] Poore RIHS.

231.20. this] his RIHS.

231.22. Jewell] jewell RIHS.

232.4. *wash?*)] ∼?‸ O+.

233.7. wofully‸] ∼, RIHS.

233.7–9. and . . . seas] MHS omits.

233.31. *us*] ns RIHS.

234.1. the] their RIHS.

234.8. *in*] MHS=.

234.15. *An*] *a* MHS, and at 234.28.

235.2. Gunnes‸] ∼, RIHS.

235.8. *It*] MHS±; *Is* O.

235.10–11. in company] in a company MHS.

235.11. hundred;]∼, O±; ∼. MHS.

235.18. They] RIHS, CH do not paragraph.

235.26. *us*] mee RIHS.

236.8. This] The MHS.

236.10. chiefest] chiefs MHS.

236.11. theirs,] MHS; ∼‸ O±.

236.20. Wetompâchick] Wetom âchick RIHS.

236.20. . . . . *Friends*] MHS omits.

236.27. *made one with*] *mad with* O+.

236.30.–237.3. . . . blood] MHS omits.

236.30. people,] ∼‸ RIHS.

236.33. house] honse RIHS.

236.33. men] Men RIHS.

237.3. knife] Knife RIHS.
237.5. *Captive*] TR; *Captaine* O±.
237.18. *slaine.*] MHS±; ∼? O.
237.22. field] battle MHS.
237.25. seldome$_{\wedge}$] ∼, RIHS.
237.32. Kúnnish] CH omits accent.
238.4. *dying.*] MHS±; ∼? O.
238.13. *consider.*] ∼? MHS.
238.17. *say*] *saye* CH.
238.28. *Dogs,*] Dogs; RIHS.
238.29. *then:*] then, RIHS.
239.1. (*That*] $_{\wedge}$∼ O±; (That RIHS.
239.3. *flames,*] ∼. O±; flames$_{\wedge}$ RIHS.
239.7. *Men,*] Men$_{\wedge}$ RIHS.
240.5. Both . . . Women] and sometimes MHS, which inserts "The women paint their faces with all sorts of colours" immediately following, from "XXV.", 219.14.
240.13. of the Pine] of pine MHS.
240.21–23. . . . clothing] MHS omits.
240.21. Letters,] ∼,) RIHS.
240.22. painting] ∼$_{\wedge}$ O±; ∼, RIHS.
241.8. griefe,] ∼. TR.
241.9. Fore-Fathers$_{\wedge}$] ∼, RIHS.
241.16. *Paints;*] ∼, O±; Paints. RIHS.
241.17. *hearts*$_{\wedge}$] hearts, RIHS.
241.25. *betimes,*] betimes$_{\wedge}$ RIHS.
242.4. Mauchinaúi] CH omits accent.
242.5. Wuttunsín] Wvttunsín RIHS.
242.13. Ncussawóntapam] CH omits accent.
242.17. In these cases] When they are sick MHS.
242.22. constrained$_{\wedge}$to$_{\wedge}$] ∼$_{\wedge}$∼, O±; ∼, ∼$_{\wedge}$ MHS; RIHS omits "to".
242.23. I beleeve] MHS omits.
242.24. them$_{\wedge}$] ∼, RIHS.
242.29. Nchésamam] Mchósamam RIHS.
242.29. *sore*] *sure* MHS.
242.30. Machàge] Nachàge RIHS.
243.5. Puttuckhúmma] CH omits accent.
243.6. nototámmin] nototam mim MHS.
243.7. Which is onely] Their only drink MHS.
243.7. extremities,]∼$_{\wedge}$ RIHS, CH.

243.8–9. . . . &c] MHS omits.

243.17. This . . . Visit] All their refreshing in their sickness is the visit MHS.

243.20. often] MHS omits.

243.22. dead:] ∼, RIHS.

243.24. takes] take MHS.

243.27–29. . . . . *pox*] MHS omits.

244.11. *An*] *a* MHS.

244.33. . . . . *Blood*] MHS omits.

244.34. *Flixe*] *flux* MHS.

245.3. . . . . *Priest*] MHS omits.

245.7. These] MHS omits.

245.7. (like *Simon Magus*)] MHS omits.

245.10. Cures,] ∼‸ CH.

245.11. them,] ∼‸ RIHS+.

245.12. times] time MHS.

245.15. times;] ∼, RIHS+.

245.16. nothing,] ∼‸ O+.

245.20. Máskit] CH omits accent.

245.21–22. O prints as two lines, separating "*physicke*" and "*Drinke,*" but MHS is right in joining the two. Other editors follow O.

245.23–26. . . . us] MHS omits.

245.24. for, having] ∼, (∼O+.

246.3. evill] eivill RIHS.

246.8. *speech,*] speech.) RIHS.

246.10. *cracks,*] ∼; O±; cracks, RIHS.

246.11. *it's*] its' RIHS.

246.18. *refresh't*)] ∼, O±; refresht,) RIHS.

246.19. *Love*] love RIHS.

246.19. *zeale*] Zeale RIHS.

247.4. Neenè] CH omits accent.

247.25. Wullóasin] wuttoasin MHS.

247.27. nlôasin] ntoasin MHS.

247.30. *Kutchímmoke*] MHS prints thrice.

248.1. husband,] ∼‸CH.

248.3. Chepassôtam] Chepasotam MHS.

248.6. Chépeck] chèpeck RIHS.

248.7. *A*] *the* MHS.

248.13. accidentally] accidently TR.

248.16. so . . . men] MHS omits.

248.20. *my*] *the* MHS.

248.25. *Mockuttásuit*] Mockkutta uce RIHS.
248.25. chiefest] chief MHS.
248.25–26. up and] up in mats and coats and MHS.
248.26. wise] wife CH.
248.29. lament,] ~; MHS±.
249.4. Yea,] ~‸MHS±.
249.7. sonne] Sonne RIHS.
249.12. looke,] ~‸O+.
249.15. death] Death RIHS.
249.15. death] Death RIHS.
249.26. *Worlds*] worlds RIHS.
249.26. *men*] Men RIHS.
249.28. Indians,] ~‸ RIHS.
250.2. *New;*] new, RIHS.
250.8. from *Whom*] from whom RIHS.
250.9. *Whom*] whom RIHS.
250.13. Blessing‸] ~.) O±; blessing,) RIHS.

Commentary

83.13–23. a rude lumpe] In this passage Williams describes the genesis of *A Key* in some detail, alluding to the tradition that the bear cub was born a formless lump which was then licked into shape by its mother (cf. Donne's Eighteenth Elegy, *Love's Progress*). One can conjecture that the drawing together on the voyage to England was only a Narragansett vocabulary, and that he added the moral observations and poems after he had decided to publish and after he had the opportunity to compare the manners of the Indian, the New English, and the Old English.

83.16. *charges*] public and private missions and duties. He extends the commercial metaphor of *dearely bought*.

84.2. *French* and *Dutch* Plantations] that is, between Quebec and Nieuw Amsterdam, thus New England as opposed to New France or New Holland.

84.6. my abode] the present cite of Providence, Rhode Island.

84.12. season] Throughout the book Williams uses the idea that God will convert the Indian if and when He wants to. He has in mind the beautiful third chapter of Ecclesiastes, which begins, "To every thing there is a season," and which in its ninth verse asks the laborer, "What profit hath he that worketh in that wherein he laboreth?"

84.14. *Leaven*] See Matt. 13:33: "The kingdom of heaven is like unto leaven, which a woman took, and hid in three measures of meal, till the whole was leavened."

84.26–27. *Abergeny men*] Aborigines. "These in the Southerne parts be called Pequants, and Narragansetts; those who are seated West-ward be called Connectacuts, and Mowhacks: Our Indians that live to the Northward of them be called Aberginians . . ." (Wood, pp. 59–60).

84.27. *Heathen*] "I shall therefore humbly intreat my countrymen of all sorts to consider, that although men have used to apply this word *Heathen* to the Indians that go naked, and have not heard of that One-God, yet this word *Heathen* is most improperly sinfully, and unchristianly so used in this sence" (*Christenings,* p. 31).

85.1. severall] different.

85.7. in opposition] instead of.

85.20. observed] The past tense would indicate that this section at least was written in London, possibly as the book was going through the press.

85.33. *Dutch* Governour] William Kieft (1638–46). Williams had other reasons than Kieft's theories of Indian origins for not liking the man. When Williams embarked at Manhattan Kieft was in the midst of a four-year war with the Algonquins which resulted in part from his friendship with the Iroquois.

85.35. about] in the vicinity of.

86.1. under favour] with the reader's permission.

86.6. *annoint*] "for the anointing oil of the Lord is upon you," Lev. 10:7 (see also *Christenings,* p. 33).

86.8. *Dowries*] "And Leah said, God hath endued me with a good dowry" (Gen. 30:20).

86.12. seperate their Women] "according to the days of the separation for her infirmity shall she be unclean" (Lev. 12:2).

86.18. *Nature* and *Tradition*] What the Indian lacks is Revelation. Tradition may err, as for Williams it does in the case of the Papists, but Nature and Revelation cannot (see *Fox,* p. 50). And since the Indian lacks Revelation it is only in the area of Nature that he is without error: "I Reply, First, What is the Light of Nature, but that Light in which every man comes into the World with (as the *Foxians* speak) a Light differing from that Light which Beasts, wilde and tame, and Birds, and Fishes have: And a Second Light differing from what is Supernatural, as that Light revealed from Heaven in the Holy Scriptures, and infused into the Souls of Men by the Holy Spirit or Power of God. What is the Light of Nature in Man, but that Order which the most Glorious Former of all things hath set (like Wheeles in Clocks or Watches) a going in all his Creatures?" (*Fox*, p. 359).

86.22. the *Beare*] the northern constellation which never sets and thus a common point of natural experience for all men in the northern hemisphere. Williams would be aware that all mariners since Ulysses and all philosophers since Il Penseroso have guided themselves by it. In this context, and with the *Nature* of 86.18 in mind, that the Indians too call Charles Wain "the Bear" would be profoundly significant because it seems to argue that nature's inspiration of the European and of the Indian was identical.

86.24. Relations] stories.

86.25–26. *walking upon the waters*] See Matt. 14:25: "And in the fourth watch of the night Jesus went into them, walking on the sea." For Williams, a dimly remembered tradition or a Satanic perversion of Revelation, and thus the "broken" aspect of the "Resemblance."

86.33. *Corne*] maize. In the seventeenth century all cereal grain was commonly referred to as "corn." In the King James version of the Bible, for example, Ruth is said to glean "ears of corn" (Ruth 2:2).

87.13–14. so much pretended] claimed. The conversion of the native was repeatedly declared to be the "principal end" of New England Plantations, but as Williams implies below by contrasting his methods with theirs, and in the following address to them, there are oceans of difference between principle and practice, between verbal ends and actual means: "I pray it may be remembered how greatly the name of God is concerned in this affair, for it cannot be hid, how all England and other nations ring with the glorious conversion of the Indians of New England. You know how many books are dispersed throughout the nation, of the subject, (in some of them the Narragansett chief Sachems are publicly branded, for refusing to pray and be converted;) have all the pulpits in England been commanded to sound of this glorious work, (I speak not ironically, but only mention what all the printed books mention,) and that by the highest command and authority of Parliament, and churchwardens went from house to house, to gather supplies for this work. Honored Sirs, Whether I have been and am a friend to the natives' turning to civility and Christianity, and whether I have been instrumental, and desire so to be, according to my light, I will not trouble you with; only I beseech you consider, how the name of the most holy and jealous God may be preserved between the clashings of these two, viz.: the glorious conversion of the Indians in New England, and the unnecessary wars and cruel destructions of the Indians in New England" (*Letters,* pp. 271–72).

87.20. divers] several.

87.35. *Wequash*] The report is in *First Fruits* (p. 249). In a letter to Governor Winthrop, written before the Pequot expedition, Williams recommends the services of two Pequot guides, "Wequash and Wuttackquiackommin, valiant men . . . who have lived these three or four years with the Narragansetts . . ." (*Letters,* pp. 18–19, 21–23).

88.4. Mr. *Fenwick*] George Fenwick (1603–57) was among a group of gentlemen who in 1632 were awarded forty leagues of territory west of the Narragansett River. In 1639 he took up residence at Saybrook, and in 1644 he sold the fort there to Connecticut. He returned to England where he became a member of the Long Parliament, an officer in the Parliamentary Army, and was nominated to the High Court of Justice appointed to try Charles. He did not serve on that court.

88.10. bequeathed] recommended to the protection of as guardian.

88.11. closed with] engaged in earnest conversation with, in the sense of wrestled with.

88.11. told] reminded.

88.31. put an edge] sharpen or make pointed.

88.33. wonderfull conversions] The irony is made more evident by comparing this to another passage: "Now secondly, for the Catholicks conversion, although I believe I may safely hope that God hath his in Rome, in Spaine, yet if Anti-christ be their false head (as most true it is) the body, faith, baptisme, hope (opposite to the true, Ephes. 4.) are all false also; yea consequently their preachings, conversions, salvations (leaving secret things to God) must all be of the same false nature likewise. If the reports (yea some of their owne *Historians*) be true, what monstrous and most inhumane conversions have they made; baptizing thousands, yea ten thousands of the poore Natives, sometimes by wiles and subtle devices, sometimes by force compelling them to submit to that which they understood not, neither before nor after such their monstrous Christning of them" (*Christenings,* pp. 35–36).

88.36.–89.1. briefe Additionall discourse] In a note appended to the 1643 edition of *A Key* Williams again mentions this tract: "I have further treated of these *Natives* of *New-England,* and that great point of their *Conversion* in a little additionall *Discourse* apart from this." When Trumbull prepared his edition of the book the tract was thought to be lost, although extracts from it and references to "Of the name Heathen" were found in Robert Baylie's *Dissuasive from the Errours of the Time* (London, 1645) (see Trumbull, pp. 12–13). In 1881, however, the pamphlet was fortuitously uncovered by Henry Martyn Dexter, and subsequently included in volume 7 of *The Complete Writings* as *Christenings make not Christians, in a Brief Discourse concerning that name "Heathen," commonly given to the Indians.* As both Williams's references to *Christenings* in *A Key* and the proximity of their composition suggest (*Christenings,* pp. 26–27), the two works share a common origin; *Christenings* provides an extension of ideas presented in *A Key.*

89.3. *Japhet*] Gen. 9:27.

89.7. *Malachi*] Mal. 1:11.

90.21. *leafe*] an error for page.

91.1. *copious*] Contrary to the stereotyped opinion that the

Indian, like other primitive people, had a brutish language scanty in vocabulary.

93.6. *Salutation*] polite greetings, but by extension good manners generally. See his discussion of Indian manners contrasted to Quaker practices in *Fox,* pp. 308–10, and of true and false civility in *Bloudy Tenent,* p. 225.

94.29. *hard by*] near.

96.9. meane] lowly.

96.11. *Luk.* 6. 22.] "Blessed are ye, when men shall hate you, and when they shall separate you from their company, and shall reproach you, and cast out your name as evil, for the Son of man's sake." The autobiographical allusion seems evident.

96.9–18. Names] In their mutual respect for names, Primitive and Puritan see eye to eye, while Williams's intense concern with diction and Papist formalities makes him doubly appreciative of the "natural" response to names. For a general account of the primitive attitude toward names see James George Frazer, *The New Golden Bough,* ed. Theodor H. Gaster (1959), pp. 187–96. For a further discussion of the subject by Williams see *Fox,* pp. 448–50. And for an excellent example of his onomastic vituperation, consider the following: "It may be wondred why the Popes when made or created by an humane & Devilish *Fiat,* they change their Name, and why the Quakers guided by the same *Hellish Spirit* and *Fancy,* are so dainty and tender about owning their Old names: The Histories say, the *Original* with the Popes was with him who was *Os porce,* or Swines snout, by Name, and was not thought fit being raised so high to bear so low and sordid a Title. If it were so then, yet it is nothing now but their *horrible pride* being in their Conceits so high, so Infallible, so perfect, to scorn to be like other men that are but Hogs Snouts, *&c.*" (*Fox,* pp. 205–206).

98.1. to doe good for evill] "But I say unto you, Love your enemies, bless them that curse you, do good to them that hate you, and pray for them which despitefully use you, and persecute you" (Matt. 5:44). The point being that the natural virtue of the Indian is very close—Williams does not say exactly *how* close—to the Christian virtues which Jesus defines in the Sermon on the Mount.

99.18. *Americans*] Williams's favorite name for the Indians, emphasizing his belief in their native right to the land. In this context, consider the phrasing of the title of the book itself.

100.25. Msíckquatash] In modern use as succotash. "they seldome or never make bread of their Indian corne, but seeth it whole like beanes, eating three or foure cornes with a mouthfull of fish or flesh . . ." (Wood, p. 71).

101.9. *dresse*] prepare.

103.4. rheume] the discharge associated with the common cold.

103.9. Tabacco] *Wuttammâuog,* meaning literally "what they drink." In the earlier seventeenth century both Indian and English spoke of "drinking" tobacco. Wood glosses *Coetop* as "will you drinke Tobaco" (p. 105). *Mourt's Relation* describes Massasoit: "behind his neck hangs a little bag of tobacco, which he drank and gave us to drink . . ." (p. 57).

103.12. *naught*] bad.

103.25–26. sweet meat] confection.

103.29. *snapsacke*] knapsack, duffle-bag.

104.2. Mohowaúgsuck] The name by which the Iroquois, and more specifically their most eastern nation, the *Kayingehaga,* were known to the New England Indians and the English and Dutch settlers. The Dutch form of the word was *Mahakuaas* or *Maquas.* "These are a cruell bloody people, which were wont to come downe upon their poore neighbours with more than bruitish savagenesse, spoyling of their Corne, burning of their houses, slaying men, ravishing women, yea very Caniballs they were, sometimes eating on a man one part after another before his face, and while yet living . . ." (Wood, p. 60).

104.21–22. that call themselves *Christians*] For Williams's definition of the true Christian, see *Christenings,* p. 33, and *The Examiner Defended,* p. 225.

104.27. *wholesome* beare *and* wine] Because he considered them to be gifts of God, the Puritan did not condemn these products of natural fermentation. "Wholesome" defends the point of view as well as it distinguishes beer and wine from less wholesome—distilled—forms of alcoholic beverages.

104.30. part *to*] divide among.

105.1. *rich to his*] God provides the material needs of his elect in abundance.

105.4. Ravens] The prophet Elijah, fleeing from the wicked King Ahab, found himself alone in the wilderness, but God provided for him: "And the ravens brought him bread and flesh in the morning, and bread and flesh in the evening: and he drank of the brook" (1 Kings 17:1–6). Williams implies autobiographical parallels, and aptly describes the dark-skinned Indians in terms of those parallels.

106.10. *without the doores*] outside.

106.13. been fearefull] In a neat bit of advertising for his book Williams suggests that the English in this case had nothing to fear from being hospitable to the Indians, and that this kind of misunderstanding can be avoided through familiarity with the Narragansett language.

106.15. lye abroad] sleep outside.

107.24. a threatning from God] an instance in which the Indian and Puritan agree.

107.25–27. Psal. 119.] This is a paraphrase of verses 62 and 147. *Prevented* is used in the sense "anticipated," thus, "I rose before dawn." The "zealous" David is the speaker of verse 139: "My zeal hath consumed me, because mine enemies have forgotten thy words."

108.1. travailed] travelled, but in the sense of a difficult journey.

108.9. Barke] a small sailing vessel.

108.16. *newes*] the Gospel as "good tidings," related to the latin *evangelium.*

108.18. soft Beds] The equation of the soft bed with the vice of luxury is proverbial. The Indian shares in the Spartan or old Roman virtues by way of his "Boord or Mat."

112.10. 100000] The editor of MHS comments, "*By combining the Indian numbers together, the author continues the enumeration to one hundred thousand.*

But this was probably much further than the natives went themselves" (MHS, 1st ser., III, p. 210). Whether Williams is correct or not, however, his purpose clearly is to demonstrate the capabilities of the natural man who uses grains of corn in his reckonings instead of Europe's artificial aids. The Narragansetts would need a good harvest in the age of the computer.

113.14. *tell*] count, with a pun, announce.

113.17. amazed] hopelessly confused, as lost in a maze.

114.8–9. *Old men*] *Kichize* "characterized old age as entitled to respect, and without associating the idea of decrepitude which belongs to *mattaûntam* and *hômes*" (Trumbull, p. 55, n. 45).

116.20. *vild*] Before 1650 this word was in use with two distinct meanings: 1) wild; 2) vile. Williams uses a word already growing archaic to bridge the gap between the natural wildness of the Indian and the moral wildness (vileness) of the unfaithful Christian.

116.20. Nicolâitans] Nicolas, "a proselyte of Antioch," (Acts 6:5) was reputedly the founder of a heretical sect there. John the Divine's injunction against their beliefs (apparently including communal marriage) is to the point: "But this thou hast, that thou hatest the deeds of the Nicolaitans, which I also hate" (Rev. 2:6).

118.2. Hangings] tapestries, and a pun. The festive atmosphere surrounding public executions in seventeenth-century London is well known.

118.9. *Burching*] birch, birchen.

119.23. dialls] sundials.

121.13. dresse] "wherein they exceede our English husbandmen, keeping it so cleare with their Clamme shell-hooes, as if it were a garden rather than a corne-field, not suffering a choaking weede to advance his audacious head above their infant corne, or an undermining worme to spoile his spurnes" (Wood, p. 100).

121.14–15. labour] work, but a pun related to the childbirth discussion.

123.26. *Stay*] wait.

124.17. *chidden*] reprimanded.

128.31. who love societie] It is worth considering how great a part Williams's observations of Indian society played in his argument for separation of Church and State. "Hence it is that so many glorious and flourishing *Cities* of the World maintaine their *Civill* peace, yea the very *Americans* & wildest Pagans keep the peace of their *Towns* or *Cities;* though neither in one nor the other can any man prove a true *Church* of God in those places, and consequently no spirituall and heavenly peace: The Peace *spirituall* (whether true or false) being of a higher and farre different nature from the Peace of the place or people, being meerly and essentially *civill* and *humane*" (*Bloudy Tenent,* pp. 72–73).

129.13. Mat. 20. 7.] "They say unto him, Because no man hath hired us. He saith unto them, Go ye also into the vineyard. . . ."

130.12. now] An indication that this observation was written after his arrival in London.

130.13. degenerated] "Another complayned of other *Indians* that did revile them, and call them Rogues and such like speeches for cutting off their Locks, and for cutting their Haire in a modest manner as the New-English generally doe; for since the word hath begun to worke upon their hearts, they have discerned the vanitie and pride which they placed in their haire, and have therefore of their owne accord (none speaking to them that we know of) cut it modestly . . ." (*The Day-Breaking,* p. 22).

131.10. the stone] The pain associated with passing a kidney stone through the urinary tract, the most excruciating that the fallen flesh is heir to and without remedy other than nature, was much feared in seventeenth-century England.

131.28. the man] "The last day of the week Wequash the Pequot guide, near hand, slew his countryman Sassawwaw, a Pequot, also Miantunnomue's special darling, and a kind of General of his forces. There was yesterday some tumult about it, because Wequash lives with Canonicus, and Miantunnomu pursues the revenge and justice, &c.

By the way, although Wequash it may be have treacherously almost slain him, yet I see the righteous hand of the Most High Judge, thus: Sassawwaw turned to the Narragansetts and again pretends a return to the Pequots, gets them forth the last year against the Narragansetts and spying advantage, slew the chief Pequot Captain and whips off his head, and so again to the Narragansett: their treacheries exceeds Machiavelli's, &c" (*Letters* pp. 38–39).

132.21. *Salomon*] "How much better is it to get wisdom than gold! and to get understanding rather to be chosen than silver!" (Prov. 16:16).

132.30. *swarfish*] swarthy.

132.31. *Blackamore*] Negro.

133.1. *blacke man*] "Indians . . . who seeing a Black-more in the top of a tree, looking out for his way which he had lost, surmised he was Abamacho or the Devill, deeming all Devils that are blacker than themselves; and being neare to the plantation, they posted to the English, and intreated their aide to conjure this Devill to his owne place, who finding him to be a poore wandring Black-moore, conducted him to his Master" (Wood, p. 81).

133.13. *personall*] personable, physically attractive.

133.18. *Acts* 17.] Williams paraphrases verse 26.

133.19. *Ephes.* 2] verse 3.

134.10. *Athenians*] "(For all the Athenians, and strangers which were there, spent their time in nothing else, but either to tell or to hear some new thing.)" (Acts 17:21).

134.28. emphaticall] A comment upon the oratorical excellence rather than the verbal poverty of the Indian. Another example of the copiousness of their language.

135.22. *Herod*] "And upon a set day, Herod, arrayed in royal apparel, sat upon his throne, and made an oration unto them. And the people gave a shout, saying, It is the voice of a god, and not of a man. And immediately the angel of the Lord smote him . . ." (Acts 12:21–23).

136.22.–137.4. *Obs.* faithfulnesse] Williams has altered the actual experience: "having got Canonicus and Miantunnomu with their council together, I acquainted them faithfully with the contents of your letter, both grievances and threatnings; and to demonstrate, I produced the copy of the league, (which Mr. Vane sent me,) and with breaking of a straw in two or three places, I showed them what they had done. In some their answer was, that they thought they should prove themselves honest and faithful, when Mr. Governor understood their answers; and that (although they would not contend with their friends) yet they could relate many particulars, wherein the English had broken (since these wars) their promises, &c." (*Letters,* pp. 55–56).

137.18. for believing or obeying] "for light of Nature leadeth men to heare that onely which Nature conceiveth to be good for it, and therefore not to heare a Messenger, Minister or Preacher, whom *conscience* perswades is a false *messenger* or *deceiver,* and comes to deceive my soule, as Millions of men and women in their severall respective *religions* and *consciences* are so perswaded, conceiving their owne to be true. . . . And however they affirme that persons are not to be compelled to be *members* of *Churches,* nor the Church compelled to receive any: Yet if persons be compelled to forsake their Religion which their hearts cleave to, and to come to *Church,* to the *worship* of the *Word, Prayers, Psalmes,* and *Contributions,* and this all their dayes: I aske whether this be not this peoples Religion, unto which submitting, they shall be quiet all their dayes, without the inforcing them to the practice of any other Religion? And if this bee not so, then I aske, Will it not inevitably follow, that they (not onely permit, but) enforce people to bee of no Religion at all, all their dayes? This toleration of Religion, or rather irreligious *compulsion,* is above all *tolerations* monstrous, to wit, to compell men to bee of no *Religion* all their dayes. I desire all men and these worthy *Authors* of this Modell, to lay their hands upon their heart, and to consider whether this *compulsion* of men to heare the

Word, (as they say) whether it carries men, to wit, to be of no *Religion* all their dayes, worse then the very Indians, who dare not live without *Religion* according as they are perswaded" (*Bloudy Tenent,* pp. 287–90).

137.30. sword-men] Trumbull quotes from Morton's *New England Canaan:* "The Salvages of the Massachusets . . . did call the English planters *Wotawquenange* which in their language signifieth *stabbers* or Cut-throats. . . . A Southerly Indian, that understood English well . . . callinge us by the name of *Wotoquansawge,* what that doth signifie, hee said hee was not able by any demonstration to expresse." Trumbull suggests that Morton "queerly confounds" the two names. But the apparent ambiguity is surely resolved when one finds Williams pointing out that the Indians call all the "English Swine" cutthroats (Trumbull, p. 86, n. 125, and below, 182.16).

138.7. you want *firing*] Of biographical interest is Williams's arrival in England in the midst of the great coal and wood shortage which resulted from the occupation of Newcastle by anti-Parliament forces (see Winslow, pp. 185–86).

138.18. *hollow*] shout.

140.2. and the *English* also] The quality which enabled the author to act as ambassador to both the English and the Indian was his refusal to compromise in matters of principle, ironically the very quality which led to his banishment: "I abhor most of their customs; I know they are barbarous. I respect not one party more than the other, but I desire to witness truth; and as I desire to witness against oppression, so, also, against the slighting of civil, yea, of barbarous order and government, as respecting every shadow of God's gracious appointments" (*Letters,* p. 327).

142.21. pleased *God* to appoint] An emphasis upon both the naturalness and rightness of primitive response to the fact of creation: "So that I Affirm, that the *two great Lights* of *Heaven,* the *Sun* and *Moon,* and all the *lesser Lights* the *Stars* are *Words* and *Preachings,* and *preachers of God to us:* Every wind and Cloud, and drop of Rain and Hail, every Flake of Snow, every Leaf, every Grass, every drop of water in the Ocean, and Rivers, yea, every Grain of Corn, and Sand on the Shore, is a Voice or word and witness of God unto us" (*Fox,* p. 445).

146.10. righteous *sentence*] The inverted word order may be confusing. Read "*sentence* is righteous."

146.14. Sun] The standard pun on Son.

150.11. Refuges] In his recommended list of measures to be taken before the attack on the Pequots, Williams includes the following: "That the assault would be in the night, when they are commonly more secure and at home, by which advantage the English, being armed, may enter the houses and do what execution they please. That before the assault be given, an ambush be laid behind them, between them and the swamp, to prevent their flight, &c." (*Letters,* p. 18).

151.11. Winter night) The most memorable being, of course, those endured during his "fourteen weeks" flight from Salem in the winter of 1635–36: "When I was unkindly and unchristianly, as I believe, driven from my house and land and wife and children, (in the midst of a New England winter, now about thirty-five years past,) at Salem, that ever honored Governor, Mr. Winthrop, privately wrote to me to steer my course to Narragansett Bay and Indians, for many high and heavenly and public ends, encouraging me, from the freeness of the place from any English claims or patents. I took his prudent motion as a hint and voice from God, and waving all other thoughts and motions, I steered my course from Salem (though in winter snow, which I feel yet) unto these parts, wherein I may say Peniel, that is, I have seen the face of God" (*Letters,* p. 335).

152.3. to feare and goe back] "I went up to Connecticut with Miantunnomu, who had a guard of upwards of one hundred and fifty men, and many Sachems, and his wife and children with him. By the way (lodging from his house three nights in the woods) we met divers Narragansett men complaining of robbery and violence, which they had sustained from the

Pequots and Mohegans in their travel from Connecticut; as also some of the Wunnashowatuckoogs (subject to Canonicus) came to us and advertised, that two days before, about six hundred and sixty Pequots, Mohegans and their confederates had robbed them, and spoiled about twenty-three fields of corn, and rifled four Narragansett men amongst them; as also that they lay in way and wait to stop Miantunnomue's passage to Connecticut, and divers of them threatened to boil him in the kettle.

These tidings being many ways confirmed, my company, Mr. Scott (a Suffolk man) and Mr. Cope, advised our stop and turn back; unto which I also advised the whole company, to prevent bloodshed, resolving to get up to Connecticut by water, hoping there to stop such courses. But Miantunnomu and his council resolved (being then about fifty miles, half-way, on our journey) that not a man should turn back, resolving rather all to die, keeping strict watch by night, and in dangerous places a guard by day about the Sachems, Miantunnomu and his wife, who kept the path, myself and company always first, and on either side of the path forty or fifty men to prevent sudden surprisals. This was their Indian march" (*Letters,* pp. 120–21).

152.25. not to exceed] A lesson in natural justice which has a parallel in Luke 6:36–38: "For with the same measure that ye mete withal it shall be measured to you again."

156.29. *Job.* 35.] "But none saith, Where is God my maker, who giveth songs in the night" (verse 10).

157.10. there . . . here] Again, the place of writing would appear to be England, even though one would not deny the author license for the sake of art.

157.27. *a cold*] cold. See "Tom's a-cold," *King Lear,* 3. 4. 80.

158.27. That Judgment] "O ye hypocrites, ye can discern the face of the sky; but can ye not discern the signs of the times?" (Matt. 16:3).

159.6. Sodome] The city destroyed by God with its neighbor, Gomorrah. The archetypal example of communal sin and divine vengeance. Williams paraphrases Gen. 19:23–28.

159.13. *That* Rocke] "And did all drink the same spiritual drink; for they drank of that spiritual Rock that followed them: and that Rock was Christ" (1 Cor. 10:4).

160.9. Cardinall] most important.

161.13. *Eccles.* 1. 6.] In announcing that "all is vanity" the Preacher uses the wind as a prime example: "The wind goeth toward the south, and turneth about unto the north; it whirleth about continually, and the wind returneth again according to his circuits."

161.31. the wings of those *Winds*] "And he rode upon a cherub, and did fly: yea, he did fly upon the wings of the wind" (Psalms 18:10).

163.14. *Heath-cocks*] Trumbull quotes from Nuttall's *Ornithology:* "formerly . . . so common on the ancient bushy site of the city of Boston, that laboring people or servants stipulated with their employers, not to have the Heath-Hen brought to table oftener than a few times in the week" (Trumbull, p. 113, n. 184). "Heathcockes, and Partridges be common; he that is a husband, and will be stirring betime, may kill halfe a dozen in a morning" (Wood, p. 31).

163.20. *Matth.* 13.] verse 4: "And when he sowed, some seeds fell by the wayside, and the fowls came and devoured them up."

163.21. mysticall] supernatural, symbolic.

164.5. the Crow] The crow seems here to be described as a totemic bird.

164.16. take great pains] are very careful in stalking.

164.16. any] as many as possible.

164.31. store] quantity.

165.18–23. Princelike courage] the Kingbird (?).

165.31. singing Birds] For the austere Puritan, song birds have a good deal less utility than food birds and so are given short shrift.

165.32–33. *Martins* vineyard] Now known as Martha's Vineyard, an island in Massachusetts Bay near Nantucket.

169.5. *Barbary*] barberry.

169.7. *Sasèmineash*] probably the cranberry.

169.19. *Hurtle-berries*] sometimes known as whortleberries.

170.17. barne] put into barns, granaries.

170.30–31. *Concordiâ. . . .*] Sallust, *Jug.*, X.

172.4. *Barnes*] W. D. Ely (*A Keyhole for Roger Williams' Key,* Providence, 1892) argues with much erudition and eloquence that in both 172.4 and 172.5 the word should be *beanes.* Partly for linguistic reasons and partly for historic, he demonstrates the importance of beans in the seventeenth-century New England economy, and suggests that Williams could not have overlooked so significant a commodity. But beginning with 166.17 of chapter XV and running through this chapter is the biblical progression of sowing, reaping, and gathering into barns. One concludes, in disagreement with Ely, that here is a clear case in which the author allows art to supersede nature.

172.12. witness] A paraphrase of Acts 14:17, in which Williams asserts the priority of the natural world as a testament to the Creator. All men have access to the Book of the Creatures, even if some have arbitrarily been denied the Word.

172.20. *Scripture*] Gen. 1:28.

173.22. *Manittóoes*] Without necessarily deifying the animal, the Narragansetts thus paid respect to the *mana* they felt in him. Again the totemic idea which Williams could not have understood.

173.28. *Ockqutchaun*] the groundhog or woodchuck (Trumbull, p. 128, n. 221).

174.7. some Deitie] In one of the Indian traditions concerning the Deluge, the hare has the part assigned by Genesis to the dove. According to Heckwelder the Delaware and Mohican Indians would not eat rabbit or groundhog on the grounds that "they did not know but that they might be *related* to them" (Trumbull, p. 128, n. 223).

174.31. many reports] See Trumbull, p. 129, n. 229; and Wood, p. 96.

180.7. Qunnamáug] long fish.

180.10. Aumsûog] alewives.

180.12. Missúckeke] striped bass.

180.23. harping Iron] harpoon.

181.5. Osacóntuck] Trumbull conjectures that this fish is either the pollack, the whiting, or the cusk (Trumbull, p. 137, n. 247).

181.7. Mishcùp] scup or porgy.

181.18. *Whales*] The Narragansett word comes from a root meaning "he blows."

182.5. Sickìssuog] the long clam. The word has its root in a word meaning "spittle." "When the tide ebs and flowes, a man running over these Clamm bankes will presently be made all wet, by their spouting of water out of those small holes. . ." (Wood, p. 37).

182.17. Poquaûhock] the round clam or quahaug.

183.22. *winter fish*] frost fish or "Tom Cod."

183.26. Qunôsuog] pickerel or long nose.

184.6. Habacuck] "and holdest thy tongue when the wicked devoureth the man that is more righteous than he? And makest men as the fishes of the sea, as the creeping things, that have no ruler over them?" (1:13–14) "*Habacucks* Fishes keep their constant bloody game of *Persecutions* in the Worlds mighty *Ocean;* the greater taking, plundring, swallowing up the lesser: O happy he whose portion is the *God* of *Iacob!* who hath nothing to lose under the *Sun,* but hath a *State,* a *House,* an *Inheritance,* a *Name,* a *Crowne,* a *Life,* past all the *Plunderers, Ravishers, Murtherers* reach and furie!" (*Bloudy Tenent,* p. 424).

184.12. *earthie element*] Of the four elements—earth, air, fire, and water—the fish was of course designed to live in water as its element and could not survive in any of the others. The implication is that man's element is earth.

185.10. a little Apron] Adam and Eve, after the fall and their concomitant loss of innocence, "sewed fig leaves together, and made themselves aprons" (Gen. 3:7). The Geneva Bible, which Williams like Milton seems to have preferred to the King James version, prints "breeches" for aprons.

186.17–18. . . . *suam*] "*nunc in pellicula, cerdo, tenere, tua*" (Martial, *Epig.* 3. 16). Williams was obviously quoting from memory.

186.19. skin] the skin in which he was born; pun, the beast's skin he wears.

187.15–23. English clothes] In a letter to Winthrop of July 1654, Williams says, "I have long had scruples of selling the natives aught but what may bring or tend to civilizing; I therefore neither brought, nor shall sell them, loose coats nor breeches" (*Letters,* p. 261).

188.3. *tush*] scoff, O.E.D. But Williams seems to be employing it in the sense "to make a fuss."

188.10–13. *Exod.* 32.] "And when Moses saw that the people were naked, (for Aaron had made them naked unto their shame among their enemies,)" verse 25.

189.3. Manìt] "may be nearly translated by 'that which surpasses,' or 'that which is extraordinary' " (Trumbull, p. 147, n. 268).

189.7. *Heb.* 11. 6.] "But without faith it is impossible to please him: for he that cometh to God must believe that he is, and that he is a rewarder of them that diligently seek him."

190.2. thirty seven] "I find what I could never hear before, that they have plenty of Gods or divine powers: the Sun, Moon, Fire, Water, Snow, Earth, the Deer, the Bear, &c., are divine powers. I brought home lately from the Narragansetts the names of thirty-eight of their Gods, all they could remember, and had I not with fear and caution withdrew, they would have fallen to worship, O God, (as they speak) one day in seven, but I hope the time is not long that some shall truely bless the God of Heaven that ever they saw the face of English men" (*Letters,* p. 88).

190.11. *house God*] Similar, as Williams suggests, to the Roman Catholic church's patron saints, but by implication identical to the pre-Christian Roman *lares* and *penates*.

190.20. they suffered Death] For a complete account of the affair, see Bradford, pp. 299–301.

191.11. . . . *Deum*] Cf. Psalm 148.

191.22. They are Gods] "The common use by the Indians of these words, and their application, by 'general custom,' to every thing excellent, or extra-ordinary, hardly authorize the inference which Mr. Williams drew, of belief in an omnipresent Deity" (Trumbull, p. 151, n. 274). Needless to say, Trumbull is perfectly correct in his assessment of Roger Williams's bias.

192.20. *Ephes.* 5. 11.] "And have no fellowship with the unfruitful works of darkness, but rather reprove them."

193.15–19. plausible Earthly Arguments] Arguments appropriate only to temporal and material issues and arguments which appeal to man's "earthly" nature. While the attack is specifically upon Catholic practices, all "hireling ministers" are included (see *The Hireling Ministry*, p. 164).

193.24. not to disturb] "Againe, that no persons *Papists, Jewes, Turkes*, or *Indians* be disturbed at their *worship*, (a thing which the very *Indians* abhor to practice toward any.)" (*Bloudy Tenent*, p. 252).

193.33. *Michachunck*] "Possibly, Mr. Williams was mistaken as to the affinity of this word with one 'signifying a looking glass' " (Trumbull, p. 154, n. 282).

195.19. *Five thousand yeers ago*] It is difficult to conclude whether Williams was a fundamentalist who could date the creation by means of Old Testament genealogy from Adam down, or a sophisticated thinker accommodating himself to the primitive mind.

197.11. they have it from their Fathers] The Indian idea of the creation differs from the Genesis story essentially in the relative fallibility of Kautantowit. Jehovah destroyed the first men because they became imperfect, the Indian god because he himself erred in his creative act.

197.20. Will you lie Englishman] "Sir, concerning your intended meeting for reconciling of these natives our friends, and dividing of the Pequots our enemies, I have engaged your name, and mine own; and if no course be taken, the name of that God of Truth whom we all profess to honor will suffer not a little, it being an ordinary and common thing with our neighbors, if they apprehend any show of breach of promise in myself, thus to object: do you know God, and will you lie? &c . . . . Yet surely, amongst the barbarians, (the highest in the world,) I would rather lose my head than so practice, because I judge it my duty to set them better copies, and should sin against mine own persuasions and resolutions," (*Letters*, pp. 92, 104).

197.29–32. . . . *up to Heaven*] Trumbull provides the following beautiful literal translation of these lines: "All this one God they-who-know, this God they-who-love and they-who-fear, to heaven they-go, forever they-sweet-minded-are (*weeteantámwock*), of-him God in-his-house" (Trumbull, p. 158, n. 288).

199.1. may well know more] For Williams, conversion must be preceded by voluntary conviction, and the only way to convince the Indian is by recourse to experience and reason: "When we deal with *Indians* about *Religion,* our work is to prove unto them by Reason, that the *Bible* is *Gods Word,* for by Nature they are much affected with a kind of Deity to be in Writing: That all their Revelations, and Visions, and Dreams (in which the Devil wonderfully abuseth them) are False and Cheating. That this Scripture or Writing we pretend to, is from God by their own experience, because it agrees with their own Consciences, reproving them for those sins their Souls say they are guilty of: That the terrible Majesty of Gods Justice in punishing Sinners so shines in it, and also his infinite goodness and mercy in finding out such a way of Mediation, and such a Mediator that their Souls cannot but adore Infinite Justice and Mercy in it" (*Fox,* p. 447).

199.5. easily have brought the Countrey to] "for our *New-england* parts, I can speake uprightly and confidently, I know it to have been easie for my selfe, long ere this, to have brought many thousands of these Natives, yea the whole country, to a far greater Antichristian conversion then ever was yet heard of in *America.* I have reported something in the Chapter of their Religion, how readily I could have brought the whole Country to have observed one day in seven; I adde to have received a *Baptisme* (or washing) though it were in *Rivers* (as the first *Christians* and the Lord *Jesus* himselfe did) to have come to a *stated Church meeting,* maintained priests and formes of prayer, and a whole forme of *Antichristian* worship in life and death. Let none wonder at this, for *plausible perswasions* in the mouths of those whom naturall men esteem and love: for the power of prevailing forces and armies hath done this in all the *Nations* (as men speake) of *Christendome.* Yea what lamentable experience have we of the *Turnings* and *Turnings* of the *body* of this Land in point of Religion in few yeares?" (*Christenings*, p. 36).

199.9. I *Thes.* 1. 9.] "For they themselves show of us what manner of entering in we had unto you, and how ye turned to God from idols to serve the living and true God."

199.21. *Heb.* 6. 2.] An allusion which relates to Williams's idea of true conversion. He paraphrases verses 1–6 in which the suggestion is made that an imperfect conversion—one according to forms only—is worse than no conversion at all: "Therefore leaving the principles of the doctrine of Christ, let us go on unto perfection; not laying again the foundation of repentance from dead works, and of faith toward God, Of the doctrine of baptisms, and of laying on of hands, and of resurrection of the dead, and of eternal judgment. And this will we do, if God permit. For it is impossible for those who were once enlightened, and have tasted of the heavenly gift, and were made partakers of the Holy Ghost, And have tasted the good word of God, and the powers of the world to come, If they shall fall away, to renew them again unto repentance; seeing they crucify to themselves the Son of God afresh, and put him to an open shame."

199.31–32. *ere long be burnt*] While Williams is not specifically a chiliast, he does, however, frequently view the contemporary situation in America and England from the apocalyptic point of vantage: "there will be new Heavens and a new Earth shortly but no more Sea. (Rev. 21.2.) the most holy God be pleased to make us willing now to bear the tossings, dangers and calamities of this sea, and to seal up to use upon his own grounds, a great lot in the glorious state approaching" (*Letters*, p. 93). See also the concluding poem of *A Key*.

200.9–10. have created out of the nothing] Compare Milton:

Nor had they yet among the Sons of *Eve*
Got them new Names, til wandring ore the Earth,
Through Gods high sufferance for the tryal of man,
By falsities and lyes the greatest part
Of Mankind they corrupted to forsake

God thir Creator, and th' invisible
Glory of him that made them, to transform
Oft to the Image of a Brute, adorn'd
With gay Religions full of Pomp and Gold,
And Devils to adore for Deities:

[*Paradise Lost* 1. 364–74]

200.14. 2. Thes. 1. 8.] "In flaming fire taking vengeance on them that know not God, and that obey not the gospel of our Lord Jesus Christ."

200.23. *where shall stand the Christian false?*] "We knew that the Sons of Men were justly divided all the world over into two Sorts, First, The wild and Pagan, whome God hath permitted to run about the world as wild Beasts all this great fourth Part of the World, and in some of the other three.

They acknowledge a great supream God and Deity, Maker of all things, yet they acknowledge (as other famous *Civilized Nations* formerly have done) that there be many other Petty-Gods and Deityes in Heaven and Earth, yea within their own Bodies, yea whatever is extraordinary, excellent or strange to them, they are presently apt to ascribe a Deity unto it, though it be but *Beast, Fowle &c.* and say it is a *God.* It is commonly known that as their garments hang loose about their Bodyes, so hangs their *Religion* about their Souls: So that (to my knowledge) they are so far from hindring any to come to God, that when they have seen the grave and solemn *Worship* of the *English,* they have often said of themselves and their own, that they are all one *Dogs* in comparison of the *English.*

The second sort of men are the *Civill* brought to *Cloaths,* to *Lawes &c.* from *Barbarisme:* these also the infinite Wisdome of God have pleased to leave to variety of wayes of *Worshipping* the *Heavenly Majesty.*

Amongst others we find four most known and eminent,

First, The *Jewish Worship* famous from Gods own appointment by *Moses &c.* 2. The *Turkish,* famous for spreading from *Mahomet* to most of thirteen parts of thirty in the World.

3. The *Popish,* famous for spreading over *Europe* and other western parts of the world. 4. The *Protestant* famous for so wonderfull a *Revolt* and Seperation from the Popish. All these four profess one God and supream *Deity:* but they differ in two things, 1. In the *Prophet* or Meanes by whome God speaks to man; the *Jews* cry up *Moses,* the *Turks Mahomet,* the *Papists* the *Pope,* the *Protestants Christ Jesus* in the Scriptures . . ." (*Fox,* pp. 258–59).

202.1. *subject*] "I have heard this greatly questioned, and, indeed, I question whether any Indians in this country, remaining barbarous and pagan, may with truth or honor be called the English subjects" (*Letters,* pp. 275–76).

202.16–17. absolute Monarchie] In a letter of 1656, addressed to the General Court of Massachusetts, Williams speaks to the issue: "And that your wisdom may see just grounds for such your willingness, be pleased to be informed of a reality of a solemn covenant between this town of Warwick and Pumham, unto which, notwithstanding that he pleads his being drawn to it by the awe of his superior Sachems, yet I humbly offer that what was done, was according to the law and tenor of the natives, (I take it) in all New England and America, viz.: that the inferior Sachems and subjects shall plant and remove at the pleasure of the highest and supreme Sachems, and I humbly conceive that it pleaseth the Most High and Only Wise to make use of such a bond of authority over them, without which, they could not long subsist in human society, in this wild condition wherein they are" (*Letters,* pp. 300–01).

202.28. *naught*] an evil man.

202.31. cukkúmmoot] In 1675, Williams wrote Governor Leverett to report a conversation of his with a sachem in which he attempted to persuade him not to join King Philip in his war on the English: "I told the young prince . . . all their war is commootin; they have commootined our houses, our cattle, our heads, &c., and that not by their artillery but our weapons" (*Letters,* p. 375).

203.12. it hardens] Jehovah is recorded frequently to have

hardened the hearts of the reprobate, thus effectually preventing their conversion. The most important instance for Williams's purposes occurs in Exod. 14:14: "And I will harden Pharaoh's heart, and he shall follow after them; and I will be honored upon Pharaoh, and upon all his host; that the Egyptians may know that I am the Lord. And they did so." Williams relies upon the standard Puritan idea that they were the latter-day Chosen People fleeing from Egypt (England) into the Promised Land (America). Compare Milton:

This my long sufferance and my day of grace
They who neglect and scorn, shall never taste;
But hard be hard'n'd, blind be blinded more,
That they may stumble on, and deeper fall;
And none but such from mercy I exclude.

[*Paradise Lost* 3. 198–202]

204.15. . . . *Thefts*] This is central to Williams's argument concerning the limits of civil enforcement of the decalogue. "First, There are no generations of men, nor never were in the world, but by the dark light of nature, have condemned these four sins, *viz. Murther, Adultery, Theft, Lying,* as inconsistent to the converse of man with man: But all the Generation and Nations of men, have most constantly differed, and varied into many thousand differences about the true *God,* and his waies of worship, &c" (*The Examiner Defended,* p. 263).

204.18. *leese*] lose.

207.4. they perish wonderfully] "wonderfully" here, of course, signifying "at an amazing rate." To discover how different from common opinion Williams's attitude was—at least with regard to the Narragansetts—one has only to read the following representative reaction to visitation of the plague upon the New England Indian: "Thus farre hath the good hand of God favoured our beginnings; See whether he hath not engaged us to wait still upon his goodnesse for the future by such further remarkable passages of his providence to our plantation in such things as these:

1. In sweeping away great multitudes of the natives by the small-pox, a little before we went thither, that

he might make room for us there" (*First Fruits,* p. 246). This was published the same year as *A Key.* In 1637, Williams writes Winthrop about a conversation he has had with Canounicus about the plague: "At my first coming to them Canonicus (*morosus aeque ac barbarex senex*) was very sour, and accused the English and myself for sending the plague amongst them, and threatening to kill him especially.

Such tidings (it seems) were lately brought to his ears by some of his flatterers and our ill-willers. I discerned cause of bestirring myself, and staid the longer, and at last (through the mercy of the Most High) I not only sweetened his spirit, but possessed him, that the plague and other sicknesses were alone in the hand of the one God, who made him and us, who being displeased with the English for lying, stealing, idleness and uncleanness, (the natives' epidemical sins,) smote many thousands of us ourselves with general and late mortalities" (*Letters,* pp. 16–17).

207.6. *Travell*] childbirth, with its connotation of pain, travail. The dialogue which follows is a graphic indication of the speedy ease of delivery which Williams discusses in the observation below.

213.4. hardened to a britle temper] An error of the author or of his printer. The purpose of tempering metal is to make it more elastic, and consequently less brittle.

214.3–4. Aprons (or small breeches)] A bow to Indian fashion, to the Geneva Bible, and by way of this translation an emphasis upon the Adamic condition of the Indian.

214.8. their Maker] their Creator, and by extending the monetary metaphor which develops into an elaborate pun in chapter XXV, he who gives value to his creation by stamping his seal upon it.

215.13. *Chapmen*] traders.

216.9. sad coulour] dark.

216.24. *rent*] ripped. "and the veil of the temple was rent in the midst" (Luke 23:45).

217.5. counterfeit] Trumbull quotes from Josselyn's *Voyages* about the Indian making their bead money "out of certain shells, so cunning that neither *Jew* nor *Devil* can counterfeit" (Trumbull, p. 181, n. 322).

217.8–9. cautelous] cunning.

218.1. beate all markets] shop around carefully.

218.9. *spans*] A span is the distance between the tip of the thumb and the tip of the little finger, conventionally taken as nine inches.

218.25. haply] perhaps.

218.27. *Tell*] count.

219.17. *serve me so*] treat me in this manner.

222.24. Owe no thing] Romans 13:8.

222.28. *such* English *then*] Although the attack is a general one, there may well be a specific target: "One kindness (yet according to true justice) let me be bold to request. I have not yet got a penny of those two unfaithful ones, James and Thomas Haukins, of Boston, concerning whom myself and wife have formerly troubled you." And, most significantly, Williams continues by reminding John Winthrop of his role of Elijah: "yet I have not wanted, through his love that feeds the ravens, &c" (*Letters,* p. 15).

224.10. drive the woods] beat the thickets and drive the game in an agreed direction.

225.31. . . . *sumus?*] From Martial, *Epigrams* 13.94. Williams elsewhere uses this epigram to conclude the following passage: "On the other side by that great red *Dragon,* whose bloudie *Followers,* Devils and men of all sorts and Nations, but especially the *Roman* bloudie *Emperor,* and *Roman Popes* (with *Lyon*-like Furie, and *Fox*-like craft) have suck'd the *Bloud* and broke the *Bones,* and devoured the *Flesh* of so many hundred thousand, thousands of the *King* or *Kings* his spiritual *Hinds* and *Roes* in this their bloudie hunting. So that aptly (I had almost said *Prophetically*) wrote one of their own *Roman Poets* of the lamentable condition of the *harmlesse Deer* above other Creatures . . ." (*Bloody Tenent,* p. 34).

227.31. *Prov.* 25.] The author appears to be paraphrasing several verses together here, but especially 11:27, "He that diligently seeketh good procureth favor," and 20:4, "The sluggard will not plow by reason of the cold; therefore shall he beg in harvest, and have nothing," adapting both to the Indian context (see also *Experiments,* pp. 69–70).

229.7. *Rushes*] "They have two sorts of games, one called Puim, the other Hubbub, not much unlike Cards and Dice, being no other than Lotterie. Puim is 50. or 60. small Bents of a foote long which they divide to the number of their gamesters, shuffling them first betweene the palmes of their hands; he that hath more than his fellow is so much the forwarder in his game: many other strange whimseyes be in this game; which would be too long to commit to paper" (Wood, p. 90).

229.10. sweating] "Hubbub is five small Bones in a small smooth Tray, the bones bee like a Die, but something flatter, blacke on the one side and white on the other, which they place on the ground, against which violently thumping the platter, the bones mount changing colours with the windy whisking of their hands too and fro; which action in that sport they much use, smiting themselves on the breast, and thighs, crying out, Hub, Hub, Hub; they may be heard play at this game a quarter of a mile off" (Wood, p. 90).

229.12. vanities] profane activities which at best waste time.

229.31. Thunderbolt] "That which is by some called the rain-stone or thunder-bolt, was by the antients termed *Ceraunia* . . . . Bootius (*de Gemmis,* lib. 2, cap. 261) reports that many persons worthy of credit, affirmed that when houses or trees had been broken with the thunder, they did by digging find such stones in the places where the stroke was given. Nevertheless, that fulminous stones or thunderbolts do always descend out of the clouds, when such breaches are made by the lightning, is (as I said) a vulgar error" (*Remarkable Providences* pp. 80–81).

One can only conjecture about Williams's awareness of the position of the thunderbolt in Greek mythology, but the parallel to the Narragansett *Manitoo* is most interesting: "The thunderbolt was to the primitive Greek not the symbol or attribute of the god, but itself the divine thing, the embodiment and vehicle of the god." (See Jane Ellen Harrison, *Themis,* pp. 59–62).

230.8. *I will burne my Rushes*] An echo of Faustus's "I'll burn my books!"? (Marlowe, *The Tragical History of the Life and Death of Doctor Faustus* 5.2., 190).

230.20–21. foot-ball playing] "For their sports of activitie they have commonly but three or foure; as footeball, shooting, running and swimming: when they play country against country, there are rich Goales, all behung with Wampompeage, Mowhackies, Beaver skins, and black Otter skinnes. It would exceede the beleefe of many to relate the worth of one Goale, wherefore it shall be namelesse. Their Goales be a mile long placed on the sands, which are as even as a board; their ball is no bigger than a hand-ball, which sometimes they mount in the Aire with their naked feete, sometimes it is swayed by the multitude . . ." (Wood, pp. 90–91).

230.31. Embleme] In the poem which concludes this chapter Williams develops the emblematic aspects of man's fondness for gambling.

231.1. *Keesaqúnnamun*] "Perhaps from *Kesuckquànd,* the Sun God,—or from *kesukun* (which has the same radical,) 'it is ripe, mature.'—'A kind of solemn public meeting,' with a 'mixture of devotion and sports,' is not a bad description of an old-fashioned 'Thanksgiving Day,'—though not of the strictest puritan type" (Trumbull, p. 197, n. 349).

231.10. danceth] It is recorded with approbation that David danced (2 Sam. 6:14), but he danced "before the Lord," while the Indian dances "in the sight of all the rest," which is clearly a vanity.

231.22. Jewell] Recall here, as at 232.5, Othello's "one whose hand,/(Like the base Indian) threw a pearl away /Richer than all his tribe" (5.2., 346–48).

231.25. post over] hurry through. Cf. Milton's Sonnet XIX: "And post o're Land and Ocean without rest."

232.4. Phil. 3. 8.] ". . . I have suffered the loss of all things, and do count them but dung, that I may win Christ."

233.6. *Northern storme of warre*] The most violent New England storms come from the north, and so violence of war. And in the summer of 1643 the Civil War was raging in the north of England.

233.7. wittily] aptly.

233.8. Lord Jesus chide] Matt. 8.26.

234.12. gallant] fashionably outfitted, perhaps directed at the Cavaliers.

234.23. the *French*] "These Indians are the more insolent, by reason they have guns which they dayly trade for with the French, (who will sell his eyes as they say, for beaver) . . ." (Wood, p. 63).

235.5. *To contribute*] i.e., to contribute men and supplies.

235.10. a great Prince] See XI, 152. 1–3.

235.13. by course] in periodic watches.

233.16. Life-guard] A picked body of soldiers whose duty it was to protect the king, particularly in battle.

235.16. compassed] surrounded.

235.18. patheticall] emotional.

236.8. mocking] the formally conceived and deliberately hurled taunts of the foremost heroes on each side, in a tradition which Williams would recognize as going back to the *Iliad* among the Greeks and to the story of David and Goliath (1 Sam. 17) in the Old Testament.

236.32. fired] set afire.

237.15. Pequttôog] In translating the Indian word literally as "The Destroyers are destroyed," Trumbull (p. 203, n. 360) underplays the autobiographical nature of Williams's rather exciting narrative of the Pequot War contained in this chapter. The modern reader may be somewhat confused that a God-fearing Christian like Williams could also be completely bloodthirsty on occasion, but our Puritan forebears were a hard lot: "In giving us such peace and freedome from enemies, when almost all the world is on a fire that (excepting that short trouble with the Pequits) we never heard of any sound of warres to this day. And in that warre which we made against them God's hand from heaven was so manifested, that a very few of our men, in a short time, pursued through the wildernesse, slew and took prisoners about 1400 of them, even all they could find, to the great terrour and amazement of all the Indians to this day: So that the name of the Pequits (as of *Amaleck*) is blotted out from under heaven, there being not one that is, or (at least) dare call himself a Pequit" (*First Fruits,* p. 246).

237.20–30. farre lesse bloudy] The attitude seems to have changed from the early part of the book. This may be partly due to Williams's own involvement in this particular war, and partly to the artistic exigencies of the book, which seem to demand a development of attitude. This is the way in which Ola Winslow describes a battle in which an Indian disastrously imitated the white man's military ways: "The two armies, totalling some fifteen hundred Indians, met on Sachem's Plain. Miantunomi, clad in medieval armor, unwisely lent him by Samuel Gorton, was called out in the open for a personal interview with Uncas. In the sight of both armies, Uncas, having the smaller force, challenged Miantunomi to single combat, but Miantunomi refused, giving the expected answer, 'My men came to fight, and they shall fight.' At this point, by pre-arrangement with his chieftains, Uncas threw himself on the ground, and the Mohegans fell upon the Narragansetts, who though twice their number, were so taken by surprise that they fled in confusion. Miantunomi, hampered by the armor, never meant for an Indian, was captured, his own brother was killed, two of Canonicus' sons were wounded, thirty of his best warriors killed, with the remainder of his army put to confused flight" (Winslow, pp. 212–13). The armor-burdened Indian Sachem would later insist on the value of "leaping and dancing" on the battlefield.

238.1. *stout*] brave.

239.4. *Sure 'tis a Mystery!*] (See *The Hireling Ministry,* pp. 158–59).

239.5–7. *Rev.* 2. 6.] An error for 6:4.

240.16. Mëtewis] identified by Trumbull as plumbago or graphite.

241.24. *Fained Inventions*] vain products of the imagination.

242.20. bleeding case] dire straits.

242.26. *Bind*] bandage.

243.8–9. drop of other comfort] Although he was violently opposed to the fire water methods of either trading or conversion, Williams sympathized with the Indians' lack of any medicinal alcohol. Consequently, although he was undoubtedly an instigator of the prohibition law of Rhode Island, he later approached the colony for "leave to sell a little wine or stronge water to some natives in their sickness" (*Letters,* p. 180, n. 4; see also p. 333).

243.17. Visit of Friends] One of the corporal works of mercy of which natural man is capable, and for the performance of which Jesus promises salvation (Matt. 25:34–40).

243.22. so terrible] For a most graphic description of the horrors of smallpox among the Indians, see Bradford, pp. 270–71.

243.29. *the Pox*] smallpox, as opposed to the Great Pox, or syphilis.

244.27. the *French* disease] syphilis. The Indians had their guns from the French as well. The French returned the compliment by naming it the English disease, while by a historical irony it may be that both races continued to contract the disease from the Indian.

244.34. *Flixe*] flux, dysentery.

245.7. *Simon Magus*] The sorcerer turned Christian (Acts 8), who attempted to buy the Apostles' power to cure through the Holy Ghost, and for which he was rebuked by Peter. The sin of trafficking in sacred things is for this reason called "simony."

245.20. *Plaister*] plaster.

245.21. *physicke*] medicinal.

245.31. to try and arraigne] Affliction was regarded as the constant factor in the human condition as a result of the fall. But it could be demonstrated from the case of Job that affliction was probative as well as punitive, and so the doctrine of the patient undergoing of affliction is central to any theologically oriented discussion of suffering in the seventeenth century. See, for example, Milton's Sonnet XIX. One would wish that Williams's lost "discourse" entitled "Jobs trialls and Patience" had survived (See Winslow, p. 271).

246.8. Davids *speech*] Possibly a reference to Psalm 39.

246.12. *Like Grashopper*] Aesop's fable of the industrious ant and the improvident grasshopper who found himself without food in the winter because he had spent the summer in leaping and singing, vain pursuits. See also Prov. 6:6–8.

247.3–8. . . . . *gone*] The dialogue provides the standard death-bed scene so popular in the Christian *memento mori* tradition. Cf. Donne's "Valediction: Forbidding Mourning."

247.16. lay on soote] In the Old Testament the application of dust and ashes was regarded as symbolic of repentance and mourning.

247.29. consolation to the living] Another of the corporal works of mercy.

248.30. teares] "The glut of their griefe being past, they commit the corpes of their diceased friends to the ground, over whose grave is for a long time spent many a briny teare, deepe groane, and Irish-like howlings, continuing annuall mournings with a blacke stiffe paint on their faces . . ." (Wood, p. 98).

249.3. to rot with the dead] "Wherefore it is their custome, to bury with them their Bows and Arrows, and good store of their Wampompeage and Mowhackies; the one to affright that affronting Cerberus, the other to purchase more immense prerogatives in their Paradise, according to Wood. Significantly Williams ignores the possibility that the Indian believes in eternal punishment as well as in reward. One need only continue the above quotation to demonstrate that his is an unusual position: "For their enemies and loose livers, who they account unworthy of this imaginary happines, they say, that they passe to the infernall dwellings of abamocho, to be tortured according to the fictions of the ancient Heathen" (Wood, pp. 98–99).

249.6–7. having buried his sonne] This, along with Williams's presence in Manhattan during the Dutch Indian war there, is one of the most exact means we have of dating the author's departure for England in 1643 (see Trumbull, p. 217, n. 386).

249.15. shall not see death] Col. 3:1–4.

249.22. *The soules mortalitie*] An attack on the Mortalist heresy, one of whose supporters was John Milton.

250.2. *New* Earth] Fittingly, the book ends with an evocation of the apocalyptic vision: "And I saw a new heaven and new earth: for the first heaven and the first earth were passed away; and there was no more sea" (Rev. 21:1).

250.6. *Alpha* and *Omega*] "I am Alpha and Omega, the beginning and the end, the first and the last" (Rev. 22:13).

250.15. to Us and Them] The Indian *and* the English *can learn* from *each other*.

A Selected Bibliography

I. *Works Cited in Abbreviation*

A. By Roger Williams

The Complete Writings of Roger Williams. 7 vols. New York, 1963. With the exception of vol. 7, this collection is a reprint of *The Writings of Roger Williams.* Narragansett Club Publications, 1866–74. Vol. 7 contains new material and an "Essay in Interpretation" by Perry Miller.

(*Bloody Tenent*) *The Bloody Tenent yet More Bloody* (1652), *The Complete Writings,* vol. 4.

(*Bloudy Tenent*) *The Bloudy Tenent, of Persecution, for cause of Conscience, discussed* (1644). *The Complete Writings,* vol. 3.

(*Christenings*) *Christenings Make not Christians, or a Briefe Discourse concerning that name Heathen, commonly given to the Indians* (1645). *The Complete Writings,* vol. 7.

(*The Examiner Defended*) *The Examiner defended, in a Fair and Sober Answer to The Two and twenty Questions which lately examined the Author of Zeal Examined* (1652). *The Complete Writings,* vol. 7.

(*Experiments*) *Experiments of Spiritual Life & Health, and their Preservatives In which the weakest Child of God may get Assurance of his Spirituall Life and Blessednesse And the Strongest may finde proportionable Discoveries of his Christian Growth, and the means of it* (1652). *The Complete Writings,* vol. 7.

(*Fox*) *George Fox Digg'd out of his Burrowes, Or an Offer of Disputation On fourteen Proposalls made this last Summer 1672* (*so call'd*) *unto G. Fox then present on Rode-Island in New England* (1676). *The Complete Writings,* vol. 5.

(*The Hireling Ministry*) *The Hireling Ministry None of Christs, or A Discourse touching the Propagating the Gospel of Christ Jesus* (1652). *The Complete Writings,* vol. 7.

(*Letters*) *Letters of Roger Williams. 1632–1682. Now First Collected* (1874). *The Complete Writings,* vol. 6.

(*Queries of Highest Consideration*) *Queries of Highest Consideration,* Proposed . . . *To the Commissioners from the Generall Assembly* (*so called*) *of the Church of Scotland; Upon occasion of their late Printed Apologies for themselves and their Churches* (1644). *The Complete Writings,* vol. 2.

B. By Others

(*Advertisements*) Smith, John. *Advertisements for the unexperienced Planters of New England, or anywhere &c.*, (1631), in *Travels and Works of Captain John Smith (1580–1631)*. Edited with a Biographical and Critical Introduction by A. G. Bradley. Edinburgh, 1910, 2: 917–66.

(Bradford) Bradford, William. *Of Plymouth Plantation*. Edited with commentary by Samuel E. Morrison. New York, 1952.

(Callender) Callender, John. *An Historical Discourse on the Civil and Religious Affairs of the Colony of Rhode-Island and Providence Plantations* (1739). RIHS *Coll.* 4 (1838): 45–176.

(*Cotton's Letter*) Cotton, John. *A Letter of Mr. John Cottons Teacher of the Church in Boston, in New-England, to Mr. Williams a Preacher there* (1643). *The Complete Writings of Roger Williams,* vol. 1.

(*The Day-Breaking*) *The Day-Breaking, if not The Sun-Rising* of the *Gospell With the Indians in New-England* (1647). MHS *Coll.* 3rd ser., 4 (1834): 1–23.

(*Description*) Smith, John. *A Description of New England; or, Observations and Discoveries in North America* (1616), in *Travels and Works of Captain John Smith (1580–1631)*. Edited with a Biographical and Critical Introduction by A. G. Bradley. Edinburgh, 1910, 1: 173–229.

(*First Fruits*) *New England's First Fruits* (1643), in MHS *Coll.*, 1st ser. 1 (1806): 242–50.

(*The Generall Historie*) Smith, John. *The Generall Historie of Virginia, New England, and the Summer Isles* (1624), in *Travels and Works of Captain John Smith (1580–1631)*. Edited with a Biographical and Critical Introduction by A. G. Bradley. Edinburgh, 1910, bk. 6, 2: 695–784.

(Jantz) Jantz, Harold, ed. *The First Century of New England Verse*. New York, 1962.

(*Magnalia*) Mather, Cotton. *Magnalia Christi Americana; The Ecclesiastical History of New-England; from its First Planting, in the Year 1620, unto the Year of Our Lord 1698*. With an Introduction and Notes by Thomas Robbins, and Translations by Lucius F. Robinson, 1852. Reprinted New York, 1967, 2: 495–507.

(Meserole) Meserole, Harrison T., ed. *Seventeenth-Century American Poetry*. New York, 1968.

(Miller) Miller, Perry. *Roger Williams. His Contribution to the American Tradition* (1953). New York, 1962.

(Morgan) Morgan, Edmund S. *Roger Williams: The Church and the State*. New York, 1967.

(*Mourt's Relation*) Edited from the original printing of 1622, with Introduction and Notes by Dwight B. Heath. New York, 1963.

(*Remarkable Providences*) Mather, Increase. *Remarkable Providences Illustrative of the Earlier days of American Colonization* (1684). With Introductory Preface, by George Offor. London, 1890.

(Trumbull) Trumbull, J. Hammond, ed. *A Key into the Language of America.* The Complete Writings of Roger Williams, vol. 1.

(Tyler) Tyler, Moses Coit. *A History of American Literature 1607–1765* (1878). Reissued New York, 1949.

(Winslow) Winslow, Ola Elizabeth. *Master Roger Williams: A Biography.* New York, 1957.

(Winthrop) Winthrop, John. *Journal, History of New England, 1630–1649.* Edited by James K. Hosmer. New York, 1908, 2.

(Wood) Wood, William. *New England's Prospects* (1634), Edited by H. W. Boynton. Boston, 1898.

(Wroth) Wroth, Lawrence C. *Roger Williams* (Marshall Woods Lecture, Brown University). Providence, 1937.

II. *Primary Sources*

Clarke, John. *Ill Newes from New-England.* 1652.

Fox, George. *A New-England Fire-brand Quenched.* 1678.

Hariot, Thomas. *A Brief and True Report of the New Found Land of Virginia.* 1588.

Higginson, Francis. *New England's Plantation.* 1630.

Hubbard, William. *A Narrative of the Troubles with the Indians in New-England.* 1677.

Johnson, Edward. *A History of New-England, from the English planting in the Yeere 1628 until the Yeere 1652.* 1653.

Megapolensis, Johannes, Jr. *A Short Sketch of the Mohawk Indians in New Netherlands.* 1644.

Morton, Thomas. *New English Canaan.* 1637.

III. *Secondary Sources*

Austin, John O., ed. *The Roger Williams Calendar.* Central Falls, R.I., 1897.

Backus, Isaac. *A History of New England, with Particular Reference to the Denomination of Christians called Baptists.* 2 vols. Newton, Mass., 1871.

Bercovitch, Sacvan. "Typology in Puritan New England: The Williams-

Cotton Controversy Reassessed." *American Quarterly* 19 (Summer 1967): 166–91.

Bradstreet, Howard. *The Story of the War with the Pequots Re-Told.* In Conn. Tercent. Commiss. Com. on Hist. Pubs. Vol. 5. New Haven, 1933.

Brockunier, Samuel Hugh. *The Irrepressible Democrat: Roger Williams.* New York, 1940.

Calamandrei, Mauro. "Neglected Aspects of Roger Williams' Thought." *Church History* 21 (Sept. 1952): 239–59.

Caldwell, S. L. "Roger Williams as an Author." *The Baptist Quarterly* 6 (Oct. 1872): 385–407.

Carpenter, Edmund J. *Roger Williams: A Study of the Life, Times and Character of a Political Pioneer.* New York, 1909.

Chapin, Howard M. *Documentary History of Rhode Island.* 2 vols. Providence, 1916–19.

———. *Roger Williams and the King's Colors.* Providence, 1928.

———. *The Trading Post of Roger Williams.* Providence, 1934.

Child, Mrs. Anne P., ed. *Whatcheer, A Story of Olden Times.* Providence, 1857.

Chupack, Henry. *Roger Williams.* New York, 1969.

Colcord, W. A. "What Were the Principles for Which Roger Williams Was Banished." *Liberty* 2: 19–21.

Covey, Cyclone. *The Gentle Radical: A Biography of Roger Williams.* New York, 1966.

Denison, Rev. Frederic. *Soul-Liberty: A Historical Poem.* Mystic, Conn., 1872.

Dexter, Henry Martyn. *As to Roger Williams, and His "Banishment" from the Massachusetts Plantation.* Boston, 1876.

Diman, J. Lewis. *Address.* Ceremonies at the Unveiling of the Monument to Roger Williams. Providence, 1877.

Dos Passos, John R. "Roger Williams and the Planting of the Commonwealth in America." In *The Ground We Stand On.* New York, 1941.

Easton, Emily. *Roger Williams: Prophet and Pioneer.* New York, 1930.

Eaton, A. M. *Roger Williams: The Founder of Providence; The Pioneer of Religious Liberty.* Providence, 1908.

Eaton, Jeanette. *Lone Journey.* New York, 1944.

Elton, Romeo. *Life of Roger Williams, The Earliest Legislator and True Champion for a Full and Absolute Liberty of Conscience.* Providence, 1853.

Ely, W. D. *A Keyhole for Roger Williams' Key; or, a Study of Suggested Misprints, in its 16th Chapter.* Providence, 1892.

———. *Roger Williams' Key: Beanes vs. Barnes.* Providence, 1894.

Emerson, Everett. *John Cotton.* New York, 1965.

Ernst, James E. *Roger Williams, New England Firebrand.* New York, 1932.

Frank, Joseph. *The Beginnings of the English Newspaper (1620–1660).* Cambridge, Mass., 1961.

Freeman, Rosemary. *English Emblem Books.* London, 1948.

Gammel, William. *Life of Roger Williams.* Boston, 1845.

Garrett, John. *Roger Williams: Witness Beyond Christendom.* New York, 1970.

Greene, Theodore P., ed. *Roger Williams and the Massachusetts Magistrates.* Boston, 1964.

Guild, Reuben A. *Roger Williams, The Pioneer Missionary to the Indians.* Philadelphia, 1892.

Hall, May E. *Roger Williams.* Boston, 1917.

Harkness, R. E. "Roger Williams—Prophet of Tomorrow." *Journal of Religion* 15 (1935): 400–425.

Hines, Donald M. "Odd Customs and Strange Ways, The American Indian c. 1640." *Western Review* 7 (1970): 20–29.

Hirsch, Elizabeth Feist. "John Cotton and Roger Williams, their Controversy concerning Religious Liberty." *Church History* 10 (March 1941): 38–51.

Hodges, Almon D., Jr. "Notes concerning Roger Williams." *N.E. Hist. & Gen. Reg.* 53 (1899).

Johnson, Lorenzo D. *The Spirit of Roger Williams.* Boston, 1839.

Johnston, Thomas E. "A Note on the Voices of Ann Bradstreet, Edward Taylor, Roger Williams, and Philip Pain." *Early American Literature* 3 (Fall 1968): 125–26.

King, Henry M. *John Eliot and Roger Williams.* Providence, 1918.

———. *The True Roger Williams.* Providence, 1907.

Knowles, James D. *Memoir of Roger Williams.* Boston, 1834.

Masson, David. *The Life of John Milton.* 7 vols. New ed. London, 1896.

Merriman, Rev. T. M. *The Pilgrims, Puritans, and Roger Williams, Vindicated: and His Sentence of Banishment ought to be Revoked.* Boston, 1892.

Miller, Perry. *The New England Mind: The Seventeenth Century.* Cambridge, Mass., 1939.

———. *Orthodoxy in Massachusetts (1630–1650).* Cambridge, Mass., 1933.

Moore, LeRoy, Jr. "Roger Williams and the Historians." *Church History* 32 (Dec. 1963): 432–51.

Morgan, Edmund S. "Miller's Williams," *New England Quarterly,* 38 (1965): 513–23.

———. *The Puritan Dilemma: The Story of John Winthrop.* Boston, 1958.

Mudge, Rev. Z. A. *Foot-prints of Roger Williams: A Biography.* New York, n.d.

Murdock, Kenneth B. *Literature and Theology in Colonial New England.* Cambridge, Mass., 1949.

Newman, Louis Israel. "Roger Williams, the Bible and Religious Liberty." *Opinion* 12 (March 1942): 6–7.

Parks, Henry Bamford. "John Cotton and Roger Williams Debate Toleration 1644–1652." *New England Quarterly* 4 (Oct. 1931): 735–56.

Parrington, Vernon L. *Main Currents in American Thought.* Vol. 1: *The Colonial Mind.* New York, 1927, pp. 62–75.

Piercy, Josephine K. *Studies in Literary Types in Seventeenth Century America.* New Haven, Conn., 1939.

Polishook, Irwin H. *Roger Williams, John Cotton and Religious Freedom.* Englewood Cliffs, N.J., 1967.

Potter, George R. "Roger Williams and John Milton." RIHS *Coll.,* 13 (Oct. 1920): 113–29.

Richman, I. B. *Rhode Island, Its Making and Meaning.* New York, 1902.

Rossiter, Clinton. *Roger Williams on the Anvil of Experience.* n.p., 1951.

Silverman, Kenneth, ed. *Colonial American Poetry.* New York, 1968.

Simpson, Alan. "How Democratic Was Roger Williams?" *William and Mary Quarterly* 13 (Jan. 1956): 53–67.

Stead, George Albert. "Roger Williams and the Massachusetts Bay." *New England Quarterly* 7 (June 1934): 235–57.

Straus, Oscar S. *Roger Williams: The Pioneer of Religious Liberty.* New York, 1894.

Strickland, Arthur B. *Roger Williams: Prophet and Pioneer of Soul-Liberty.* Boston, 1919.

Swan, Bradford F. *Gregory Dexter of London and New England, 1610–1700.* Rochester, N.Y., 1949.

Sylvester, Herbert Milton. *Indian Wars of New England.* 3 vols. Cleveland, 1910.

White, Elizabeth Nicholson. *Mary Barnard, Wife of Roger Williams.* n.p., n.d.

Wroth, Lawrence C. "Variations in Five Copies of Roger Williams' *Key into the Language of America.*" RIHS *Coll.* 29 (Oct. 1936): 120–21.

Vaughn, Alden T. *New England Frontier: Puritans and Indians 1620–1675*. Boston, 1965.

Ziff, Larzer. *The Career of John Cotton: Puritanism and the American Experience*. Princeton, 1962.

John J. Teunissen is professor of English and head of the department at the University of Manitoba. He received his B.A. (1960) and M.A. (1962) from the University of Saskatchewan and his Ph.D. (1967) from the University of Rochester.

Evelyn J. Hinz is a Killam post-doctoral research scholar at the University of Manitoba. She received her B.A. (1961) and M.A. (1967) from the University of Saskatchewan and her Ph.D. (1973) from the University of Massachusetts.

The manuscript was edited by Marguerite C. Wallace. The book was designed by Mary Jowski. The typeface for Linotype Baskerville is based on the original design by John Baskerville in the 18th century; and the display face is Caslon Old Style designed by William Caslon in the 18th century.

The text is printed on Warren's Olde Style Antique paper and the book is bound in Columbia Mills Llamique cloth on sides and Bayside Vellum cloth on spine over binders' boards. Manufactured in the United States of America.